CW00939621

PRAISE FOR
DISMANTLING THE INNER SCHOOL

Dismantling the Inner School is a gem of reminders, ideas, insights, and wisdom for life learners and anyone else who cares about children and society.
- Wendy Priesnitz
Editor, Life Learning Magazine

David H. Albert's *Dismantling the Inner School* combines humor, wit, and comedy, along with common sense and plain good parenting. A must for those exploring homeschooling and for those who want a better option for their youth beyond the traditional educational framework available in our country. Albert opens his readers' eyes to the possibility of raising a generation that thinks outside the box and still manages to show that one size definitely cannot and will not fit all. Entertaining as well as enlightening.
- LT Bentley

DISMANTLING THE INNER SCHOOL

DISMANTLING

THE

INNER SCHOOL

Homeschooling & the Curriculum of Abundance

David H. Albert

HUNT PRESS • LOS ANGELES

Copyright © 2011 David H. Albert

All rights reserved. No part of this book may be reproduced or
transmitted in any form or by any means, electronic or mechanical,
except for the purpose of review and/or reference, without permission
in writing from the publisher.

Published by Hunt Press, Los Angeles, California.

www.huntpress.com

Printed in the United States of America

ISBN 978-0-9850206-4-4

10 9 8 7 6 5 4 3 2 1

FIRST EDITION

The ultimate purpose of education is to learn to treat each other better.
- (I said that).
David H. Albert

Do not teach all children the same thing, or in the same way. For if you do so, they will learn that they do not need each other, and the world will split apart.
- subiyay,
late spiritual leader of the Skokomish Tribe

Man is born to live, not to prepare for life. And life itself, the phenomenon of life, the gift of life, is so thrillingly serious!
- Boris Pasternak,
Dr. Zhivago

Nullius in verba[*]

---

[*] "Take no man's word for it." It is the motto of the (British) Royal Society, founded in 1660 "for the promoting of physico-matheticatico experimental learning."

Table of Contents

Foreword

IF YOU'RE A parent, an educator, or anyone interested in learning, in becoming smarter, more creative, more imaginative, David Albert's *Dismantling the Inner School: Homeschooling and the Curriculum of Abundance* will delight you, stimulate you, and frighten you right out of your drawers. David is The Happy Revolutionary, happily opening wide the doors of our educational system and freeing the prisoners – all of us, we discover – happily unnerving the wardens, the guards, the keepers of the keys, happily sabotaging conventional wisdom – almost everything we've been taught about growing and learning – and finally, with great glee to say nothing of pure common sense – leading us by example to what we didn't know we already knew, wisdom, and the ability to learn and to teach.

(A disciple of John Holt, David too defines intelligence as the ability to deal not with what one knows, but with what one does not know. How does a person behave, Holt asks, in a situation new to her? David is a disciple too of Ivan Illich, the author of 1971's *Deschooling Society*. Not surprisingly, David is one of the leading advocates of homeschooling).

Like John Holt and and Ivan Illich, of whom he is a disciple, David is for deschooling society, de-institutionalizing it, shucking the present system like a bad ear of corn. He takes pains to show us just how harmful it is, how progressively stupid it makes us, and how that stupidity – ignorance far from bliss – leaves our kids, ourselves, and our communities frustrated, stressed out, unhappy, and unfulfilled.

Answering a teacher's boring questions, following a teacher's boring directions, undergoing a relentlessly deadly education inspired by the dullest, most unimaginative, and, yes, most uninspired authorities the modern world has ever known, anonymous employees ensconced in the cubicles of the Educational Testing Service, leaves us, our kids and communities, David also suggests, fodder for any charlatan's imagination; a nation of sheep; submissive; in other words, cruel, or at least a party to cruelty. Think Robert McNamara offering up kids to the slaughter in Viet Nam, the "mean girl" in middle school, the demagogic politician serving his own interests instead of that of the community. By the time we question them, or they question themselves, it's after the fact. "I have to live with what I've done," says Colin Powell, after presenting the false evidence of weapons of mass destruction in Iraq, a lie that itself caused mass destruction. He believed what he was told. He followed directions. He didn't know any better. I blame our educational system. He only learned to answer questions, not to ask them, and certainly not to ask his own.

Educated as one of the elite, a man of a thousand degrees, David shows us too how Western education made *him* stupid, and how "stupid" harmed him. So not only he advocate deschooling society, he shows us the absolute necessity of "dismantling" the school inside us, our "inner school."

Simply, we must "unlearn" to truly learn, to be true to ourselves, to our own feelings, thoughts, needs, and interests. David teaches us, again through example, how to unlearn and consequently how to learn. Indeed, time is of the essence, he says. Therefore, take it. Get rid of the internalized bells ringing, the rigid schedules and state-sponsored linear curricula inspired by fears of what you'll "miss" (most of which you forget anyway), concentrate on what you're good at (that's where you'll be spending your life), see failure as the natural process of elimination on your way toward eventual success. He identifies the "bricks", the old scaffolding, the institutional myths, the old hand-me-downs of conventional education as you learn from him to unlearn, then to learn.

If intelligence is, among other things, as David suggests, courage, humility, focus, centeredness, perspective, a sense of humor, intuition, analytical thinking, creativity, inventiveness, imagination, empathy – all of which are what it takes to be smart, to face the unknown, to make something positive out of it – have schools not really taught us this? Is David right?

Totally, Dude. Absolutely. I taught for 40 years. If you walk into almost any classroom in America and ask the students what they truly are interested in learning, they fall back on "math," "history," "English," "science". To them, learning is schooling and school is learning. They've been brainwashed to the point where they can no longer distinguish one from the other. Since school by and large is boring, meaningless and shallow, and schooling is learning, then learning itself is pretty much boring, meaningless, and shallow, and schooling is learning, then learning itself is pretty much in their minds a ruse, a joke. It is a joke that a skilled, shallow intelligence can "get", but then ultimately, what is it they've gotten? David got it, and like most who do – like McNamara, our " best and brightest – to say nothing of those who don't, those who like me who just sat there eight hours a day in despair or screwed off – he ended forgetting who *he* was, what *he* needed or wanted.

Like Colin Powell, like the rest of us, David forgot *his* questions. Who wouldn't, when you've got to answer a teacher's all day throughout your childhood and adolescence. Microphones are now being used in classrooms because teachers talk so much they're losing their voices. Steal them, I saw, and develop your own.

Or as David puts it, "Have fun. Learn stuff. Grow."

He shows us how to do it, how to become a great student and consequently a great teacher.

I spoke recently to the "gifted" students (a label itself preening with vanity) at a high school in Atlanta, all seniors. Yes, their grades were "A's", their SAT scores in the statistical stratosphere, their elite college and university acceptance letters practically in the mail. With such success, the trade-off, as David reveals, is more often than not in originality, creativity, and a mind of one's own.

Originality, creativity, a mind of one's own. For this, I told them, "competence", even "excellence:, was not enough. No, to be truly "gifted", to be "great", you must be inspired. And to be inspired, you have to be true to yourself, your own thoughts and feelings, which means you must learn to know yourself, what your thoughts and feelings are, what your real needs and aspirations are, what your real questions and problems are. I tried to show them through example after example, of which related to their own lives, that an open heart is an open mind, that the personal is the universal, that Denial fogs up the window and blocks the view, that Truth is liberating.

Afterwards, a kid towards the rear of the auditorium raised his hand. His smile was charming. You can tell the way the kids turned to look at him that they liked him. His name, he offered, was Jeffrey.

"Mr. Schein," he asked, "Could you expound on the distinguished, prominent nature of Southern literature pre-Margaret Mitchell?"

"No," I replied.

He seemed delighted.

"Are you really interested in the answer to that question?" I asked.

"Of course not."

"So it's meaningless, since you don't really care about the answer."

"Right," he said, grinning. "Exactly."

"So where did it come from?"

"My teacher gave it to me."

And where was his teacher?

Sitting right next to him, I noticed, as he turned slightly to his left.

And his question? What was *his* question? Where could he find it?

In *Dismantling the Inner School".*

That's where all of ours can be found.

Bernie Schein
December 31, 2011

Walking

IF I MAY say so myself, I'm a pretty adept walker. Nothing special, or worth writing home about, but my feet usually get me where I want to go. I slouch a bit, probably more than I used to (Mrs. Hochstein, my third grade teacher, wouldn't approve), and haven't taken any big hikes lately, and I haven't worn a backpack in a long time. Maybe a little slower than I once was (my nickname in college was "Fast Eddie", though honestly it didn't have anything to do with foot speed). But the legs work, and the feet carry me in a reasonably straight line. I might be a little flat-footed, but there's nothing remotely Chaplinesque, and, by my walk, I would certainly never be mistaken for Popeye, even if I had any biceps to speak of (and I don't). I am an able-bodied pedestrian, a pretty solid "B" walker.

Now I must admit I wasn't always this way. In fact, I can hardly begin to tell you how many times I failed walking. Just couldn't get it. Flunked repeatedly. Some of the time, I couldn't even get up on my feet, and some of the time I was too scared to even try, and some of the time, well, I probably decided, in my own way, that there was no particular place I wanted to go, so why make the effort? Failure. Fell down a couple of dozen times during test weeks. It took me months, when for some, it only took days. Scores of "Fs." No one had to send a note home to my parents – they witnessed the whole thing. My mother bought me a pair of shoes with "cookies" in them (and this was long before shoe retailers had websites).

I did eventually learn from my mistakes, of course, and although I never became the two-legged terror of the neighborhood, and would always remain more noun than verb, there has, at least until now, never been a time when my walking has failed me. Perhaps my sights have been lowered, and my Himalayan touring days are certainly over, but I have few regrets.

The reality is, as the late British educator Robin Hodgkin – himself a renowned trekker and climber – once wrote, "Every skilled act, many of which now seem easy and automatic, started as an achievement in the face of difficulty and danger." The analogy with walking may seem to some overly simplistic, but I think it is the very simplicity of how we go about learning to walk that reveals the engines behind virtually all learning quests. If I was decent at marketing, I'd call it the "Not-(Yet)-So-Fat Albert's Five-Step Homeschooling Recipe for Learning Success (and Hair Loss Elixir)™" (but I'm not). You can find it in the next chapter.

Don't get me wrong. I'm really happy you've picked up my book. Maybe even bought it new! But the reality is that if you take my recipe to heart and apply it to your own experience, you won't *have to* read the rest of this book. So it will be a guilty pleasure. You're absolved in advance. Read. Try it – you'll like it. Write me a letter.

But before you settle in, grab the kids, get out of the house, and go for a good long walk. Take the dog, and be sure to smell the flowers. Or splash in a puddle. Or make a snowman. I'll still be here when you get back. Promise!

Ah, it's great to be homeschooling!

"Not-(Yet)-So-Fat Albert's Five-Step Homeschooling Recipe for Learning Success (and Hair Loss Elixir)™"

- The truth of my inner development encounters physical, cultural, and social opportunities for action;

- *My inner drive, though of limited competence, meets up with the space and freedom where this truth can realize its expression;*

- Models for action presented to me provide for the development of goal orientations;

- A bit of encouragement and a modicum of coaching can help me feel assured that I am on the right path and assist me in discovering tools and techniques which are not as yet, to me, intuitive; and

- Success in pushing back one of the frontiers provides some of the inner knowledge that commitment and courage will allow me to advance in pushing back others.

Learning Happens from the Inside Out

My website and e-mail address:

www.skylarksings.com

david@skylarksings.com

Dismantling the Inner School

NOW THAT YOU'RE returned from your walk and are sitting down with a nice cup of tea, it's time for me to get the show on the road.

So where to start? I could go softly and ease you in, capture you in my magic web before you think it necessary to escape. Bait you with honey. Reaffirm you in your predilections. Maybe seduce you with a nice little poem, or a salutary quotation.

Nah! Forget that. Let's just go for the jugular and let the chips fall where they may. Give you a chance to leave if you choose (I hope not!) If you decide to stay, provide you with some strong medicine.

I think I've run out of bad and jangling metaphors, so it's time to get down to it. Ready?

Schools make the kids dumb and dumber.

I know what at least a few of you might be thinking. "Here's this nefarious homeschooling author and he begins his book, which I'd really been looking forward to reading 'cause of what my friends told me about him, with a cheap shot. On what basis can this guy possibly make such a wild, categorical, and irresponsible claim? And even if there is some truth to the argument, why make it here?"

Obviously, these thoughts have crossed my mind as well, or you wouldn't be reading them. You'll soon find out, I hope, that it isn't a cheap shot, and that folks much more knowledgeable about such things than I am are the ones making the claim. But, in any case, I throw myself on your mercy, with the following pleadings:

- I am more than aware that the vast majority of parents are not prepared to homeschool their children, and that, as a society we have a stake in the future of all of our children, not just those fortunate enough to be homeschooled.

- More to the point, in my experience, when it comes to education, most everything about school, broadly speaking, is wrongheaded. However, if we can understand in some detail precisely what it is that schools get wrong, we stand a better chance of not stumbling into the same mistakes.

If you live in a community anything like mine, you have witnessed the annual drill. The data on those high-stakes tests are released to the local press. A bunch of public officials put on their fancy clothes and hold a press conference. Grades are higher than ever, they say. The schools are doing a great job (though there is still room for improvement). And if only "we" (meaning they) had more money!

Now, no attempt will be made to follow the same kids year-over-year to try to discover whether what happened in the classroom actually made any difference. That's not required in the Race to the Bottom. There will be occasional outliers, but on the whole, it is predictable that in the charts displayed in the local newspaper, scores by school will reflect local real estate values, the higher the values the more robust the scores. In fact, tens of millions of dollars could be saved in testing (and in preparation for it) simply by assigning scores to individual students by average family incomes in the surrounding community, and they would rarely be too far off. (By the way, if one really wanted to know what children were learning in school, wouldn't it be wiser to have them take a test *without* any special preparation? Could save millions that way, and lots of headaches!) There won't be any mention of the real statistical anomalies: I have seen it demonstrated, using arcane psychometric procedures, that in the U.S. every state is above the national average in elementary school test scores. Don't ask me how that is possible – the new math is not my strong suit.[1] As a result, according to recent polls more than three-quarters of Americans are satisfied with their own local public schools, even while the same percentage have been led to believe that public education is collapsing.

It would seem that the idea of things schoolish always getting better and better isn't a new one. Since the introduction of intelligence testing in the U.S. and elsewhere in the early years of the 20th Century, scores on so-called "objective" criterion-referenced tests have increased in a consistent manner. IQ scores have improved roughly three points per decade, which, if true and taken at face value, means our grandparents and great-grandparents were on the whole a bunch of morons, imbeciles, and idiots who couldn't tie their shoes, and those were the days before Velcro.[2] Until the 1990s, test scores had to be re-centered every 15 years or so to reflect improved performance. The "Flynn Effect", named after American-born New Zealand psychologist and philosopher James R. Flynn who first described the phenomenon, mostly reflects a change in cognitive demands made on the population, and, secondarily, enhanced performance in the "bottom half", resulting at least in part from improved nutrition (before 1950), smaller family size, and other environmental conditions, and especially increased exposure to and value

---

[1]   Also, don't dare ask how the tests were graded, or who graded them. For a rollicking yet at the same time extremely sobering read from an 'insider', see Todd Farley's *Making the Grades: My Misadventures in the Standardized Testing Industry.* Sausalito, CA: PoliPoint Press, 2009.

[2]   All three terms – morons, imbeciles, and idiots – are technical terms defined by Henry Herbert Goddard in 1910 to describe those who perform poorly on IQ tests, in varying degrees.

placed upon scholastic skills, scientific and managerial reasoning, and habits of mind.[3] [4] There is, however, little evidence that this ostensible increase in "intelligence" has made people more competent or effective in coping with the demands of everyday life.

In fact, there are some scientists who believe the process of improving intelligence *and* of coping with the demands of living (I don't quite understand why these should be different) ground to a halt in the late 1980s/early 1990s, not just in the United States, but in other "well-schooled" nations as well. In 2006, I came across the work of Professors Michael Shayer and Philip Adey of Kings College at the University of London. Adey and Shayer have been following the results of tens of thousands of children on intelligence tests over the past 30 years.

---

[3]   Flynn asserts that the seemingly improved performance reflects changing social priorities and/or altering cognitive demands made on our minds, and hence is entirely environmentally induced. And, according to Flynn, environment explains *all* intergroup differences, and as the present generation has no real genetic advantage over the last generation, the huge IQ gains are purely the effect of environment and testify to how potent it really is. He uses the example of a typical IQ test question, "What do dogs and rabbits have in common?" In the 19th Century, a common answer might be, "Dogs are used to hunt rabbits," which would receive no points on a modern IQ test, where the "correct" answer would be "Both are mammals." The emphasis would now be on classification and abstract reasoning. There is no reason to believe, according to Flynn, that our grandparents didn't know that dogs and rabbits are both mammals, only that this kind of knowledge would have been considered less valuable or would have had a lower priority. (I wonder how many kids today would know that dogs were once used to hunt rabbits). Flynn states, "The best data (since 1947) show we have gained almost nothing in terms of general information, everyday vocabulary, and arithmetical reasoning, but have made huge gains in classification, seeing logical relationships between symbols, and on-the-spot problem solving." Flynn, James R., *What is Intelligence?* Cambridge, UK: Cambridge University Press, 2009)

      Sorry, I can't resist the poetical: "Our meddling intellect/Mis-shapes the beauteous forms of things:– /We murder to dissect." – William Wordsworth, "The Tables Turned" (1798). At least I've kept it to the footnotes…so far.

[4]   Very recently, biologists and epidemiologists have weighed in on the intelligence debate and posited a new explanation for differences in intelligence across nations, and within nations (differences among individuals are only implied). The "parasitic stress hypothesis" builds on findings that exposure to infectious diseases at an early age are the single most powerful predictor of average national IQ (more so than the effects of education, national wealth, or a host of other variables). Even within the U.S., states with highest exposure to infectious disease have the lowest average IQ. The two explanations posited are that, 1) During episodes of infection, human energy resources are temporarily lost to the brain as they are consumed by the immune system, or 2) Because of the frequency of infection, developmental pathways are permanently changed and more energy is invested into immune function rather than into brain growth. See Eppig, C., Fincher, C., and Thornhill, R. "Parasitic Prevalence and the Worldwide Distribution of Cognitive Ability," *Proceedings of the Royal Society – Biological Science*, Vol. 277 No. 1701, December 22, 2010; Hassall, C. and Sherratt, T. "Statistical Inference and Spatial Patterns in Correlates of IQ," *Intelligence* 39, 2011.

And their findings? Eleven-year-old children are, "now on average between two and three years behind where they were 15 years ago" in terms of cognitive and conceptual development.

Now these are no fly-by-night researchers. Professors Shayer and Adey have for decades been two of the foremost and most highly respected lights in British education. Their work is funded by the Economic and Social Research Council, Britain's leading think tank on educational matters. I could go on and on about their credentials, but perhaps it is enough to say that as far as mainstream educational researchers go, these guys are at the top of the heap.

"It's a staggering result," stated Shayer, "But the figures just don't lie. The results have been checked, rechecked, and peer reviewed." "It is shocking," said Adey, "The general cognitive foundation of 11- and 12-year-olds has taken a big dip." "The test," noted cognitive scientist Denise Ginsberg, measures both general intelligence and "higher level brain functions." "It is nothing less than the ability of children to handle new, difficult ideas."

The results caused experts all over England to question whether the standardized national tests they have been using are of long-term benefit to learning, and cast doubt, according to Paul Black, another educational luminary at King's College, London, on the usual claims that standards are in fact improving.

The articles I read indicated that the study was to be published in late 2007 in the *British Journal of Educational Psychology*. Since I don't usually accept what I read in newspapers or magazines or on the Web at face value, I did what any self-respecting homeschooler would do – I looked the authors up on the Internet at King's College, and contacted them directly. They were gracious enough to send me an advance copy of the study, and were intrigued (and pleased) that a homeschooling advocate from the United States would communicate with them. Without going into too much detail, there were large drops in competency between 1976-2000. But – and more striking – the declines accelerated beginning in 2000, even as schools were implementing test-normed "higher standards" in England, adhering to large-scale "National Numeracy and Literacy" projects.

In press accounts, Professors Adey and Shayer were somewhat circumspect when it comes to explaining this observed mass cognitive retardation. (Yes, you can quote me if you like: "School is the leading preventable cause of mental retardation.") Shayer noted, "I would suggest that the most likely reasons are the lack of experiential play in primary schools, and the growth of a video-game, TV culture. Both take away the kinds of hands-on play that allows kids to experience how the world works in practice and to make informed judgments about abstract concepts."

Professor Adey went a bit further. "By stressing the basics – reading and writing – and testing like crazy, you reduce the level of cognitive stimulation. Children have the facts but they are not thinking very well. And they are not getting hands-on physical experience of the way materials work." Both stressed the need for increased conversation with adults (who, it is assumed, are more likely to model higher-order thinking).

In the article itself, it is evident that Adey and Shayer are aware of some of the contradictions suggested by their work. They are part of the child development tradition that Jean Piaget pioneered related to the formation of intelligence. Piaget believed that it is the whole everyday environmental experience of the child that drives cognitive development, with schooling possibly playing only a minor part of the process. But today, it is now a given within the educational orthodoxy, both here and abroad, that school *should* play a more significant role. And the evidence now suggests that it does – *negatively*.

Of course, Adey and Shayer are still school people, and it is therefore not surprising that they seek solutions in the schools themselves. The article concludes, "Perhaps the next major Government objective in education should be to address the question: in focusing teachers' attention on the specifics of the 3Rs only, what has been lost from the earlier primary practice of attending to development of the whole person of the child?" Now, candidly, I must have been out of school during those decades, for I can't seem to remember *anyone* attending to my whole person. Perhaps it was better this way, as I think I probably benefited greatly from benign neglect. Anyway, despite Adey and Shayer's research conclusions, they remain focused on where the *teachers'* attention should be, rather than that of the *kids*. Realistically, and given who their employers are, maybe that is expecting too much of them.

But we and our children don't have to live inside the box, either literally or figuratively. In the spirit of learning from the demonstrated success of schools in retarding children's intellectual development, and school being the leading preventable cause of learning disabilities[5], we can at least take the hint. Want your kids to be better at math? Throw out the workbook pages, and let them play in puddles, bake some cakes, grow some vegetables (I can guarantee you'll be reading more from me on that score), assist you with map directions. Want them to read well? Let them help you with the shopping, choose the videos, sort the mail, and provide them with enough experiences – and good books! – so they'll want to make use of the reading skill. Oh, and here I make common cause with the two professors, lots of good conversation – precisely what they will never get sitting in those little chairs behind those little desks never to be seen anywhere else in the real world.

This reminds me how privileged I have been to homeschool my two kids, for as the author of the groundbreaking book *Children's Mind*, Margaret Donaldson reminds us, the basic problem in education "is to understand how something that began so well can often end so badly."[6]

---

5   I think I should copyright that one separately.
6   Donaldson, Margaret. *Children's Minds*. London, UK: Fontana Press, 1978.

I USED TO say that the hardest thing about homeschooling is deciding to do it. Well, for many of you, you've gotten past that (and I hope to bring the rest of you along). Give yourself a pat on the back, if you can still reach. If not, a knee will do.

But wait, there's more, and we all know it. Good thing, because I'm just getting warmed up. Let's do a little more exploring.

A FRIEND OF mine, a homeschooling mom in the San Francisco area, related the following incident to me. She had gone to a local corner grocery with her five-year-old son at 11 o'clock in the morning and, it being a "school day," the shopkeeper asked the boy where he went to school.

"I homeschool," the boy replied proudly.

"Oh, I see," said the shopkeeper. "Can you count to ten?"

Homeschool mom's first response, of course, was to be offended. How dare a perfect stranger feel entitled to go about testing her five-year-old simply because they went shopping together at 11 o'clock in the morning? The nerve! What an outrage! How would *he* like to be tested by anyone who happens to cross his path?

Had this gone on much longer, there would have been red and black smoke emerging from her ears and nostrils. But then she looked down at her son. He was taking too much time to answer the question. "Come on, Billy," she thought, "You can count to ten. I know you can." Her palms began to sweat. It was not her son who was being tested, but herself! Legs a little rubbery. Her self-esteem, her very identity as a homeschooling parent was on trial, and might be found wanting. "Come on, Billy," she would have prayed, except she wasn't the praying sort, "Answer the man."

Billy had his hands in his pocket, and was seemingly bashfully looking down at the floor. At last he picked up his head, looked at the shopkeeper, and in a small, thoughtful voice, asked,

"Would you like me to count to ten in English, French, German, Russian, or Japanese?"

ONCE YOU START homeschooling with your son or daughter, you quickly discover that almost everyone seems to think the kids are fair game for testing, and that you are just inwardly begging for their advice. Uncle Harry, who dropped out in the 11th grade, was never asked to provide words for the Scripps-Howard Spelling Bee, so he feels this is his opportunity. Aunt Bertha wants to know if little Jimmy knows his vowel sounds; her sister Aunt Emma wants to know about subtraction. Grandpa Milton insists that Bobbie read the front page of the newspaper (a nice thing to do if Grandpa's eyes are becoming dim); Grandma Hazel asks her if she knows the capital of Kyrgystan ("Hint," she whispers, "it begins with 'A'"; "Oh, Grandma," Bobbie shouts out, "I think you have it confused with Kazakhstan. The capital of Kyrgystan begins with a 'B'.") You grit your teeth, try to avoid arguments, and hope the kids know enough to get the relatives, and the neighbors, off their backs.

That's the easy part. After all, if little Susie performs like a trained seal, the worst thing you will experience is an occasional knowing nod, and the conversation will quickly turn to something else (as in Cousin Alice finding it necessary to inform you about the new gifted program at her local school, which is only 650 miles away).

If you've managed to avoid these little pin-pricks, don't worry, the grappling hooks aren't far behind. You have now entered a world in which virtually everyone has become an education expert. Your older brother Robert, who drinks himself into a stupor nearly every chance he gets, and was divorced by his wife after she grew tired of being kicked, punched, and slapped around, wants to know how Jimmie is ever going to be properly "socialized." Your sister Molly, who hated every minute of school and let you know it while growing up, and to this day can't balance her checkbook, wants to know if you are teaching Alexandra the "new math" or the old variety. (You are pretty sure that she doesn't know either). Mom, who never cared a lick about what you did in school back in the Dark Ages, has now become the reincarnation of Horace Mann and insists on knowing why you don't simply join the PTA and reform the local school system. As he cuts your six-year-old's hair, Benny the Barber, who, it seems, can't read and only looks at the pictures in *The Enquirer*, wants to make sure that Joey knows his phonics, and asks whether you are worried about college. Mrs. McGillicuddy, the next-door neighbor with blue hair and who has been teaching at the local elementary school since she was a blonde, just gives you "the look" when she sees you out on the front lawn and Annie riding around on her bicycle during "school hours."

I know, it grows tiresome. Wearying even. And there's going to be another ten or so years of this! How are you ever going to stand it? Isn't there a South Sea island somewhere where you can move so that they'll leave you in peace?[7]

To be honest with ourselves, however, there is more operating than you allow yourself to know. The reality is that, with the possible exception of Mrs. McGillicuddy, there is little that is likely to be malicious in what are, at bottom, expressions of concern. The vast majority of folks who confront you and your son and daughter this way remember quite vividly the horror that school was, at least occasionally, even if they are slow to admit it to

---

[7]   Candidly, it is a lot better than it was 20 years ago. When you mention homeschooling these days, an increasing number of people just sigh and indicate wistfully that they now wish they had done it with their own kids, or express their hopes that their grandchildren will be homeschooled.

themselves (and, hence, slower to admit it to you). This being a major challenge to their imaginations, most will have little idea what your day or that of your children actually looks like, and have difficulty getting their heads around the idea that the clones of Mrs. McGillicuddy are not required for the learning enterprise.

But it's still difficult, and the reason it is difficult is that all those clones of Mrs. McGillicuddy live inside us. Otherwise, it would be a simple matter to say to our friends and family, "Thank you for your concern. I'm really glad that you care so much about us and our educational choices, and we'll take your suggestions under advisement." And that would be that.

And it is not simply that our former teachers – good or bad (and, looking back at it, I'm not always sure I can identify the difference) – still have their mitts on us. Some of you figured it this out much sooner than I did – I being particularly slow on the uptake – there is a man behind the curtain, and he spent years building a school inside our heads. And for years, even decades after we left the physical confines, many of us remain stuck in our minds behind those little desks, coats in the closet, waiting for the next assault of *education*.

So if we are ever going to make peace with ourselves, and provide an education truly worthy of the name for our children, we are going to have to find ways to dismantle the inner school, brick by brick. If you are a slow learner like me, and allowed the mortar to fully harden, some of this is going to be the business of a lifetime.

It's time to identify the bricks, and get out the chisel.

Brick One: Learning Starts on the First Day of School

THE YELLOW SCHOOL bus, belching blue-black smoke out of its exhaust, turns the corner, and is lumbering its way up the street toward you. There you are, holding your mother's hand tightly (though perhaps not as tightly as she is holding yours), with a backpack strapped to your hunched shoulders, unicorn lunchbox in hand, new sneakers on your feet. This is the first day of school – the first such day in *your whole life* – and you are excited, and fearful, and happy, and sad, and confused, and brave (maybe) all at the same time.

And mom is transmitting the same vibe. The door to the bus squeaks open, you both let go, and up you go to your seat. You are free, and scared, and surprised there is no seatbelt, and the door shuts, and you wave at mom, and she gets smaller and smaller until the bus turns the next corner. And then she is gone.

Over the next several weeks, you may have made friends on the bus, or sat by yourself. You might have thrown up a few times, or sung silly songs, or both. You might have been bullied or threatened or (who knows?) you might occasionally have bullied or threatened others. (Even bullies have a mom).

You might have shared snacks (though I hope you'd been warned about peanuts). You might have come home excited, bored, talkative, or uncommunicative.

But the man behind the curtain placed a little brick in your poor brain that tells you when your education began, the point at which there was a radical disjuncture from your previous experience the point at which you left your mother standing at the curb. Whether it ended well or badly or somewhere in between, this is where it all started. Or so you were led to believe.

The most common question I field from erstwhile homeschooling parents who happen to cross my path is "Where do I start?" The question is the same whether the mom asking the question (it's almost *always* mom) has a child who has never been in school, or whether she has just helped her son or daughter fly the coop.

I have learned to appreciate the question, and am excited that it represents a family – parents and children together – ready to roll up their sleeves and embark on a new adventure. The first thing I do is offer my congratulations, and I try to remind them that there is a world of experts out there (that's many of you, dear readers), and that they are soon to join 'em. And then I offer various words of encouragement and inspiration), an occasional scrap of practical advice, and a hearty "Bon Voyage…"

I'm not dissatisfied with the range of responses I've given, and folks seem to appreciate them. But as I reflect back, there was something absent, and that is this: by the time folks ask "where do I start?" they already have. I don't mean to sound overly flip or glib (if "flip" is short for "flippant," is "glib" short for ….?), but we as parents have been there to witness, encourage, provide opportunities and tools, model and mentor, and applaud the courage and commitment of our children as they push back the frontiers since the day they first opened their eyes. Yet, it's as if somehow, on the day it is announced that one is to "start homeschooling," something fundamentally different is supposed to take place, like getting on the yellow school bus.

And, no, I am not here making a distinction between "curricula-based" versus "unschooling" approaches to education. Indeed, the very problem with conceiving of these as representing some kind of basic dichotomy is that they are both defined by our notions of what education and, specifically, "school" are supposed to be like, or at least were about for us. Regardless of our predilections or philosophies, our kids started living and learning at the same time. Furthermore, we all carry with us a knowledge, sometimes hard won, that: 1) We learn better when we are allowed to follow our leadings and passions; 2) The tasks that allow us to learn better are those that meet up with the truth of our inner development; and 3) Our experience of the world has led us to believe (sometimes wrongly, it turns out, but we can be forgiven) that certain kinds of knowledge or information or tools are likely to serve our children well, now and in the future, regardless of how they acquire them.

The rest is just a balancing act, which makes homeschooling an art rather than a science.

But you and your child don't have to wait to get on the yellow bus. You are already on it. Only the destinations are going to be a lot more exciting.

Brick Two: You are Going to Miss Something Important (and Ruin Your Kids for Life!)

NERVOUS HOMESCHOOLING MOMS (and occasionally dads) e-mail me, call me up, or even come to see me for help. The kids are usually a little older. The parents are nervous. It's not like things are going badly. In fact, since they took little Johnnie out of school, he seems to be so much happier. He is finally his old self again. The scars seem to have healed over, and he can barely remember being poisoned by Mrs. McGillicuddy's sucralose-laden missives. He is reading again, something that seemed to have been snuffed out by two years in the box, collects beetles, and likes to do wheelies on his bicycle with his friends.

So I'm trying to figure out what is wrong. Homeschooling parents don't usually approach me to tell their success stories, at least not with such concerned looks on their faces, or trembling in their voices. And then I know what comes next. It has nothing to do with Johnnie.

"Everything seems to be going okay," homeschool mom sighs, in a way which clearly indicates that she doesn't really believe it. "But I am really worried. I don't know what it is, exactly, but I'm sure somehow that we are going to miss something important."

I know the feeling. Exactly. And very personally. You see, I spent 21 years in formal "education," trying to make sure all the holes were plugged. I learned early that I was to be considered a piece of Swiss cheese, and the holes were to be plugged, whether with the proper way to do long division, or with Russian language tapes. And I learned that lesson all-too-well. As everyone else I knew was getting narrower and narrower (and, in some cases, more career-driven), my "interests" (really, my "needs") were getting broader and broader. I went to the finest schools, finishing up with Oxford University and a prestigious program at the University of Chicago that required masters' level equivalence in four different fields. Somehow I figured that if I couldn't find what was missing by going there, chances are it wasn't to be found. Luckily, I managed to get them to pay me to do it, and I met more than my share of extraordinary people, for which I am grateful.

I did learn a lot of esoterica and, even if there are others who find the detritus (my younger daughter learned that one) and foraminifera (I picked this word up when I was 10; you'll have to go look it up) that floats around my poor brain as both somewhat intimidating and less than exhilarating at the same time, it has kept me in a semi-permanent state of bemusement all these years.

Some folks, I have discovered, actually enjoy my dinner conversation; others might question my sanity; most will find me relatively harmless, even if I am an acquired taste.

And there are people who will look at my educational journey with envy. After all, I could study what I wanted, spend as much time as I wanted at it, and not have to worry about putting food on the table (yet). For all intensive purposes, I would seem to have all the possible trappings of educational and academic freedom.

Except I did not. For with all those rewards piled on me, and with my incessant (one might even suggest "valiant") attempts to fill all those Swiss-cheese holes of which the man behind the curtain made me all-too-aware, it took me my entire youth to figure out that no amount of information could ever fill the spiritual hole created from having learned to be unfree. In short, I had become a prisoner of my own mind, and it has taken me the better part of my adult life to tie the bedsheets together and shinny down the drainage pole and make my escape. And to be entirely fair to myself, now that I am at liberty, I have come to appreciate the maxim of the 19th Century female astronomer Maria Mitchell, who wrote, "We have a hunger of the mind. We ask for all of the knowledge around us and the more we get, the more we desire."

So I am in position to offer you an ironclad guarantee. *You will miss something.* Even something important. If you are lucky, the kids won't hate you for it forever (you could, of course have escaped all culpability if the kids were in school). If it makes you feel any better, put a dollar in the therapy fund for every dollar in the college one.

The man behind the curtain wants to make sure we are prepared for the next test. With all the emphasis on being prepared for the next test, the educational equivalent of bingeing and purging which leaves us equivalently weakened as healthy human beings as a result, it is hard to keep our minds and hearts focused on the truth: education is neither a series of way-stations, nor even a destination, but the voyage of a lifetime. And if there is a place our kids need to go, we hope to have equipped them with the confidence that comes with being true sailors tacking into the unknown.

Brick Three: There are "Special" Places for Learning, "Special" Times, and there is "Special" Equipment

FOR HER FIRST birthday, my older daughter Aliyah received a raft of presents, most of which were soon forgotten. One of them, however, we have saved in a box of keepsakes.

It wasn't a present at all, but the silver mylar wrapping paper in which one of the presents arrived. It was a source of virtually endless fascination. It crinkled, and uncrinkled; it reflected light unevenly like a collection of broken mirrors; it could be rolled up in a ball and then would slowly unroll itself; other things could be hidden in it, or under it, or placed on top of it. No doll, no ball, no stuffed animal could match the pleasure provided by this mylar sheet. The inventors (who I assume were as intrigued as Aliyah was) should be proud.

But we've all seen this. The one-time trip to the science museum (never again requested) turned out to be less memorable than the frogs and tadpoles that somehow turned up in the swimming pool in the backyard. The conversation in the car leads to an exploration of how leaves know when it is time to change color, and how they do so. Reading from a book is much less intriguing than the signs in the supermarket, or on the highway, or on the video case, or the back of the cereal box. The math problems in the workbook pale in comparison to figuring out the proportion of ingredients needed to bake a cake, or computing gas mileage (if you happen to have a car that doesn't do it for you).

This is the curriculum of childhood. Opportunities everywhere meet up with the truth of our inner development. And once they do, it really doesn't matter a whole lot in the global scheme of things whether these opportunities are pursued to a higher level with the aid of books, workbooks, prepared curricula, or just in the course of daily living. And the "special places," "special times," and "special equipment" are determined by the child as her curiosity is unleashed.

Let's recognize that while modern schools as we know them were first developed as a tool for preparing the vast majority of children for a life in burgeoning, highly regimented, industrial enterprises (and to ensure that we wouldn't rebel against them), for many children, schools – strange as it may seem – were an enriched environment of sorts. Indeed, the legacies of Montessori and Steiner (Waldorf Schools), and the largely unfulfilled hopes of progressive educators like John Dewey, were to provide openings into a larger world to which many children would never otherwise have had access. But this is no longer the case, provided (a big "if") a child has the support of her family (and tacit support of a larger community) to grow into the wider world that awaits her, even as school environments have become ever more narrowly focused, having been taken over by the standardistas and testocrats. [8]

When I look back over the time I spent in the box and reflect as well on the experience of my friends' children who are in school, I am struck perhaps most of all by the people we *didn't* meet. We didn't meet the street-musician, and hence begin a lifelong love affair with the violin or ukulele. We didn't meet the judge who might have energized our interest in the Bill of Rights. We didn't meet the neighbor who *really* knew how to bake a cake. We didn't meet the wildlife ecologist at the park who could have taught us how to channel our interest in animals. We didn't meet poets, philosophers, investment bankers, wedding planners, welders, home-brewers of beer, accountants, composers, owners of small presses, game developers (there weren't any when I was growing up), sportscasters, videographers, cabdrivers, or comedians. They were all around us, of course, but we were *in school*. Occasionally, a few might show up for "career day," or there might be a "field

---

[8]   Let it be known that I spent a good part of my professional career in the public health end of the alcohol and drug treatment field. There are at least 10-12% of families so affected by substance abuse where the kids are likely better off in school, and I hypothesize that there are at least another 10% of parents who actively dislike children, where the kids are also likely better off in school. Some 24% of American children are growing up in poverty, with many experiencing hunger on a daily basis. It's a choice between frying pan and fire. Please don't read this as an argument for schools as we know them; if anything, it is plea for greater early childhood support for families *outside* of the school environment, and for greater societal value to be accorded to children.

At this point, the expected thing is for me is to say I have the "utmost respect" for schoolteachers. Well, I don't. I have known my share of really dedicated ones, and I bow to them. I know others who think they are doing the best they can in mostly providing surrogate care for children while their parents are out making others rich, and rolling over and playing dead as the corporate steamrollers flatten them and their charges. Still others are just collecting a paycheck. It is extraordinary how little resistance there has been in the past two decades from the teaching "profession" as a whole to the corporate gangsters as they are mowed down. Maybe they have indeed become so flattened to the pavement that they are unable to turn their heads and look around.

trip.." But on the whole, it seemed like there was a conspiracy to keep us away from the adult world. And now, the way our society organizes so-called "extracurricular" activities, the conspiracy extends into the "non-school hours" as well.

In the organizing of "special places," "special equipment," and "special times" for learning, how much learning is in reality being denied?

Brick Four: There is Someone Who is More Expert When It Comes to Your Children Than You Are

"PAY NO ATTENTION to that man behind the curtain. The Great Oz has spoken."

I am a great believer in science. Essentially, it is a form of religion, the core dogma being that, over time, we can learn from our mistakes, provided of course they don't kill us along the way. The heart of the scientific method is scientific error. We observe, we hypothesize (and it isn't really a hypothesis – or science — unless it is falsifiable – that is, there is a way to prove it untrue), we test, we form conclusions, and we move on.

Progress in science by its very nature is, generally speaking, slow. The really big ideas – those of Copernicus, Galileo, Newton, Darwin, Einstein, and their ilk – take a long time to test, and scientific consensus takes a protracted time to develop and, often, even longer to change. And it is worth reminding ourselves that science does *not* advance primarily through the addition and accumulation of facts, but by replacement. The scientist becomes discomforted by the reality that the data no longer fit the prevailing theory, and so casts about for a better explanation to displace the earlier one which, in the give-and-take among scientists, is (and often not without great struggle) discarded.

"Education" – the "management" of learning and the management of child rearing – however, is way down the scientific food chain. And so, lacking clear scientific backing, but often reflecting or responding to institutional pressures and demands, there are constant efforts to browbeat the general public into submission.

The following is advice taken from an *Instructions to Mothers* brochure provided to new mothers by the Research Hospital of Kansas City in 1949:

> *"Don't listen to careless advice of friends and relatives. Do as your physician advises. He knows more about you and your baby than they do."*

Contained in the pamphlet is advice to awaken the baby for regular feedings, including in the middle of the night; handle the infant as little as possible; don't pick up the baby to show to relatives and friends; don't pick up the baby when it cries, as normal infants cry some every day to obtain exercise, and infants are quickly spoiled by handling; and the baby should never sleep with you or any other person.[9]

Now if you are graybeard (or at least gray mustache) like me, and kept track of child rearing advice, you've seen it turn from that provided above, to Dr. Spock (advising mothers that "you know more than you think you do," but insisting, without a shred of scientific evidence to back him up, that babies should not sleep on their backs, to attachment parenting, with hundreds of variations along the way.

It has been even worse in the education arena, with scores of national commissions, blue-ribbon panels, and schools of education churning out thousands of Ed. Ds, almost all of them built around notions of how children might or might not "perform" better in schools, or be better "managed" (and, in a tradition dating back to the early days of industrialized education, how teachers might be best managed as well). Very, very few studies exist regarding how the kids might have done if offered opportunities outside of schools or instead of schools, and all of them assume without question (and without any science behind the notion whatsoever) that separation from parents as soon as possible is the best way forward. The psychologists, psychiatrists, and pharmaceutical companies seem to have jumped on for the ride.

None of them know *your* kids. It is my firm belief that nature has equipped almost every parent with virtually everything we need to know about our children, and provided most of our children with the means to communicate their needs and desires, if we just learn to listen well enough. A little extra knowledge can sometimes be a good thing, and, as we know, sometimes dangerous as well. We can learn from the scientists (very little from the child managers, in my experience), from our families, and from other parents. We can also learn from other cultures and societies which, when it comes to children, perhaps have taken a less destructive turn if for no other reason than that they seem to value children more highly, and are less likely to view children as something other than, as Barbara Kingsolver notes, "a sort of toxic-waste product: a necessary evil, maybe, but if it's not our own we don't want to see it or hear it or, God help us, smell it." [10]

You are an expert in your own children – you know them better than anyone else. Throw out the rules and guidance (including mine) when they don't fit with your experience, give your kids a home of safety and security from which they can go out and explore the world, and I can almost guarantee that people will be flocking to *you* for advice.

---

[9]   Cited in Rogoff, Barbara, *The Cultural Nature of Human Development.* Oxford, UK: Oxford University Press, 2003.
[10]   Kingsolver, Barbara. *High Tide in Tucson.* New York, NY: HarperCollins, 1995.

Brick Five: If You Don't Learn Things on Time and On Schedule, It Doesn't Count (or Worse!)

AS I REMEMBER, it worked something like this: On Monday, the teacher taught the math lesson. I may already have known what she was teaching, but no matter. On Tuesday, I was sick, or the teacher was sick. On Wednesday, we had assembly. On Thursday, we reviewed the lesson. On Friday, we had a quiz. Usually, I did just fine. Not so for many of my classmates. Maybe they weren't listening. Maybe there was a mini-crisis at home. Maybe they had a bellyache, or hadn't eaten breakfast (or dinner the night before, and were perpetually hungry). Maybe they were just plain bored. No matter. The quiz would come back with a bunch of little red x's, and small cuts to their self-esteem. Never mind that they might have done just fine on the following Tuesday, or Friday, or next week, or the next month; it was time to move on. If they knew it on the following Tuesday, it didn't count. There was to be no forgiveness. Repeat this exercise hundreds of times over 12 years and, for many, it was (and is) death by a thousand cuts. For some, it was a miracle to escape with some modicum of self-respect intact.

This was the smallest of the small tracks. In fact, there were larger ones. Every year, the man behind the curtain placed us on the starting line, supposedly beginning the race equal, on the same spot, bits in our mouths, ready to charge. Of course, we all know in retrospect that this is untrue. But the education schedule (not the learning schedule, because no one knows in advance exactly what we would learn) was set by the education managers and teachers *without them having met even a single one of us*. And if we didn't "keep up" (keep up with what?) or we "fell behind" (fell behind what?), we had only ourselves to blame (when did blame make its way onto the track?), though it soon became fashionable to indict parents, television, rock 'n' roll music, a culture of permissiveness, (on rare occasions, poverty and hunger), sex, drugs, video games, cell phones, and now the teachers themselves. The recent craze for standardized testing, with teachers voluntarily or involuntarily called upon to cheat, has only added another set of tracks, only now with entire schools, and school systems, condemned, with, as of this writing, 82% of American public schools to be declared failures by the federal government. Whose idea was it precisely to pair "blame" with "education," and to do so incessantly?

The Derby metaphor impacts homeschoolers as well, with lists made of what each child needs to know at each grade level. Of course, no one really can say *why* she needs to know this or that in third grade rather than fifth (as I remember, Egyptians in third (only dead white ones; were there any live ones?), Eskimos in fourth (no Aleuts need apply), and Central and South American Indians in fifth – who made up this schedule and on what scientific principle was it based, exactly?[11]); why algebra should be introduced in the

---

11   For decades I've wondered what principle of scientific educational management had them choose these, and in that precise order? The best I can figure out is that, given that my school was a real melting pot (New York City), this would ensure none

eighth grade rather than when a child is age 4-7 (you'll read more from me on that score later); or why there should even *be* grade levels other than for administrative efficiency, and to ensure enough of our children fail so that they will be satisfied with, indeed thankful for, a job at Wal-Mart.

So what do we know? Well, we think we know that it is easier to learn a second language well if one begins before the age of five. And if one learns a second language then, a third or a fourth (or a fifth or sixth) becomes very much easier. Ask my friends in India. Meanwhile, I took up learning Tamil (a language of South India) at the age of 61, complete with its 247-letter alphabet. I think I'm doing just fine – there are no tests, except my ability to engage in a decent conversation (I'm not there yet). We also know that, generally speaking, learning is not linear; it happens in fits and starts, rather like children's growth in height or shoe size.

Step off the racetrack. Smell the flowers on the infield, and then go galloping off on side excursions that will turn out to be ever-more interesting. You and your child have *plenty of time*. And, more often than not, you will find out that the side excursion leads to the real destination, and that, on one or more of these excursions, your children will meet up with themselves.

of us had ever met any of these folks (especially true for the dead white ones), and so the teachers were safe from any firsthand contradiction, or complaints from parents. And hence the teachers wouldn't really have to know very much (I've often wondered whether my third grade teacher actually knew that Egypt was in Africa), would they? But if you don't like that explanation, why not ask any schoolteachers you know and see if they have a better one?

Brick Six: There are Such Creatures as Average Children

TO A HAMMER, everything is a nail. To a statistician, everything is a bean.

It's time for one of my own little side excursions, if you'll grant me leave and a little patience. One of the most important figures of the 19th Century may have been Charles Darwin, but few people recognize the impact on our lives of his cousin Francis Galton. It is said of him that he was a true genius and polymath: anthropologist, tropical explorer, travel writer, geographer, inventor, meteorologist, and, for purposes that I will be addressing here, statistician, psychometrician, and eugenicist. He may also have lived most of his live on the verge of insanity, and we know he experienced at least two nervous breakdowns. He spoke of the link between genius and madness, to wit, "Men who leave their mark on the world are very often those who, being gifted and full of nervous power, are at the same time haunted and driven by a dominant idea, and are therefore within a measurable distance of insanity." As a civilization, we would have done well to have heeded his words.

Galton was obsessed with two grand ideas: the need to measure absolutely everything, and the inheritance of human mental characteristics. In statistics, he is responsible for the terms *correlation, regression toward the mean,* and the popularization of *normal distribution* and *standard deviation.* To simplify to the point of being simplistic, he proposed that normal random variables would distribute themselves statistically along what we have come to call a "bell curve.." And he invented a bean machine, called a *quincunx,* to demonstrate normal distribution (creating a bell curve). You should look that one up (it makes a great Scrabble word, and can net you as many as 108 points if you manage to place it on the Triple Word Score). This set of ideas is usually considered the most significant breakthrough in statistics in the 19th Century.

Why should we care? Well, Galton decided to apply his statistical paradigms to human characteristics. For example, it seemed to him logical (and borne out by limited data) that height would fall along this normal distribution. (He'd never met a particular population where a certain segment or caste had been subject to poor nutrition for several generations – hence stunting their growth – which would have resulted in a large bulge on the lower end of the curve). He next decided to apply this principle to human intelligence. But since human intelligence remained undefined, and no test for it yet existed, Galton and his intellectual descendants for the next 100 years have been devising tests whereby "intelligence" (a single, unitary characteristic) in a human population would fall along a bell curve. That the curve and distributions were unstable over time was just one of those little nasty inconveniences that either had to be explained away or, failing that, the tests needed to be *improved.*

The intellectual debates have been hot and heavy since then, but I think it worth returning to an examination of the initial idea. No evidence whatsoever independent of the tools themselves constructed to show a normal distribution of human intelligence exists anywhere to indicate human intelligence falls along a bell curve. It is an entirely theoretical construct, subject to what is called *reification* (also known as the fallacy of misplaced concreteness), whereby an abstraction or hypothetical design is treated as if it were a concrete, real event, or physical entity. In other words, it is the error of treating as a "real thing" something which is not a real thing at all, but merely an idea.

It has had deadly consequences. Following on the heels of his cousin's work, Galton put forward the notion that intelligence is hereditary, follows a normal distribution, that there is a racial and social class intelligence hierarchy, and that, while human intelligence as a whole could not be enhanced through environmental changes, it could be improved through selective breeding. He suggested that the Chinese be encouraged to immigrate to Africa because of their racial superiority; he encouraged eugenic marriages – early marriages among people of "high breeding" to improve the race, with incentives to increase the number of their children (an idea that dates back as far as Plato's *Republic*). Those not gifted with the required intelligence would be expected to repress their urge to procreate, or be considered 'enemies of the State'. Schools would take on the role of collecting and regularly updating eugenic information on the 'stock' of the nation. It wasn't long before others, especially in the United States, would expand upon this idea and take it in a more sinister direction: not only would the breeding among the inferior masses (read: people of non-northern European descent), as determined by their scores on intelligence tests, be discouraged; their access to better and/or higher education would be blocked as well. This became a key idea in the development of American education and social policy, with its vestiges still existing to this day[12], and it took an even deadlier turn in Germany.[13] [To those who think teaching sex education in schools is a new development, the teaching of racial and sexual hygiene (preventing the "lesser" among us from breeding with those of better quality) was a regular and required part of the public school curriculum in many states through much of the early and mid-20th Century.]

Why should you care? Simply this: the reality is that *there are no average children* independent of efforts to standardize them and rank them on the school

---

[12]   Steven Selden's *Inheriting Shame: The Story of Eugenics and Racism in America* (New York, NY: Teachers College Press, 1999) is an excellent introduction to the issues raised here. For a much fuller examination of this entire idea, written in a delightful style, though not without controversy, read Stephen J. Gould's masterwork, *The Mismeasure of Man* (Revised and Expanded Edition), New York, NY: W. W. Norton, 1996. I will suggest an alternative framework for beginning to think about intelligence later in this book, in "The Curriculum of Abundance", where you will see this and the following reference again.

[13]   For a harrowing account of how racial purification laws in Germany leading up to the Holocaust relied upon the leadership of the American eugenics movement, often with the backing of America's foremost educators, see Edwin Black's *War Against the Weak: Eugenics and America's Campaign to Create a Master Race*. New York, NY: Dialog Press, 2008.

assembly line. This should be obvious enough when one observes that children develop at variable rates, that their environments differ, and that different cultural expectations and practices produce different results.

Nowhere does this become more apparent that when one takes an extensive cross-cultural perspective. We think children lack 'developmental readiness' to handle knives or fire safely by themselves? Among the Efe in the Congo, infants routinely use machetes safely; in New Guinea, children handle knives and fire with care by the time they can walk. In Central Africa, children ages 3-4 can cook their own meals over an open fire. In Oceania, children begin to take responsibility for caring for other children, tending their own garden plots, and taking their produce to market to sell (and handling all cash transactions) by age four. In West Africa, children from ages 20 months to age six travel in packs, the older ones feeding the younger ones and caring for them, with no adults involved. We even find differences within highly developed societies in schools. In India, as already noted, many parents assume that children are prepared to learn three (or more) languages by age five.

So which children are "average" – those who can't be left alone under penalty of law before the age of 14 (England), or 3-4 year olds who feed and care for four-month-olds without adult supervision? (Polynesia)?[14]

Children's performance (and maybe even what we like to call their development) depends in large measure on circumstances that are routine in their family and the cultural practices surrounding them. Children can develop skills because they want to be like older siblings, but only in cultures where they spend significant time with older siblings, which is unlikely to happen much in cultures with compulsory school attendance. In cultures where young teens play an important role in the community, teen angst is virtually unknown. And there are powerful variations in children's lives when they spend most of their time witnessing adult activities.

All this is by way of saying again that there are no such creatures as average children. They all have their own internal development trajectory, particular proclivities develop at different rates, and all of this is mediated by family and community practices and cultural environments. Once you've removed your children (and, mentally, yourselves) from the school conveyer belt, you don't have to compare anymore. You've stepped off the bell curve, out of the world of the neo-Galtonian bean counters, and entered a world which is much wider and more exciting! Once you have banished the ghost of the average child, you will have made it easier to see your own child's individual genius, and can then spend your energies focusing upon how best to nurture it.

---

[14]   Rogoff, Op cit.

Brick Seven: "Socialization" Only Happens in a Group of Age-Restricted Peers

THIS YEAR WE acquired a new family member: a delightful Welsh Terrier puppy named Remy. We purchased him from a 13-year-old homeschooler in Kansas who is breeding Welsh terriers to pay for her college education.[15] Since he is a terrier (easily misspelled as "terror") and thus has a strong mind of his own, we took special pains in socializing him.

So what did we do? Well, housebreaking came first, which is a matter of training him to tell us when he needs to go. Then a few simple commands: "Come, Sit, Down, Wait, Off, No! Drop It." (We are, of course, still working on those, and probably will be forever – he is, after all, a terrier, and thus while he may understand entirely, he will insist on making his own decisions). Not to chase automobiles. Then to stay off the furniture (we lessened our strictures around that once he stopped chewing – our furniture is perfectly suited for dogs). Off the kitchen table (we are still struggling to convince him that we don't approve of "Bury the Baguette"). Then we needed to acquaint him with the other pets, get him to cease jumping up every time Ugo the canary starts to sing, and teach him not to scratch at Echo the eight-year-old bunny's cage. (Echo, by the way, thinks he is a dog; Remy is not convinced). And then, when he gets his crazy puppy energy, to go outside to run it off! Digging is okay (we couldn't stop it in any case), just not in my flower garden.

Of course, that wasn't enough. We made sure he got to sniff lots of visitors, and learn not to jump up on them (at least not too much!), and to be especially careful with children (and allow them to pet him, which didn't take too much convincing). And then it was off to the dog park. He needed to learn to behave himself around other dogs, big ones and little ones. Fierce ones with loud barks. Older ones who would put him in his place. Puppies. Frisky ones. Fluffy ones and bald ones, and ones who drool. Larger ones who want to throw their weight around. Others who simply like to lie down and be climbed over. (He managed to stare down that bully of a Jack Russell, and they went gallivanting off together). He also needed to learn to respond to other owners in ensuring the dog park would be a safe place for everyone (dogs and people together). Later, we might start agility training, as Remy is a very athletic guy and loves to show off.

So we socialized him. He got to spend time around all kinds of dogs and all kinds of people because he would be spending his life around all kinds of dogs and all kinds of people. He learned some necessary rules to make our lives, and his, easier. He managed to rein in what are likely some of his natural instincts. And now he'll be a great pet and companion, and a friend to many.

Socialization of children *does happen* in a group of age-restricted peers. The question really is what kind of socialization and toward what end?

---

[15]   If you are interested in one, write me (david@skylarksings.com) and I can put you in touch.

School socialization is essentially a management strategy, a creation of the man behind the curtain, and it imparts certain ideas, habits, and values. It teaches children that they are not to participate in adult activities, and to devalue intergenerational activities. It teaches them that they should not expect to learn from children or youth older than themselves, and that they are not to engage in helping those younger than themselves (or anyone else, for that matter). It socializes them to the idea that their time is not their own, and space is not their own. It teaches them that the proper locus for cooperation is narrow and confined, though social punishment is acceptable when individuals break arbitrary rules. It teaches them to devalue empathy (see "The Tenth Intelligence," later in this book). It teaches them not to question, and they can be sure that they will only be asked questions for which the teacher already knows the answer. It socializes them to the idea that they have no learning needs above and beyond those which are dictated to them. In fact, it denies that most needs and desires (even the need to go to the bathroom when one feels the call) even exist. It teaches them to devalue their own thought processes, and to devalue difference. Most of all, it teaches them that rebellion is hopeless, resistance futile, and that, through some inscrutable process of which they are never made aware, they get what they deserve.

This is socialization taking place. Frankly, I think we do a better job with Remy. What is especially noteworthy is that this school socialization flies in the face of what we as a culture often claim to be our most deeply-held values, and ones we recognize, and even celebrate, in adults. We praise those who learn from others and make it possible for others to learn from them. We appreciate those who make good use of their own time and space and resources, who take responsibility for themselves, yet cooperate and collaborate with others. We value empathy and those who are able to express it and act upon it. We hold in high regard those who think for themselves, who question deeply and seek wisdom. We applaud those who value and celebrate diversity. We honor those who resist injustice, who work for change even in the face of overwhelming odds and often at great personal cost to themselves, and commend those who put the needs of others before their own more mundane comforts.

Maybe we admire all of these qualities because, deep down, we can sense that these qualities are a true expression of our common humanity, but that, given our own socialization, often have difficulty finding their fullest expression.

I've sometimes had this dystopian (don't go look it up if you don't have a dictionary handy: it's simply the opposite of utopian) vision of my office: all the cubicles filled by other 62-year-olds who can't get up from their chairs and desks, can see but never talk to each other, all involved in exactly the same task, and with my boss making the rounds eight hours every day, asking questions for which she already knows the answers. It's not a place I'd like to work, it's unlikely to be a place I'd learn very much, and I seriously doubt very much would really get accomplished.

But it raises an interesting question that homeschooling parents, or all parents for that matter, might want to address for themselves. If you kept your highest values for your children in the forefront of your mind, and banished the man behind the curtain, what would you really want their socialization to look like? I'm not going to short-circuit your thought process by providing you with an answer. I will have failed mightily if, by the end of this book, I haven't socialized you to think this through for yourself.

Brick Eight: What You Teach is What They Learn

THE APPLICABILITY OF research studies undertaken in schools is always limited. The studies are rarely able to account for the impacts of particular interventions as opposed to the effects of the general school environment, or, as we have already seen, they usually work within relatively narrow cultural assumptions about child and learning development. And, given the usual suspects of sponsors and funders, this should not be surprising.

Still, I gasped when I saw the headline in the August 8th, 2011 edition of *Science Daily*: "Schoolchildren Can Also Learn Complex Subject Matters on Their Own, Researchers Find."[16] My first response was a big, "Well, duh, where's the beef?" Then I looked at the grammar and syntax of the sentence. What's with the "also"? Was it assumed that everyone *except* schoolchildren could learn complex subject matter on their own?

The research undertaken by the Technical University of Munich of 1,600 eighth-grade students across Germany (sponsored by the German Ministry of Education) purports to demonstrate that schoolchildren can independently develop strategies for solving complex mathematical tasks, with weaker students proving just as capable as their stronger classmates. Weaker students did not require more guidance from teachers on the tasks, as researchers expected they should. The study thereby stressed the importance of self-directed learning.

That's fine. I like to have my own prejudices confirmed by the school people. But then I began to consider the matter more deeply. Why were some of the children considered "weaker" to begin with? What had happened in schools that they were so labeled? Did the children themselves consider themselves "weaker? And, given the demonstrated evidence that, under self-directed conditions, they performed just as well as the so-labeled stronger students, what had they *learned in school* that made them appear weaker? Had they been *taught* that they were weaker?

Almost 50 years ago, in his very first book *How Children Fail*, John Holt (a schoolteacher himself), profoundly asked what it was that children learned in school so that they failed to develop more than a tiny part of their capacity for learning. It is worth quoting him in full:

---

[16]   http://www.sciencedaily.com/releases/2011/08/110808104521.htm

"Why do they fail?

They fail because they are afraid, bored, and confused.

They are afraid, above all else, of failing, of disappointing or displeasing the many anxious adults around them, whose limitless hopes and expectations for them hang over their heads like a cloud.

They are bored because the things they are given and told to do in school are so trivial, so dull, and make such limited and narrow demands on the wide spectrum of their intelligence, capabilities, and talents.

They are confused because most of the torrent of words that pours over them in school makes little or no sense. It often flatly contradicts other things they have been told, and hardly ever has any relation to what they really know—to the rough model of reality that they carry around in their minds."[17]

There are few teachers of course who would easily accept the notion that what they teach is fear, boredom, and confusion. But *what you teach is not necessarily what they learn.*[18]

If you spend enough time around children – those who are not fearful, bored, or confused – you come to appreciate those *Eureka!* moments – when children discover letters on signs affixed to parking meters at just their height (and can begin to make them out); or there are certain sounds coming from pressing certain keys on the piano (we call them chords) that sound more harmonious than others; or that an unseen force (we later give it the name "gravity") prevents water from running uphill, no matter how hard they try to dam the downward path with sand; or, well, you fill in the blank yourself. This *Eureka!* process requires very little on our part – as noted, no special equipment, or "Discovery Time," just children who feel safe and secure and who are ready to go out and explore, and you are welcome to join them on this magical mystery tour.

You've also come to smile inwardly when a child first figures out that time, energy, and effort gets her where she really wishes to go, whether in learning a difficult gymnastics move or hitting a baseball, calculating large some sums in her head or making her own change at the store for a candy bar, or finally getting to play that violin piece that felt impossibly difficult only six months before. This is much about a child learning what habits of mind will propel her forward in the process of self-discovery.

---

[17]   Holt, John. *How Children Fail.* New York, NY: Pitman Publishing Co., 1964.

[18]   In "The Seven-Lesson Schoolteacher", John Taylor Gatto, a highly decorated New York City public schoolteacher for 26 years, came up with a list of seven lessons that are universally taught in school: confusion, class position, indifference, emotional dependency, intellectual dependency, provisional self-esteem, and that there is no place to hide. See *Dumbing Us Down: The Hidden Curriculum of Compulsory Schooling.* Philadelphia, PA: New Society Publishers, 1992. I am proud to have been both the book's editor and publisher.

So is there a role for "teaching"? The first rule, whatever you decide, is, as in medicine, "do no harm." For as we have already seen, teaching (at least as we witnessed it in school) has its own dangers attached to it. If you were to do nothing with your children (of course, that's a non-starter!) but spare them the lessons of fear, boredom, and confusion, they would already be far ahead in the game. I think you can also safely invite them onto the riotous carousel of our world, not only "prepared environments" meant for children (though I and, I hope, you have seen some very fine ones), but the places and times where adults engage in production and exchange, and find nourishment, refreshment, and meaning.

But learning, as Holt was fond of saying, is a product of the activity of learners. What we can provide them, both through modeling and explicitly, is an "apprenticeship in thinking."[19] We can share with them our many ways of knowing, and the ways through which we acquire knowledge – from other people, either directly or indirectly, through coaching or mentoring or simply watching; through books and media; from scaffolded practice and training (yes, nothing wrong with offering the workbooks or computer modules occasionally as an efficient way to go[20]); through movement or games; or meditation or prayer. When children are made aware of an array of choices in ways of knowing, in gathering information and knowledge about the world and about themselves, and develop in their ability to make good learning choices, they grow in confidence, ever-more ready to embrace a world that is theirs by birthright.

If there is one thing I learned in our homeschooling adventures, it is that listening is a radical act. I discovered that a willingness to allow a dialogue with my children to unfold, on its own timetable and in its own direction, unfettered to the highest degree possible by my own preconceptions and predilections, has great transformative power. (And let me tell you: being an opinionated, ever-so garrulous sort of guy, this was a difficult lesson for me). If you truly learn to listen to your children, and your heart, and then to act upon that which you hear, you will quickly find *your* need for teaching slip away, as you continue on your journeys together.

---

[19]   The term comes from the cognitive anthropologist Barbara Rogoff. *Apprenticeship in Thinking: Cognitive Development in Social Context*. New York, NY: Oxford University Press, 1990.
[20]   Your kids could do a lot worse than spending significant time with the Khan Academy. - http://www.khanacademy.org/. It's worth at least paying a visit.

Brick Nine: You Can Only Enjoy Things You are Good at…and You Should Only Pursue Things You are Good at

WITH SOME RELUCTANCE and a fistful of caveats (which I plan to explore), I am willing to admit the obvious: some people are "born" with particular gifts, talents, individual proclivities, capacities, gifts, genius, or, at Howard Gardner's insistence, "intelligences."[21] We talk about these qualities as being "innate," "God-given," "in their genes," "the result of past lifetimes," any and all explanations for phenomena we honestly can't explain. All of these expositions are examples of circular reasoning: we say the explanation for their particular genius lies in their genes (which we can't see), and the reason we say so is that we see their expression (that we can't explain).

I thought I saw these characteristics in my own kids, and I marveled. My younger daughter Meera began to show precocious pianistic prowess at age two, and her social skills – her capacity to charm virtually every one she meets (she never seems to get turned down for a job or opportunity once she gets an interview) – is something I'd like to bottle and sell (I'd save some for myself). The prowess my older daughter Aliyah demonstrated very early in her verbal dexterity was quite prodigious, and is something that finds expression in her young professorial career.

Even if you haven't experienced this in your children (or perhaps haven't noticed yet), it would be hard to deny the nature of the young Mozart, or the early Michelangelo, or the precociousness of any number of young mathematicians, physicists, and, on occasion, philosophers (these seem especially common in the East). Something would seem to be going on.

Still, I must admit some disinclination to looking at things this way. It was Thomas Edison who first argued that, "Genius is 1% inspiration, and 99% perspiration." Of course, this self-description might better characterize his unusual penchant for business, and his application of teamwork in research and mass production in distribution of his inventions, rather than to his inventiveness itself. But we would seem to get a similar, contemporary view from the writer Malcolm Gladwell, who argues that much of what we take for prodigiousness is a myth.[22] He suggests, for example, that it took Mozart some 10,000 hours of composing before producing anything of seriously lasting value, and that this was true of Bill Gates as well, who began at age 13 to tinker away for hours on end at the Lakewood School on an early, and then rare, connection to a large mainframe computer.

---

[21]   I've never seen any particular advantage in calling them "intelligences" other than a rhetorical one, and Professor Gardner, to his regret I'm sure, doesn't own the language.
[22]   Gladwell, Malcolm. *Outliers: The Story of Success.* New York, NY: Little, Brown & Co, 2008.

There is more going on than Gladwell's 10,000-hour rule, or so seems obvious to me. I could spend 10,000 hours at the violin, perhaps, and I'd likely end up pretty good, perhaps even very good, but I'd be no Yehudi Menuhin (or at least I don't think so). And there are other factors operating. Without Mozart's dad Leopold forcing him to spend the 10,000 hours (at ages five, six, seven), we don't end up with *The Magic Flute*. Without Bill Gates, Sr., already a multimillionaire, providing encouragement to 13-year-old Billie who attended perhaps the only private high school in 1968 with almost unlimited access to mainframe computer programming time – and without his mother happening to be good friends with the chief executive officer of IBM and having lunch together at just the right time – I might be writing this book using a different word processing program. Certainly, as Gladwell argues, culture, circumstance, timing, birth, and luck often account for much in the way of success.

Still, how does one account for that 1%? Well, there is what Gladwell calls "accumulative advantage." Gladwell reports, for example, how a disproportionate number of elite Canadian hockey players are born in the first few months of the calendar year. It turns out that youth hockey leagues determine eligibility by calendar year. So children born on January 1st play in the same league as those born on December 31st of the same year. Because children born earlier in the year are bigger and more mature than their younger competitors, they are often identified as better athletes, and develop more self-confidence, leading to extra coaching and a higher likelihood of being selected for elite hockey leagues. The aforementioned James Flynn argues that something similar to this effect often can be seen in twin studies purporting to demonstrate that characteristics are inherited. He gives the example of twins, separated at birth, both of whom become basketball players. Growing up in very different home environments but in a basketball-loving state, both are singled out for special attention by physical education teachers and, later, coaches because they are somewhat taller than average. Their genetic inheritance promotes specific environmental advantages being offered to them, and results in "accumulative advantage."

But what about the rest of us? Do we really learn much about ourselves and our own children by studying the "outliers"? Perhaps, but the truth may be more surprising than what we learn from studying the young Mozart.

I believe that a good metaphor for thinking about people (children and adults alike) is to envision ourselves as being born with a coiled inner spring. It is very tightly wound at birth, taut with potential energy, unwinding with greatest force in our early years, but continuing to uncoil throughout our lives. The energy from the coiled spring also rearranges and energizes the environment around it, paradoxically most notably when infants are supposedly most helpless. (We treat them like kings and queens, and they can be quite despotic! It is fortunate that their wants are few, or at least relatively easily satisfied). The child (as is true of adults as well) not only adapts to the world around her, but is an agent in the world's constructive architecture. But as we grow and change, the truth of our inner development means that we are prepared to take on certain challenges at specific times in our lives, and at other times, we just aren't there.

Often when children and adults learn (as opposed to simply being "trained"), I have found there is a shock of recognition, as if what is being learned was already known, but simply waiting to make its appearance. I expect you have had this experience as well, and witnessed it in your children if you've watched closely enough. Freed from expectations of exactly when reading is supposed to happen, reading "happens" (you'll find much more on this subject later in the book), mathematical logic impossible one month is almost second nature the next, art skills such as drawing with perspective totally absent at one point become the most obvious thing in the world at another.

What often occurs, however, is that because of outside expectations placed upon us, we become frozen in our estimation of ourselves. We believe we are "poor in math" and this is our destiny because, sometime when we were seven, it is was drummed into us that we were poor in math, and there would be no way to recover from this deficiency, which we were likely "born with." Or we are "dyslexic" (I believe there is such a phenomenon, but it is also extraordinary to me how many cases of what is often thought to be dyslexia disappear if a child is not forced to read before age nine or so, or scapegoated or stereotyped if not yet able.[23] [24]). We are told we are not musical, poor with languages, can't draw, or are sports-challenged. And we (and our children, if we are not careful) incorporate all of this unconstructive talk into our self-concept, until we come to believe it, and to live it. Sometimes, and for reasons unfathomable to us at the time, we may find ourselves situated in a caste position which subsequently (as I write about in "The Tenth Intelligence," later in this book) we find very difficult to escape.

Are there "natural" differences in abilities, proclivities, and gifts among our children (and among adults)? "Yes, but…" I reply, and with the possible exceptions of the outliers, these are perhaps not as great as we are indoctrinated to presuppose. The child who has difficulty with subtraction at seven years two months old is not "bad at math;" she simply had difficulty

---

[23]   In the world of schools, Finland is often thought to be on top of the heap. What is noteworthy about Finland is that no formal instruction begins before age 7. None in pre-preschool, pre-school, kindergarten, or first grade. Finland, no surprise to me, has the lowest number of classroom hours in the developed world, and children often go off skiing by themselves during school hours. Perhaps the main reason for their school success story is that neither students nor teachers wear shoes. See http://news.bbc.co.uk/2/hi/8605791.stm

[24]   There is an excellent new resource on dyslexia by Brock Eide and Fernette Eide, *The Dyslexic Advantage: Unlocking the Hidden Potential of the Dyslexic Brain.* New York, NY: Hudson Street Press, 2011. What is especially exciting about this book is that it is not the usual stuff about how to help a dyslexic child in coping with her a school-defined disability, but rather how to understand and nurture the natural tendencies and gifts with which dyslexic children seem to be blessed.

with subtraction when seven years two months old. If the truth of our inner development meets up with the right opportunities for action, at the right time and in the right form, in my experience, we find out that we are usually competent, at the very least, in just about everything, and perhaps "gifted" at far more than we could have imagined. In my own life, it was drummed into me that I was poor at languages – I now know that was untrue. And that I have atrocious handwriting (still true in English, but you should hear the compliments I get on my written Tamil). As I've already informed the kids, they are going to inherit the paintings I am yet to execute. And I can tell you all about mathematicians who were told, repeatedly, that they were poor at arithmetic.

Why should this matter? Simply this: 1) Great enjoyment can sometimes be found in activities at which we may not be, objectively, very good at the time, and 2) Within these activities, our children may eventually find their true gifts and passions. I know painters whose work I think is abominable who find great emotional relief in their work (and sometimes their work ends up selling for millions, so go figure); I know amateur singers who find release in voice lessons knowing that their singing is not likely to ever emerge from their own living rooms. And sometimes, the seeming "deficit" in "natural" talent, intelligence, or genius is "overcome" when a child decides to put in the time, energy, and effort to where she wants to go.

And sometimes it will lead them in different directions. My older daughter Aliyah, a better-than-mediocre singer and pretty decent violinist (I'm far, far worse!), and poor pianist and oboist, became a decorated composer. My younger daughter Meera ended up hating the constrictive group nature of pre-ballet, and found her place as a highly competitive gymnast. For both of them, the discipline required in their chosen activities has carried over into other significant areas of their adult life. Meanwhile, they had fun and pursued their chosen activities with passion and persistence, and are the better for having done so.

The flip side is that I know many people who have ended up in careers that they would not have "freely" chosen for themselves. I can't tell you how many people I have known in science– and math-related pursuits now in their forties and fifties who tell me that now they wished they had become psychologists, or social workers, or photographers, or dancers, or whatever. They had always been told they were "good" at math and science, and hence encouraged to do more math and science, and then were rewarded for doing more math and science, etc., all shades of 'accumulative advantage'. Now there is nothing unexpected in the fact that many people experience "mid-life crises." But what I do find striking is that many of those individuals knew they were on the wrong track even as teenagers, but just hadn't mustered up the self-confidence to assert themselves. When I ask why they don't change now, underneath the myriad of reasons, rationalizations, justifications, and pretexts I have heard, what seems to underlie all of them is fear (one of Holt's three great lessons of school, where the "limitless hopes and expectations" of others, now internalized as part of the inner school, "hang over their heads like a cloud."). The 'accumulative advantage' has turned on itself.

The challenges of our time are filled with complexity, and the people who will be able to navigate this world well are those who can embrace multiple challenges with passion and who are open to the myriad of possibilities that will present themselves on this wild, wonderful planet. If you learn to work hard at things you love when you are young, and to find pleasure in the results, chances are you will have a carved a psychic pathway for happiness as an adult, even as new challenges present themselves.

Brick Ten: Learning Happens by Moving Data

> *In the pursuit of learning, every day is something new acquired.*
> *In the pursuit of Truth, every day something is dropped.*
> - *Lao-Tzu*

AS ALREADY NOTED, I'm getting on in age. I am old enough to remember those heady days of the late 1950s and early 1960s when it was thought (by some, at any rate) that television was going to revolutionize education. Educational broadcasting was going to take over the airwaves. We were all going to have almost instant access to the world around us. We would learn cutting-edge science, and history would no longer be dull. In my New York City classrooms, we watched space launches in real-time, and many of us – the 'Sputnik babies' (those with IQ scores over 90) – knew that we would grow up to be nuclear physicists and build magic weapons that would defeat the evil Russians who, by some fluke that was never even remotely explained to us, had gotten to space first.

The television educational revolution didn't happen, as we all know. Yes, there was *Sesame Street* and some really nice nature programming from National Geographic, and endless documentaries about World War II. More common were the television programs that came to express and represent the culture's *zeitgeist* – *The Beverly Hillbillies, Green Acres, Hee-Haw,* and *Dallas.* And when an abortive attempt was made to bring TV into the daily classroom, a full eight of the 15 minutes was taken up with commercials. Soon that was gone as well. If you go to the History Channel on cable these days, you'll find much of it taken up with cooking or tales of aliens or *Pawn Stars,* and the Nature Channel with alligator wrestling.

But that's all about content. What I remember thinking, some 50 years ago, was how similar my classroom experience was to watching television. In fact, if I could put a rectangular border around the teacher's head, it wouldn't have been that different at all (and I imagined doing just that, complete with a 'pan out' feature for the blackboard). My teachers transmitted data packages. Where they got these data, I had no idea, and no one went out of the way to tell us. That the data were correct was something I was trained to assume and never question. Why these data were important I was never informed. Why I needed to receive this particular data package now was a question beyond asking. Who paid my teachers to transmit these data was a complete mystery. (In fact, school itself was a big mystery). But the idea seemed to be that if they could keep my eyeballs screwed to the teacher's head, mouth, and lips, and occasionally the blackboard ("David! Eyes front!"), the data would flow, as if through a pipe, from her cranium to mine, and somehow I would be the better for it. I would then be tested, which would measure the efficacy of the data transfer. In my day, it was thought that what was to be assessed this way was the receiver. Now, with our belief that we have become more sophisticated, it is thought that by testing the receiver we can also assess the effectiveness of the transmitter, and perhaps that of the pipe as well.

The data pipe analogy breaks down with even the slightest acquaintance of how brains work. Every time we take in new information, and change our knowledge of the world, the entire thinking brain has to be reorganized, old beliefs and 'misinformation' discarded (written over? taken to the dump? metaphors fail), neural pathways restructured, and new connections forged. What I wrote about science earlier equally applies to our 'little scientists,' our children. Learning doesn't advance primarily by the addition and accumulation of facts, but by wrestling with new "theories" of how the world works that help us make sense of the data, so we can throw the old theories out.

Teaching may be the activity of teachers, but learning, as already noted, is a product of the activity of learners. Perhaps it is worth pondering the possibility that we can't actually teach anyone else anything. What we can do is provide environments conducive to learning, we can ensure ready access to information, we can model our own thinking and our methods of inquiry in guided participation, and we can afford opportunities for people to put their learning to use. Whether and what is learned is up to the learner.

Learning does of course happen through TV. Much of it can be attributed to the fact that the viewer is empowered so that she can choose when to watch and what to watch (and may be equipped with a paper or electronic program guide), can change the channel, and turn the box off at will. I imagine there are millions of students across the nation who would love to be equipped with a clicker (and, I would suggest, without sarcasm, they might actually learn more as a result).

Brick Eleven: Learning is for the Kids

SO YOU ALWAYS wanted to learn to play the piano when you were a child. But you never quite managed it. Your family was too poor to afford the lessons, or there was no room in the house for a piano. Or your father insisted you play the clarinet so you could be in the marching band, or your uncle had an old accordion sitting around the house that he no longer played. Or your mother insisted that any time you might have to spend practicing would take away from your homework.

Well, let me make a suggestion. Before offering piano lessons to your son or daughter (unless they've asked), take lessons yourself. Put aside a little money, establish a place for the piano in the house, hunt down a teacher that you like and will work with an adult learner, find some music that you'd like to eventually be able to play, and make some time to practice daily. Curse (or at least complain loudly) when you hit a clunker, and keep going.

Outside of keeping your child out of the box, it may be just about the best thing you ever do in helping her along her own learning path. It will be terrific if at some point she wants to learn to play as well, and then you'll have a 'two-fer'. But don't count on it, and don't believe that would be the only way (or even the most important way) your joint learning venture will be successful. In fact, it *will* be a 'two-fer' anyway, just in a different fashion than you initially imagined.

In other times, places, and cultures, children from a very early age get to spend time observing and participating in adult activities in their families and communities. They would have living examples in front of them of how adults (or slightly older peers) approach problems, what methods or ways they use to gather necessary information, how they consult with and collaborate with others, how they deal with errors or mistakes along the way, what thought processes are engaged to find solutions, and how they would incorporate their learning for the next time around. The children would of course gain specific skills as they became older, but far more important would be the aforementioned "apprenticeship in thinking" that would be a regular part of their growing up – and, past that, an understanding of how the world, and the people in it, tick. (Warning: You're not going to find that in any pre-packaged curriculum).

Contrast that with the experience of contemporary schooling. Now I went to what were supposedly "good" schools. I never experienced a teacher learning anything. I'm sure that at least some of them were, but what it was they learned was entirely opaque to me. We had no idea how or where they received the information they thought so important to impart to us, how or where they learned it, or how they ascertained that what they were teaching us was, in fact, true. And we were well-trained to believe that everything they taught us was true because of the simple fact that it came from them. So much for preparation for life in a democratic society.

My teachers were mostly nice people (okay, there were a few ogres, but that's true in every profession, though it's a little bit suspect when they choose to work with children). I'm sure some of them were learning or engaged in otherwise interesting stuff in other parts of their lives, but we were never privy to them (with the exception of one bizarre 10th grade homeroom teacher who was writing a semi-pornographic musical based on Henry Fielding's risqué novel *Shamela*, which he'd share with us every morning[25]).

---

[25] Bless him! He was a music teacher mostly by default, I think, and he was known to walk into class, take attendance, and then sit down at the piano and play jazz for 55

And I didn't know how or what they thought, either. Did the biology teacher actually believe in evolution, and how did she really feel about the thousands of frogs she had killed? Did the English teacher who forced us to "discuss" the themes of *Silas Marner* actually love literature, even as she ruined it for the rest of us? Why was the chemistry teacher teaching us rather than working as a chemist? (And what work did a chemist do anyway? I was an "A" student in chemistry, and I don't remember having any notion). Had the Russian teacher (whom I remember liking, for what that's worth) ever gone to Russia and, if so, what did he think of it?[26]

Don't recapitulate the school experience. Learning is so much more than that. For the few years you have together with your children, turn your household into a learning community. Name your family learning community, and paint a sign and nail it on the house next to the front door. (We did, as you'll read later). Come up with a learning family motto, maybe even a song or a jingle. Set aside time each week for the whole family to share what they learned in the previous week, what was easy and what was difficult, and maybe make a notebook listing each member's most "perfect mistakes." Review it once a year so that each of you – children and adults – can see how much you've grown. Share what you know, what you don't know, and how you feel about both your knowledge and your own knowledge quest. *You* are homeschooling!

And celebrate. You get to redo your education right this time. Your kids have gifted you with a second chance.

Play that new piece you've just learned on the piano.

Brick Twelve: Learning is All About Individuals (That is, the Learning to Be Gained by an Individual Trumps Community Intelligence).

I HAVE A sense that, while as individuals we are often thought to be getting smarter and smarter (though, as noted at the beginning of this essay, even that must now be called into question), as communities we are getting dumber and dumber. It is true that we've gotten very good at building roads and bridges (though not so great at caring for them), building out the water and electrical grid, and equipping neighborhoods with cable, the Internet, and in erecting cell towers. We are wonderful when it comes to asphalt. But my general perception is that we've gotten less good at caring for one another. We are less likely to welcome the neighbors' kids into our living room, to lend out equipment or to ask for a cup of sugar, or to even know who our neighbors

---

minutes until the bell rang, without saying a word. In his later years, it is said he could do this for weeks at a time. Apparently, and unbeknownst to me then, he had played with many of the jazz greats of the 1950s.

[26]   In hindsight, I think the Russian teacher was actually a Communist, and most definitely would never have said.

are. It seems the moats around our castles (and our personal lives) have become deeper, and we change castles more often.

I am not about to wax eloquent about some Golden Age that existed in the days of Ozzie and Harriet. Each age has its own challenges, and usually its own mythologies attached to it. But my impression (which I am sure you've already picked up) is that the invasion of school mythology into so many aspects of our lives has disabled us and our communities. It has made us less flexible, less empathetic, less capable of pulling together in anything but the most formal of settings, in short, simply less intelligent. In our dogged pursuit of individual "excellence" and our insistence on a single standard for it whereby we are all expected to cultivate the same capacities at the same time, we have marginalized entire groups of people: children (who are not supposed to be seen outside of school, and what are they are doing outside after school when they should be doing homework?), the aged, the unemployed (who are most definitely supposed to remain silent), people who work with their hands or their backs or their as-yet-to-be-fully-realized artistic imaginations, those who stay home with their children, the infirm and the disabled (and those without substantial education who care for them) are far removed from our community dialogue (and often from our democratic processes as well).

The list could likely be longer, but the point being that we have been trained that the best we can do, in most areas that are critical to our lives, is simply to adjust, as atomized individuals, to circumstance and, also as individuals, to simply *make do*, as we become confined to our own little worlds. Whether things are getting better or worse in this regard, I have what are more than mere suspicions (as you will see in "The Tenth Intelligence.") What is clear to me is that public education has not done us any favors in developing our capacities for autonomous and meaningful participation in social and community life, and hence we are all less than we could be. If a child is not given the opportunity to work out for herself what is specifically and uniquely her own, she will grow up to feel that she has little to creatively contribute to the larger, evolving order of things. And for those who have a vested interest in preventing the continuing evolution of the social order, that might exactly be the point.

Sometimes we search for explanations for phenomena like these that are rather more complicated that they really need to be. I was fortunate that, through my daughter Aliyah who at 15 was studying native botanical medicine (and we have some rather hilarious stories about her distilling and preparing them), I became acquainted with *subiyay* (aka Bruce Miller), the late spiritual leader of the Skokomish Tribe in western Washington, shortly before his death. *subiyay* worked with artists, those addicted to alcohol and other drugs, naturalists and folklorists, writers and dramatists, youth and families, the elderly, those with crippling diseases and mental health difficulties, and those in need of spiritual renewal. As part of his legacy, he gave us this to ponder "Do not teach all children the same thing, or in the same way. For if you do so, they will learn that they do not need each other, and the world will split apart."[27]

Brick Thirteen: There is a Permanent Record that Will Follow You Forever

AT THE AGE of 47, my wife, Ellen, massage therapist, doula, caregiver, and homeschooling mom extraordinaire, decided to go back to school to become a hospice nurse. Early college leaver that she was, (I think of her not as a college dropout, but as someone who knew when it was time to move on to a fuller life education), she discovered that the local program she was applying to was going to require her high school *transcript*. (To be scrupulously honest, I should also note that, in lieu of said transcript, she could have taken the GED, the thought of which quite amused the both of us).

Now this was going to be interesting. It wasn't so much that she'd gone to a private, Episcopalian "alternative" high school in Maryland where they wrote "meaningful course evaluations," or that she spent a good part of one year hanging out in a public park (to be fair, it was *real* science and she spent some time in dialogue with representatives of the U.S. Geologic Survey), or that she graduated a year "early" (why was it "early" if she met all the requirements?), and spent the next year hitchhiking around Europe.

The problem was that the school no longer existed, and hadn't for almost 40 years. Contact with the Episcopal Diocese was a dead end. However, after a couple of weeks of searching, she found an individual in the Maryland Department of Education who was able to direct her to what was essentially the "State Office of Defunct Private Schools." She sent off her $25 and a form stating what she was looking for. And three weeks later, back it came, a true artifact of history.

Of course, we both marveled over the fact that the transcript existed at all, even if the school didn't. But more than that, I have repeatedly tried to imagine what it must be like to be the state worker who has to spend the majority of her waking hours diving into the bowels of the filing system (or the aging microfiches and the aging microfiche readers) to come up with people's 'permanent records'. It is easy for me to imagine the job requires a masters degree in library science; it is more difficult for me to envision the high school student whose life aspirations are to become the manager of the State Office of Defunct Private Schools. Life certainly has its twists and turns.

My wife's story contrasts greatly with my own. I have enough degrees for the both of us. But in almost 40 years in the workforce, I've never had even a single employer ask for a diploma – high school, college, or graduate school – let alone a transcript. Not one. Good thing, because I don't have any of them

---

[27]   For more about *subiyay*, visit:
http://www.seattleartmuseum.org/learn/CDROM/SongStorySpeech/Content/Modu le01_TreePeople.htm

– I think they sit in a draw somewhere at my mother's home some 3,000 miles away, if they haven't been tossed out.

I suspect it is likely that most people's experience falls somewhere in-between. What I can say for certain is that the seventh grade teacher's threat that any youthful indiscretion on my part would follow me around on my permanent record forever turned out to be false, especially as it seems that for anyone to track down one's permanent record can certainly take some doing. But there is a permanent record. It is the one written on your children's minds and hearts in the course of their life journeys. It will indeed follow them forever. And that is much of what this chapter (and book) is all about.

Brick Fourteen: Your Life Outcomes Will Be Determined By How Well (or Poorly) You Do in School

NOT TO BE mean-spirited, but the school people certainly want it to be so. It gives some added meaning to their occupations, not just as educators, but as gatekeepers for the rest of the society.

But there is more to it than that. The man behind the curtain knows that this brick is one of the cornerstones of the edifice, and without it, the entire structure quickly begins to crumble. It is difficult to defend education as it is currently practiced on its own terms, so the linkage to lifetime outcomes is critical.

We need to remember how young this idea really is. George Washington and Benjamin Franklin, both of whom greatly valued learning despite (or perhaps because of) a general lack of school-based education, would have thought this particular brick an absurdity, and an affront to the democratic ethic they were trying to build. (Franklin once noted, "We are all born ignorant, but one must work hard to remain stupid.") Abe Lincoln, who spoke of his schooling as "readin, writin, and cipherin to the Rule of Three," and who was proud of studying and nearly mastering the six books of Euclidean geometry by himself once he made it to Congress, spoke of the profitable lesson to be gained in the example of Henry Clay, "It teaches that in this country, one can scarcely be so poor, but that, if he *will*, he *can* acquire sufficient education to get through the world respectably." The man behind the curtain has been working hard for more than a century to have us forget this lesson, lest he be revealed for the charlatan he is.

In October 2011, it was reported that a high school in La Palma, California, had a system for publicly identifying and treating students differently according to the scores they receive on state standardized tests. Students who performed at the highest levels in all subjects would receive a black or platinum ID card, while those who scored a mix of proficient and advanced would receive a gold card. Students who scored "basic" or below would receive a white ID card. Students with black, platinum, or gold cards were entitled to certain privileges, such as free entrance to sporting events and discounts at local businesses. Those with white ID cards got no such privileges, and had a designated line in the cafeteria, while the elite black, platinum, and gold cardholders had a different line. The majority of students at the school, needless to say, had white cards, so one can easily envision where the lines were longest. (Shouldn't the lines for the struggling students have been made the shortest, so there would be more time for tutoring?) A school administrator reportedly advised female students at an assembly to only go to dances with boys with black rather than white cards. Now if only those of the black or platinum cardholding caste could have been convinced to breed only with other similar cardholders, and we would have a Galtonian wet dream!

Putting aside our fundamental American prejudices against such a practice, the reality is that our society *does* attempt to ration resources this way, and by doing so, bend life outcomes to conform to school performance. The simplistic notion, most charitably framed, is that the student who does well in tenth grade biology is more likely to come up with the next cure for cancer than the student who doesn't, and hence should receive more privileges and have more resources thrown in his direction, not only as a reward, but as down payment on his future contributions to society, which would certainly (it is assumed) be greater than that of the "C" student.

Our collective life experiences provide us with more than enough in the way of anecdotes to question the validity behind the notion. We all know of "A' students who went on to do great things, "A" students who became convicted felons, and "A" students who became Wall Street investment bankers (some falling in each of the former two categories, though perhaps fewer actually convicted among the latter). We all know of school failures and dropouts who became drug-addicted, homeless criminals; responsible husbands, wives, fathers, and mothers who earn a decent living and care for their families; and inventors, investors, writers, and artists who have changed the way we live, think, and dream about the world.

It is evident that some of these life outcomes (as we remember from Malcolm Gladwell) are at least partially determined by culture, circumstance (social class, race, ethnicity, family wealth), timing, birth, and just plain luck. But we all share in a greater truth: while we can't tame circumstance, we know that much in our lives is shaped by inner discipline, drive, determination, perseverance, patience, creativity, authenticity, getting along with others, courage, and love (with the last two likely being the most important of all). You may not find a curriculum for many or even any of these, but I hope (and think) I can help. Keep reading!

Brick Fifteen: School Can Fix EVERYTHING, and If Things aren't Going Well, the Solution is More of It

> *Dr. David Kibner: Would you please tell me, in your opinion, what exactly is happening?*
> *Elizabeth Driscoll: People are being duplicated. And once it's happened to you, you're part of this thing. It almost happened to me!"*
> — *Invasion of the Body Snatchers (1978)*

THE INNER SCHOOL that I have been dissecting is a direct result of what could best be called "school creep." Since industrial-style public education became the norm in the United States toward the close of the 19th Century, schools have become the chosen venue for interventions in the life of our communities far beyond their more narrowly defined educational purposes. They may never have become true centers of eugenic record keeping as envisioned by Galton, but quickly became significant centers for gathering intelligence, not just about children, but for keeping tabs on parental and community characteristics, attitudes, and practices. Schools became the lynchpins for control of communicable diseases such as tuberculosis, and for a range of public health education and intervention initiatives. I have already referenced sex education, which had its original in racial and sexual hygiene programs common in the 1920s and 1930s; HIV/AIDS education began to appear in the curricula in the late 1980s. The first city to require smallpox vaccination for children entering school was Boston in 1827, the first state Massachusetts in 1855. It was the 1930s when compulsory immunization laws for other diseases as a condition of school entry became common, and it was in this period that schools began in some communities to house public health clinics. The first school nurse was hired in 1902 in New York City, an outgrowth of the tireless work of Lillian Wald among immigrant communities.

In communities both rural and urban, schools have been used variously as centers for community entertainment, adult education and employment training, teen "drop-ins," civil defense, voting, family food distribution, military recruiting, and political debates, just to name a few. The first school lunch program was launched in 1853; Harry Truman signed the National School Lunch Act into law in 1946. Such programs have often been used as dumping grounds for surplus agricultural commodities, though in some communities now, school nutrition programs and the provision of 'feeding sites for the poor' have become the order of the day.

Individually, any or all of these activities might be considered worthy (you can choose one from Column A, and one from Column B if you like). But taken together, and looking at the funding that has been poured into them over time, it is easy to recognize "school creep." As other voluntary and publicly supported social and community institutions and associations (what de Tocqueville in *Democracy in America* saw as essential to the unique fabric of American society) wither, school and "education" casts a larger and larger shadow over our cultural, social, political, and economic lives, and our minds as well.

And what about the kids themselves? Historically, the answer to social and political problems, whether it be to the "threat" posed by the new wave of immigrants around the turn of the 20th Century, or the Soviets' challenge in winning the space race, or racial and socio-economic inequality and poverty, or the test of remaining "globally economically competitive," is more school for them – longer school days, longer school years, more school years [or pre-school years, or 'pre-preschool' years, or 'school readiness' years, or maybe even "Phonics in Utero" (as you'll read about later in this book)], schools on weekends, more "afterschool" programming (to take place in school, of course), and more homework.[28] As individual interventions, they might or might not be effective (as below, I have my doubts[29]), but there can be no denying that, taken together, they aggrandize the power of schools, sometimes at the expense of the communities they purport to serve, and at the expense of children and families as well.

Currently, one often hears the assertion that school results would improve radically if we would just get rid of summer vacation, and move toward a year-round school schedule. After all, it is contended, summer time is just a period when kids – especially poor ones – simply forget what they know and fall further and further 'behind.' A lead piece of research in the arsenal for this approach was a study conducted by John Hopkins University sociologist

---

[28]   My favorite anti-homework screed comes from an 1860 edition of *Scientific American*: "A child who has been boxed up six hours in school might spend the next four hours in study, but it is impossible to develop the child's intellect in this way. The laws of nature are inexorable. By dint of great and painful labor, the child may succeed in repeating a lot of words, like a parrot, but, with the power of its brain all exhausted, it is out of the question for it to really master and comprehend its lessons. The effect of the system is to enfeeble the intellect even more than the body. We never see a little girl staggering home under a load of books, or knitting her brow over them at eight o'clock in the evening, without wondering that our citizens do not arm themselves at once with carving knives, pokers, clubs, paving stones or any weapons at hand, and chase out the managers of our common schools, as they would wild beasts that were devouring their children." The theme was taken up in a 13-year campaign of *The Ladies Home Journal* and its Pulitzer Prize-winning editor Edward Bok who, in his editorial "A National Crime at the Feet of American Parents" (1900), argued that children were "permanently crippled" by the pressure of schooling and homework. I wish there was a Fourth Amendment protection against government intrusion into the home in the form of homework.

[29]   I am reminded of advertisements for 19th Century medicinal tonics, such as "Bonnore's Electro Magnetic Bathing Fluid," which claimed to cure cholera, neuralgia, epilepsy, scarlet fever, necrosis, mercurial eruptions, paralysis, hip diseases, chronic abscesses, and "female complaints." The evidence for the efficacy of school-based interventions in curing all of our social, political, or economic ills is often not much more robust.

Karl Alexander, and published in 2001.[30] Alexander followed 650 first graders from the Baltimore City public school system, and found that, after five years, children who came from low socio-economic class backgrounds, after starting with only a small deficit, were well behind those from higher ones. But he also found that cumulative classroom learning over the five-year period was virtually the same.[31] The difference was almost entirely a result of what happened to the reading scores of the two groups during summer vacations, with those from lower socio-economic backgrounds making virtually no progress during the four summers from first to fifth grades, while those from upper socio-economic backgrounds gaining significantly.

On that basis, it is asserted that keeping the kids (especially the poor ones) in school would help bridge the gap. But look at what the data *actually* indicates. Kids from upper socio-economic backgrounds gain most *when they are not in school, not in classrooms, not forced to read or write or complete math problems, not saddled with homework, not listening to teachers.* Something else is happening in their environments *that is not school* that accelerates their learning. Imagine what their "performance" might have looked like had they not been in school the rest of the year? And as for those children from poorer socio-economic environments: since purportedly they already learn "as much" as the wealthier ones while they are in school, the question really should be what can be done, in their homes, families, and communities *outside of school and instead of school* to improve the quality of their living and learning environments? We actually know the answers to that question as well.

For two-and-a-half years, two University of Kansas professors Betty Hart and Todd Risley recorded, transcribed, and analyzed speech in the homes of young children ages nine months to three years for an hour a month. Some 42 families participated, including families living in poverty and receiving welfare, working class families, and professional families.[32] The researchers determined that the children all had the same kind of everyday language experiences. But they found that they could predict future educational outcomes, even after correcting for other phenomena such as poverty and access to enrichment activities, based solely on *linguistic frequency*, the amount of talking that occurred, and the qualities of that speech. In extrapolating

---

[30]   Alexander, K., Entwistle, D., and Olson, L. "Schools, Achievement, and Inequality: A Seasonal Perspective," *Educational Evaluation and Policy Analysis* Vol. 23 No. 2, Summer 2001. If you ever come across schoolpeople "summarizing" the results of this research, urge them to go back and read the original study. (Most of them haven't).

[31]   "Cumulative classroom learning" was defined by Alexander et. al. as that which occurred during the school year. The researchers didn't bother to actually examine whether it simply occurred in that year, or was specifically a result of activity in the classroom. They just assumed that if learning happened, school was responsible for it. To my way of thinking, this calls the entire exercise into question.

[32]   The researchers report that none of the families included in the study were dysfunctional, severely stressed, abusive, or addicted. None were independently wealthy. No persons with disabilities were present in any of the homes.

from the data, over the first four years of life, an average child in a professional family would have the accumulated experience of almost 45 million words, in a working class family about 26 million words, and in a welfare family about 13 million words. What the researchers call "non-business talk" (non-directive, *non-teaching* talk often consisting of running narratives of experience – in other words, *conversation*) accounts for almost the entire difference in learning trajectories among children. The authors emphasize that much could be done to change these trajectories, but virtually all of those changes would have to be made in families and communities, *outside of school* and having nothing to do with direct teaching, to really make a difference. [33]

The commitment to the mythology that everything can be fixed through school, it is worth noting, is only as deep as the pockets of those who will fund it. There are now four-day school weeks springing up all over the country, in more than 120 counties in 21 states as of this writing. One district superintendent, in Deuel, South Dakota, indicates that doing so not only saved money, but the "failure rate" among students has actually declined, which he attributes to more time for teacher training and one-on-one tutoring. I would wager he could make the failure rate drop even further, if he would only take what he has already learned to its logical extension. [34]

School doesn't fix everything, and, if I am correct, actually not much of anything. What it does, as an institution and as a form of thinking, is blunt our social imaginations. And that is something that, at this point in our history, and with some of our children, dear reader, likely to live into the 22th Century (!), we truly can ill afford.

> *I hear babies cry, I watch them grow*
> *They'll learn much more, than I'll ever know*
> *And I think to myself, what a wonderful world,*
>
> *Yes I think to myself, what a wonderful world.*
> *- Bob Thiele and George David Weiss*
> *"What a Wonderful World"*

THERE YOU HAVE it. I've pulverized my bricks. Fifteen of them. It has taken me a very long time – much of the past 35 years. You may have some of the same ones, and they may vary in resistance to your own sledgehammer. You might have others – write me about them! I'd love to hear from you.

---

[33] Hart, B., & Risely, T. *Meaningful Differences in the Everyday Experience of Young American Children*. Baltimore, MD: Paul H. Brookes Publishing Co., 1995.
[34] See John Taylor Gatto's essay, 'We Need Less School, Not More," in *Dumbing Us Down*. Op. cit.

So what are you going to get in the rest of this book? Well, you'll get a little learning theory and philosophy, including an opportunity and invitation to craft an educational philosophy of your own. Some fun anecdotes. A few learning tricks of the trade you can try out and see if they work for you and your family. Friendly prompts to keep you on course. Stories – I *love* to tell stories! Occasional pontificating – I've tried to keep it to a minimum. A constant reminder, originating in the thought of the French philosopher Jean Jacques Rousseau, that "liberty is the mother of virtue." And a bit of cheerleading – you really *can* do this. I promise Fun! Whether you actually learn anything or not is totally up to you.

You will see certain themes pop up again and again as you read. I have taken pains *not* to remove repetitions of them as they occur. If you are like most homeschooling parents, you may not find yourself with the luxury of an extended time period to read this book cover-to-cover, but rather dip in an essay at a time. If you see it buzzing more than once, you can be certain I have that particular bee in my bonnet.

So here are some lodestars. You may have already picked them out, but I want to restate them for emphasis. Consider them the "take home" message. That should work – you're already at home!

Love and listening and time are the keys to an education worthy of the name – If you provide your children with these, you will quickly discover that your educational adventures – regardless of the 'method' of homeschooling you adopt for your family – will become nothing short of astounding. These are the three qualities public schools are unable to provide, and yet lie at the foundation of what it means to learn with your children.

A curriculum of patience can go a long way – Once you've stepped off the school performance treadmill, there's no rush to get anywhere. You can focus on the quality of your journey together, rather than simply the number of places visited. If it was worth learning today, it will be there to be learned tomorrow. In some cases, you'll discover it wasn't a destination worth visiting in any case. Keep busy – wallpaper the entire house! Or get some of those relaxation tapes. (Now that dates me: do any of you even remember 'tapes'?) You will discover that courage, perseverance, and patience are often what make what seems impossible roll into view.

There are no such creatures as average children – so stop comparing – My goal for my own children is that they will become responsible, life-affirming adults who can order their own lives in freedom, and find meaning and purpose in the ongoing flow of their own lives and pursuits and that of their communities. If that sounds like a high-fallutin' mission statement, it is because it is. Write your own: I doubt there is any way you'll be able to shoehorn in the word 'average', or any kind of comparison. When you hear anyone trying to compare your children with others, give them your mission statement, and watch the conversation turn.

Tiredness and happiness are not opposites – I think I originally learned this lesson from my daughter Meera. We adopted her at ten months of age, and English was not her first language. But she seemed to come equipped with an "energizer Bunny" of a motor. She'd get up in the morning, would never miss a beat, and then just keep 'going, and going, and going…' Until she'd lay down in our family bed, next to me, turn over, and say, "Daddy. Happy." And then she'd be out.

I have an old friend who had a vision almost 25 years ago that she was to adopt children with special needs from around the world. At last count, she had 16 (including one 'natural' child – anyone have a better term?) from at least five countries. Luckily for her, many of them like to cook. The family is not wealthy, but cares for the kids virtually without any government assistance though with much 'hands-on' support from family and friends, and homeschooling most of them most of the time. Hubby keeps building extra rooms onto the basement.

I will occasionally see her (as you can imagine, it's quite a chore to get all the kids onto the family bus!) Once, I remember meeting up with her at a community event.

"Diane," I said, noticing the bags under her eyes, "You look tired."

"I *am* tired," she responded, without even the slightest hint of change in her attention toward the kids she had with her.

"Don't you ever sleep?" I asked.

"Oh, David," she replied, again with her attention to the kids unwavering, "I've read my Bible cover to cover maybe four, five, or six times. Nowhere did I find a commandment that says, "Thou shalt sleep." There will be plenty of time for that later."

And you thought *you* were tired?

This is not meant to belittle your very real feelings. Homeschooling *can* be tiring, sometimes even exhausting. But remember: this special time with your children isn't going to last forever, so savor it for all that it is worth. And you will be surprised at how quickly they grow and change, and you along with them.

If it helps, replace the word "tired" with "stretching."

Have fun! Learn stuff! Grow! – *It isn't just for the kids* – Okay, that's the name of a previous book of mine. And I really mean it. You shouldn't think of homeschooling as a species of self-sacrifice. On the contrary, this can and should be among the most exciting times in your life. You get to reinvent yourself, get to do things you would never have imagined yourself doing, and grow into yourself. Give the kids a kiss, and thank them for providing you with this opportunity.

Have tea and conversation – The research is pretty clear: the best thing you can do for young children (beyond providing them with love, listening and time) is to engage them in, and surround them with, conversation. You may quickly find that it applies when the kids get older as well. But don't limit them to your conversation. Surround yourselves with interesting, exciting, caring people, bring them into your home, and have tea. Don't use the possibility that your house is a mess as an excuse. We've all seen it already. And don't be shy. Enrich your own life with conversation and it will rub off on the kids. They will learn to seek out mentors, new friends, and just engage people in their community, and they will grow as a result. You will, too.

Create your own salon. Become the Gertrude Stein of the neighborhood.

Trust children more – Toward the end of his long and productive life, with more than a dozen books under his belt, the godfather of the modern homeschooling movement John Holt suggested that all of his work could be summed up in two words: "Trust children." Given the forces arrayed against children in our culture, including the inner school we carry around inside our heads, that's an awfully stiff assignment. Perhaps a bit more than most of us can carry off with the requisite grace. So I've added a word: Trust children *more*.

It is my experience that when we get into the habit of trusting our children more, we discover that they find capacities and capabilities within themselves that they (and we) never even knew they had. Occasionally, they will make mistakes – the aforementioned *perfect* mistakes – the kinds from which they do recover and which play important roles in their development. More often, you will find your trust validated, as their learning space and their self-confidence is enlarged in the process of making the world their own. And as you trust them more, you will find that you trust yourself to an even greater degree, and recognize that you too are also a child whom you are bringing up, educating, and, in some important ways, getting to know for the first time.

I began this chapter by reflecting on how schools make the kids dumb and dumber, and then went on to explicate how those interior aspects of school – the bricks that we carry around in our minds – can get in the way of providing the best possible education for our children. And so, here's a hint: if at some point in your homeschooling adventure you find yourself stumped as to what to do next, how to respond to your children's needs, how to make their learning sing, and how to move to a higher step, a higher plane:

Figure out what they would do in school in this situation – and then do the opposite§ - It works about 90% of the time. Try it – you'll like it. When it doesn't work, pin it on me. I am willing to shoulder all of the blame. But none of the responsibility. For ultimately, as homeschoolers, that is what we have to chosen to take on for ourselves.

Learning School

Learning School
Shades of the prison-house begin to close
Upon the growing Boy,
- William Wordsworth,
"Intimations of Immortality"

IT'S BEEN MORE than 50 years since I've played school. I can't honestly say I've missed it, though I remember the scenarios quite vividly.

Since then, educators would have us believe that school has changed significantly. For the better, we are told, though obviously they could do even better if they just had more money, and, if they could do more testing, they could 'race to the top!'

Perhaps. All the experience I have of school these days is secondhand (I thank my lucky charms!) But over the years, I have watched enough children – both institutionalized and homeschooled – play school and, doing my best to look at it through their eyes, it doesn't seem to have changed all that much.

There's Marty, eight-year-old incipient bully, who always wants to be the teacher. He makes his little sister Casey sit in a chair, and not move. She is initially happy to do so, as she aims to please. Jimmy sits directly behind her, occasionally pinching her or threatening to pull one of her pigtails, making her fidget. Joey decides he doesn't want to sit in a chair, and so flops on the floor, and promptly zones out. Marty tells him to sit up straight (without success). Jimmy shoots a rubber band at Marty as the latter begins to intone, "Now children…." Casey hits Jimmy. Marty yells at her and tells her she has to stand in the back of the room. Jimmy giggles. Casey begins to cry. She whines, "This is no fun anymore." Unless Marty can figure out how to cajole or bully the three others back into "class," they will soon be on to something they all find more enjoyable.

There are many variations, as diverse as children are themselves. But, and I've seen them so many times (and other adults tell me about what they see), the themes remain the same. The teachers are masters, or at least master-wannabees, trying every method at their disposal to remain in control. The students vary: some want to befriend the teacher, others choose to subvert the teacher's authority, others sink into themselves as a way to maintain their self-respect. The teacher will use stratagems ranging from simple shaming, to divide-and-conquer, to carrots for "those who set a good example."

I have many schoolteacher friends, and my mother was a 30+-year New York City schoolteacher. They are usually very nice people, thoughtful, and tend to read more books than most folk. (I'm always hoping they'll read mine, hint, hint). Yes, I know there are occasionally sadists or savage ogres among them (most of us have had that experience), but few entered the profession for the money, but rather because they liked kids, or at least so they believed. And I think that is especially true of those who teach in the younger grades. (As for the ogres, as their charges, we were never able to inquire whether it was a product of their upbringings, or poor home life).

So why, over a more that 50-year period, do the kids pick up on the same stereotypes and scenarios? Are the myths involving school so powerful that they overwhelm the kids' personal experience? Or do they reveal a strain that runs so deep in the public education narrative that they transcend issues of educational content, school "reforms," No Child Left Behind, and whatever else passes for contemporary educational discourse?

I'd suggest that what the children's play indicates is that they, and we, have *learned school*. The first lesson is the power relationship between teacher and student that gives the former complete hegemony over the latter – body, mind, and spirit. The child learns to live in a state of unknowing – not knowing what activity comes next, what demands will be placed on her and for what purpose, and for how long. All she learns for sure is that, regardless of the good naturedness of the one in front of the room, any possibility of regaining some semblance of personal control is impossible without a concerted strategy.

And so we see the potential strategies as children play school. Submission, subversion, or resistance (active or passive). Most of us, at least initially, choose one of the three, or we might have experimented among them. Sooner or later, however, as the choice becomes habit, we forget that we ever made any choice, or did so for the purpose of retaining at least a hint of autonomy and self-respect. We become socialized to believe that these are our identities, and that how we respond to others in control defines who we are.

Gandhi once observed that one should not confuse the habitual with the natural. Submission, subversion, and/or or resistance are simply not good ways – for children or adults – to go out and meet and greet a wider world. Yes, one may pick up content that way. But they are ultimately self-defeating, as learning school warps our perspective on what we learn when it divorces us from who we really are, or potentially could be. And seeing what learning school has done both to individuals, and to our communities and society as a whole, it is far too high a price to pay.

We (and that means you!) are harbingers of a better way.

AN EXCELLENT RESOURCE for beginning to think about some of the power relationships involved in parenting and in learning and transforming them into compassionate, mutually respectful family and educational dynamics is Marshall Rosenberg's short pamphlet *Raising Children*

Compassionately: Parenting the Nonviolent Communication Way (PuddleDancer Press, 2005). Back in the early '80s, I was Marshall's first publisher, and since then, his relatively simple approach to clear communication without resort to authoritarianism or subterfuge has spawned a veritable workshop and publishing empire. If there are nonviolent communication workshops in your community, they are well worth a try. Check out his website at www.cnvc.org.

Slow Pitch

THE DAY ARRIVES. Dad takes Junior, almost turned three, out to the backyard with a plastic whiffle ball and a plastic bat. The sun gleams brightly off their matching red St. Louis Cardinal Baseball caps. Junior takes several awkward practice swings with the bat, just as he thought he had seen baseball players do on TV.

Dad backs up and underhand tosses the ball gently and slowly toward Junior. Junior takes a wild swing, and misses by about two feet, which is pretty difficult to do when you are only 29 inches tall. He smiles. Dad tries again, and again, each time tossing more gently and slowly, the ball almost hanging still in the air, with the bat consecutively missing the ball by an even greater distance. Junior is still grinning; Dad is getting frustrated.

Mom comes out the back door from the kitchen, still wearing her gingham apron.

"Can I try?" she asks, knowing how important in its own strange and messy way this event is for her husband. Dad hands her the whiffle ball. She talks soothingly to Junior, telling him to watch carefully, and then tosses the ball, as it turns out at a speed roughly twice as fast as Dad's slow pitch. Junior swings, and hits the ball right at Dad who catches it, startled. Mom does the same thing again. Again Junior swings, and this time hits the ball near the basement window. The cat, sunning herself on the ledge by the window, is offended, and moves off to find another warm spot. And the third time, Junior hits a little groundball right back to Mom.

"Time for dinner," she says, collecting the grounder and handing it to Dad, "Why don't the two of you go in and wash your hands?"

So what happened? Was it Mom's especially encouraging words? Did Dad's visions of a future major leaguer somehow cloud Junior's abilities with the bat? Was Dad a potential hurler of no-hitters, while Mom the reincarnation of the most hittable pitcher ever to make it to the majors?

All of the above are possible of course. But Dr. Terry Lewis, Professor of Psychology at McMaster University, arrived at a different conclusion, published in the July 2005 issue of *Vision Research*. Dad pitched the whiffle ball *too slowly*.

Did, too. "When you throw something slowly to a child, you think you're doing them a favor by trying to be helpful,' said Dr. Lewis, "Slow balls actually appear stationary to a child." Add a little speed to the pitch, Lewis and her colleagues suggest, and Junior is able to judge its speed more accurately, and is hence more likely to hit it.

"Our brain has very few neurons that deal specifically with slow motion and many neurons that deal with faster motion," added Dr. Lewis, "Even adults are worse at slow speeds than they are at faster speeds. And kids' neurons are immature, making the task even more challenging for them."

Sigh. I often wonder how much of my own education was hampered by the fact that so much of it was slow pitched. I don't mean that I should have been "accelerated" (whatever that actually means; if I wasn't accelerated, does it mean they were putting on the brakes? Or was coasting simply expected?), but rather that no one seemed to be ready to account for what I might actually be ready and prepared to do, or wanted to.

There are no such creatures as "average" children. There couldn't be, not with eight possible "natural intelligences" (Howard Gardner gave us a good start, but there may be more as yet unnamed), 71 different theories of "learning styles," an overabundance of learning disabilities, proclivities, talents, and gifts, many of them changing over time, all wrapped inside bodies and minds and psyches developing at various rates and with widely varying speed. Once you remove the "average," the pseudo-intellectual underpinning, from the practice of "education," the rest of it collapses like a house of cards.

With very rare exceptions, you don't need to know any of this stuff to be a successful homeschooler. Oh, it might occasionally help, and provides a common vocabulary for talking with other homeschoolers, and sometimes the ground upon which you might be given some useful advice, and a validation of your experience. But none of this says anything in particular about *your* child's needs, aspirations, hopes, and desires.

Now for the good news: if you listen hard enough, and the kids learn that you listen and act upon what you hear, for the most part they are going to tell you what they need. And get this: you were built with a very fine (and wireless) receiver, and with a little practice, you will learn to tune in on most of the signals.

Don't be surprised if, in doing so, you find that they are often less than happy with "the slow pitch." I know too many cases of children who became reluctant about reading because they did not learn early that books had any information worth knowing; whose "kiddie" telescopes were mounted so unstably that they never got to see what they were hoping to, and their interest in astronomy disappeared for a lifetime; or whose mathematical curiosity was stifled by page after page of workbook pages when they really wanted to know the math necessary to build bridges. Sometimes they need the opportunity to play with the *big kids' stuff*, just so they can plot a sense of their own development, and imagine what it would be like to walk in the big kids' shoes. Having big kids around to talk to about it can be a help, too, And, sometimes, they, and you, will discover they are ready for it, in ways you might never have otherwise expected.

Slow pitch, fast pitch…oh, maybe in the course of your journey together, you may discover that it shouldn't be any pitch at all, and that the three of you should be out playing soccer.

Phonics in Utero

I CAN BE a cranky sort of guy. Not a crank (or at least I hope you don't think me so) or on crank (in my day job, I help folks find treatment to wean themselves off the stuff), just cranky. I usually sleep okay, though I recently discovered unhappily that my dentist now mixes epinephrine with the lidocaine, and that can make me a bit loopy.

Just cranky. I don't tend to find conspiracies under every rock, but not because I don't see the agglomeration of big business and big government (most of the time, it is difficult to know where one ends and the other begins, really) wrapping their blood- and brain-sucking tentacles around us and the rest of the world ever-more tightly. Rather, they don't usually seem particularly secretive about it anymore, and perhaps that is more worrisome.

I attempt to share and ultimately dissipate my crankiness through humor. Homeschooling conventions and forums are therapy for me, so please keep the invitations coming so that I don't turn into an ax murderer, or, avowed pacifist that I am, simply a crotchety old guy ("crustified," says my younger daughter Meera, an adjective I seem to have earned when she turned the ripe old age of 14).

I have joked for years at conferences how the past-President of the United States had come to believe that if little Johnny didn't know his vowel sounds at six-and-a-half, he was destined to become a drug-addicted homeless criminal. (The current President believes the same thing – so much for partisan differences). The logic chain seems ironclad: if Johnny doesn't know his vowel sounds and 'perform at grade level', he will 'fall behind'. If he falls behind, his self-esteem will take a big hit. If he feels bad about himself, he won't learn how to succeed. If he is not succeeding, he will be left back. If he is left back, he is likely to fall in with the wrong crowd. If he falls in with the wrong crowd, he is more likely to use drugs at an early age. If he uses drugs at an early age, he is more likely to become involved with the juvenile justice system. If he becomes involved in the juvenile justice system, he will meet miscreants older than himself, and learn to commit more serious offenses. If he is arrested for a more serious offense and serves time in prison as a criminal, he is likely to find it difficult to find and hold a job. If he can't hold a job, he will become homeless. Skid Row, the shooting gallery, and the state penitentiary are all the future has in store for little Johnny for failure to properly identify the Sa, Fa, Ma, and Pa quadruplets at the appointed time. There it is – bald, clear, and terrifying, and holds parents and entire communities as willing hostages.

The prescribed solution has been to mount the kids on the school conveyor belt at earlier and earlier ages – Head Start at ages 3-5, or Early Head Start at age 2. (That research has shown it doesn't work, even on the President's own terms, would be the subject of another essay). And then, I would jest, soon they'll be teaching phonics *in uteri*, which usually provokes some arch laughter from homeschooling audiences.

Well, following one of these talks, a woman came up and presented me with a full-page advertisement cut out of *Modern Maternity* magazine. There, lying on a bed with a book, is a smiling, clearly very pregnant, blonde woman (in most of the parenting magazines I have perused, blondes seem to be the symbol of blissful future motherhood, and they all "carry their pregnancies well"), with the following headline: "You're never too young to learn. (In fact, you don't even have to be born!)" The copy reads, in part, "BabyPlus® provides your child lifelong benefits by beginning the learning process even before your baby is born. Our prenatal curriculum, comprised of 16 weeks of audio "lessons," is the first step in your child's cognitive development....We suggest you and your child begin the lessons between weeks 18 and 32 of your pregnancy. Don't miss the opportunity to provide your child this once-in-a-lifetime opportunity." (The ad, by the way, gives no indication of how the curriculum is to be delivered – for that, you have to go to the website, for which I am deliberately not providing the link, lest you fall into temptation).

At least they seem to understand that you can't get left back and be forced to retake week 29 before you are born. Detention goes with the territory. But if you don't start the curriculum early, "research" undertaken in Russia ("limited in scope and substance due to budgetary constraints during a time of profound political upheaval," says the website) seems to indicate your child will have: poorer school readiness and diminished intellectual abilities; shorter attention spans; later developmental milestones; decreased ability to self-soothe; poorer sleeping patterns beginning in early infancy; poorer nursing; and will be less alert and relaxed as a newborn. Put it together, and one can quickly see that to *not* utilize the Prenatal Education System™ – "When learning begins" proclaims their motto – is to subject your future Britney to child abuse and neglect, and a life of continuous woe.

The system costs $163.95, plus $14.95 shipping and handling, including the optional speakers and belt package "for those who feel their abdominal/physical size requires two sound sources for the use of Baby Plus®." (The blonde in the picture clearly wouldn't require it, but how could you be certain? What do I know? – my second X chromosome is missing a leg). The package is pretty inexpensive, I'd say, given that the benefits will last a lifetime. Didn't see a money back guarantee, though.

But I'm more than a little bit cranky about the product. It's not that I'm a cheapskate (well, I am frugal, but not when it comes to my kids), nor in denial about its potential. No, in fact, I'm off the hook – one of my kids was born well before the product was invented, and the other is adopted – what we are doing for her is about two decades worth of remediation for her lack of access to a technology that could have positively transformed her life, and ours. Many of you can't make identical claims, and therefore stand convicted, and it's too late to do anything about it.

With the hair stiffening on the back of my neck, and blood pressure further from registering 'dead' than is normal for me, I sought to explore how it works. As this thing goes, I'm now an expert! What BabyPlus® claims to do is introduce lessons to prenates through "the only language they understand – the maternal heartbeat." What's not to love? It's not a vitamin, it's communication, and the technology speaks the language of the heart! And the baby learns to discriminate the BabyPlus® sounds from those of the mother, and is stimulated, and along comes little Einstein, only a happy, alert, relaxed, sleeping, nursing one who performs above grade level! There seem to be lots of satisfied customers – there are a bunch of testimonials on the product website from very happy, what seem to be first-time mothers and fathers. They even posted one with a 9/11 hook from a New York City Police Officer! None reports on whether the prenatal curriculum helped their kid get into Yale – yet, but perhaps that is forthcoming.

I'm still cranky. I'm not sure I'd be more peeved if the product works or if it doesn't. Doesn't it seem to imply that the mother's heartbeat is somehow insufficient for the future well-being of the baby? I guess that's the heart of the matter for me: if parents are willing, for the sake of sonny boy of course, to surrender the language of the mother's heartbeat, what won't they be willing to surrender later to a larger societal view of "what is best for the child?" to further the child's "education?" The thing is, if I am a mother- (or father-) to-be, am I supposed to feel ecstatic or violated?

I don't have any easy answers. I do know that in 1998 the California Legislature was so concerned with how the child's "brain is organized" (as a result of relentless lobbying by a washed-up television actor who went by the endearing appellation "Meathead"), that they enacted the California Children and Families Act "to provide, on a community-by-community basis, all children *prenatal* (my emphasis) to five with a comprehensive, integrated system of early childhood development services." With a little imagination, one can imagine public health nurses going door-to-door making sure that moms-to-be are wearing their belts correctly (with the extra sound source if called for), and school officials charging those who don't wear their belts religiously with aiding and abetting the fetuses in being *truant in utero*. Actually, home visits will likely be unnecessary; implanting microchips in pregnant moms to monitor them to ensure they are 'laying the proper emotional, physical, and intellectual foundation for their children' would work just as well. I know – I'm getting ahead of myself. (I've always loved this metaphor, as it likely implies that most of them time I am actually behind myself, which means I could use some remedial assistance in catching up. I'm sure Meera would likely agree that I can be a little slow on the uptake).

Frankly, my objections appear to amount to a bunch of metaphors. "A child's womb is his castle." "A mother's womb is sacred space." "There is a sacred bond between mother and child that is not to be interfered with." "The language of the mother's heartbeat is not to be bought or sold." The rhetoric may make for good protest signs, or counter-advertising, but I hope you, dear reader, expect more from me. I certainly do.

At bottom, I think my hostility is not so much to the technology (after all, I'd urge pregnant women to take folic acid) as to guilt-tripping parents into believing that, to ensure their children's "success," they've got to mount the kids on the conveyor belt even sooner than they do now. If I question the morality of stereotyping and scapegoating "late readers" as "slow learners" (usually untrue), or the drugging of seven-year-olds because they indicate through their actions that they would rather be playing outside rather than confined to the interrogation rooms, or the social machinery of school itself as a system of tools designed to maintain and reinforce social class distinctions, why wouldn't I question the morality of a technology which goads parents to get their kids into the game that much sooner, even before they are born! for heaven's sake! whether it works or not?

I fully expect to be chewing on this at least until my next epinephrine-free dentist appointment. My crankiness is not likely to fade away anytime soon. Since I am not as of yet at rest with this matter to my own satisfaction, and I expect some of you, dear readers, are not either, I want to invite you to send me your own thoughts.

In the meantime, and imagining infinite regress and the importance of finding ways to get the XYs involved, I'm hoping against hope that someone doesn't come up to me at the next homeschooling conference with a magazine ad headlined "Sing to Your Sperm."

Fa Nichts

SO I HAD poured my heart out at that last homeschooling workshop. Lots of anecdotes and stories. Personal experiences and those of others. Theoretical constructs. I tried to make it amusing – I usually insist that I can guarantee fun, but whether folks actually learn anything is totally up to them. Worked up a bit of a sweat.

After my workshop, mom came up to my book table. There were my own books, and those of John Holt, and of my old friends John Taylor Gatto and Jean Reed. Books on deschooling, on helping kids deal with conflict and negotiate win-win solutions, on the development of compassion. I sat behind it.

She wanted to know if I had any phonics programs, or whether there were any I could recommend. Sigh. I was situated between two curriculum sellers who would have been more than happy to part with their wares (I would have preferred to have been located next to the funny Dutchman at his "Learn to Play the Ukelele" booth, but those are the breaks). I put my compassion lessons to good work. I happen to believe that the ultimate purpose of education (please sit up and take note) is to learn to treat each other better. I'm still working on it. I invited her to sit down next to me. I can be a very good listener when I try. And I was committed to trying. Publishers send me all sorts of stuff through the mails (ah, the benefits of being an infamous homeschooling author!) Some of the programs might be better than others. But I was (and am) committed to not recommending any.

You see (or maybe you don't yet), every child and every adult I have ever met first learned to read without phonics. There. I said it. I am sure there is an exception to what I have written somewhere (there always is), but honestly, as far as I am aware, I haven't met any.

That's an awfully strong and shocking statement to make, don't you think? I tend to be rather a careful sort, at least when it comes to my writing if not in speech, so why go so far out on a limb? I could have couched what I have to say in more neutral, less definitive, utterance, talk about percentages or tendencies, cite some academic references, quote an expert or two or three, and moved on. But the fact is I have such confidence in what I wrote above that I don't find it necessary. "Pride goeth before the fall," goes the old saying, and so I guess I should be ready for a big one.

So now that I've got your attention, and you are ready to catch that erstwhile homeschooling expert out, will you allow me the luxury of a little demonstration? If you will allow me….

I am about to write something on this paper.). There, I did it. Would you pronounce it, please? Oh, I see – you can't. Some of you might recognize it as something approaching a closed parenthesis, but there's no 'name' for it, is there? Now how about this. _ . Oh, you don't recognize that one either (might it be the underline key?)

Now, let's put them together. Not randomly of course – one (the first) on top of the other (the second). 2 . "Two," you say? Pronounce it carefully now – "tooo."

If I were to write this on a blackboard, or do a chicken scratch of it on a piece of paper, 99.9% of your kids would recognize it before they had learned anything about phonics whatsoever. "Tooo," they'd say, and if you asked them what two means, they'd tell you they have two eyes or two ears or two feet or two sisters or they had two bananas for lunch. And if you asked them to use it in a sentence, if they knew what a sentence was, they'd say, "I have two dogs." And if you asked them to hold up two fingers, or to count to two, it is not likely they'd find themselves particularly challenged.

So that part was easy. They were able to visually make perfectly good sense out of a particular set of visual cues, pronounce them properly and manipulate them for linguistic purposes to describe their world. In short, they were *reading*.

But let's take this a bit further. Make a set of two of these chicken scratches side by side. 22. What's that you say? No, it isn't "too-too," is it? The first one (or the one to the left to be more accurate) is now "tuh-wen-tee," while the one to the right is still "too." Yet, they look exactly the same! And if I cut out each set of chicken scratches and put the one on the right side "in front" (actually, to the left) of the other it now becomes "tuwen-tee" while the other one goes back to being "too." Works the other way as well, with the one on the left (that had been on the right), now being "tuh-wen-tee" and the other reverting back to little ol' "too." No matter how I order things, it never becomes "too tuh-wen-tee."

Amazing, isn't it? What happens when you get three sets of the chicken scratches? 222. No, that's not "too-too-too," is it? The one in the middle now becomes "tuh-wen-tee," the one to the right side is now "too," but the one on the left side is "too-huhn-dreh-d." I can shuffle them anyway I like and still come up with the absolutely non-phonetic "too-huhn-dreh-d tuh-wen-tee too." Gets really interesting when you add "wunz" into the equation. "Wun" on the left, "too" on the right equals "tuhwel-v." Reverse the chicken scratches and one reads "tuh-wen-tee wun." Blackjack! Makes "i before e except after c" sound like child's play in comparison. Except this is all "child's play," isn't it?

I hope by now this has become as obvious to you as it has to me. Children learn to make sense of visual representations and turn them into sound and into meaning without any necessary knowledge of phonemic content. But that does not mean that they don't have to learn the phonemic content of the chicken scratches. On the contrary, by forming analogies between the sound content of the known and then applying it to the unknown, they are able to match up the visual cues with words which in the aural realm they already know. (What we are dealing with in numbers, however, is that on top of the expectation of being "literate," there is the second expectation of becoming "numerate." You may know how to "read" 21 and 12 without any notion of how to subtract one from the other).

Stated another way, reading depends on a kind of fuzzy logic. If some kind of visual approximation of phonemic content doesn't match up closely enough with a known *spoken* thing, concept, or action, it remains totally nonsensical even if one can pronounce it absolutely correctly. Conversely, one can work from the sound content in the name of a known thing, concept, or action, to figure out how to read the chicken scratches depicting another thing, concept, or action similar in sound. (If I know "sheep," I can *read* "peep.")

If you have followed me up to this point, I think you have come to realize that reading represents a peculiar kind of symbolic logic, and the ability to perform these logical operations requires a "grammar of logic" that develops internally, and has little to do with instruction whatsoever. As Dr. Frank Smith, author of *Reading Without Nonsense*, and one of North America's leading experts on reading, emphasizes, children cannot be taught how to read; at best (and that's pretty rare), we make it a little more possible for them to learn.

So what about phonics? All children (with the very rare exception of those few children who learn the sound and sense of all words entirely through visual recall) have to learn phonics. *But it doesn't mean that they have to be taught it.* The problem with phonics instruction is that it is only useful at that precise moment in the development of a child's internal grammar when she recognizes that chicken scratches can have both phonemic and referential content, but before such time that she quickly recognizes what they are.

We can actually isolate when that moment is by formulating a sample "phonics equation":

BAD (ba-a-da) = SAD (sa-a-da) minus sa plus ba

This only works at such a time as basic letter sounds are already understood, and the logical grammar has developed to the degree that the child can accomplish the phonetic replacement operations. Phonics instruction offered too early – before the ability to perform the logical operations is developed – is meaningless and frustrating; offered too late – after the logical operations are fully internalized – it is unnecessary and stifling. (Boy, do I have stories about that one!)

Oh, and what about the alphabet? Glad you asked! Well, in case you were wondering, the size of the alphabet doesn't seem to matter either, at least for the kids. I am busy trying (so far not very successfully) to learn Tamil, the language of southern India. In Tamil, there are 12 vowels ("soul letters"); 18 consonants ("body letters"), one "hermaphrodite" letter, and 216 combinant letters, representing every possible combination of vowel and consonant. The kids manage to learn to read just fine, 247 letters and all, and there is no evidence that the radically larger number of letters has any impact on when they learn to read. Once the magic switch is thrown, the reading train just comes chugging on down the track.

Mostly, as most of you will soon find out if you haven't done so already, this is much ado about very little. Fa Nichts. Those of you caught up in these questions now will be surprised at what little importance they are to you two, three, or four years hence, as your children go on their way creating a world for themselves that is richer and, often, far more unexpected and surprising than anything you can currently imagine.

Home Alone – Home Together

I AM SITTING stretched out in my writing chair. As usual, there's a cup of coffee getting cold on my left side. My wife is watching the ball game (Go Mariners!). The two dogs are loafing, also as usual (why don't they go out and get a real job?) Echo the bunny is busy redecorating his cage as he often does, moving the dried grass from one location to another. The two snakes, mostly inscrutable, are doing their usual snakely things. Azul the arthritic parakeet, had to be put down two weeks ago (R.I.P), as he could no longer grip his perch, marking this as the first time in almost two decades that there isn't a member of the avian species in the house.

Devoid of children, too. This is unusual. Both kids are gone. And the phone is unlikely to ring.

Oh, wait! Here's an e-mail from Meera! She's arrived in Cairo, and, "It's sooooooo beautiful," she writes, "I wish you were here to see it with me. I guess pictures will have to do." Now I have to wait for the pictures.

Meera won a full "Youth Ambassadors" scholarship from AFS (http://www.afsusa.org/) to study intensive Arabic at a language institute in Cairo for the summer, and live with an Egyptian family there. The scholarship is paid for by the U.S. State Department's Bureau of Cultural and Educational Affairs, which arranged for pre-visits with State Department personnel and meals at the Egyptian Embassy in DC before she headed off on her adventure.

The scholarship was very competitive. They only awarded 25 of them from among about 200 applicants nationwide, all of whom had to be nominated by others in their community, and then pay $75 to apply. Then there were half a dozen essays to write, recommendations to solicit, medical papers to complete, interviews to schedule and undergo. I've joked (without, I must admit, much appreciation for the humor from the rest of my family) that I expect her to bring back a blow-up Sphinx to put under our mimosa tree.

Being 16 and in Cairo makes sense for Meera. She wants to be an accountant. That's not a non-sequitur, even if, when she informed us of her career aspirations a year ago, she was the only 15-year-old I had ever met who was enthusiastic about being an accountant when she grows up.

But not just any kind of accountant. An international development accountant. You see, Meera has a plan. She is going to be the finance manager attached to the first major international project to rebuild Gaza. We are all well aware that the world will have to cooperate just a bit to make that possible, but stranger things have happened, and she is going to be prepared to take advantage of the opportunity.

For the past four years, Meera has been working for the Rachel Corrie Foundation (www.rachelcorriefoundation.org) named after the young Olympia, Washington resident who was run over by a specially equipped American-made Israeli bulldozer as she attempted to protect the family home of Palestinian pharmacist Khaled Nasrallah. Khaled and his family have visited us in Olympia, and Meera has been involved in efforts to rebuild his home (www.rebuildingalliance.org), which was completed on May 24th this year! In the past several years, Meera has performed several benefit concerts, including one for the Israeli-Palestinian Families of the Bereaved Forum for Peace (www.theparentscircle.com) and one for the Atfaluna School for Deaf Children (www.atfaluna.net) in Gaza City. She helped administer registrations for a major international Israel-Palestine peace conference that brought the grandson of Mohandas Gandhi, Arun Gandhi, to our town, worked on the post-conference accounting, and serves as treasurer's intern for several peace groups about town. In the community of folks interested in and working for peace and justice in the Middle East, I am simply known as "Meera's dad.."

Meera has already met a future business partner. A graduate student in international development at American University was friends with Rachel Corrie while she was living in Rafah, and has dedicated his life to peaceful rebuilding in her memory. Meera met him when he was a guest at the annual Corrie Foundation dinner, and saw him again when she visited Washington, DC recently. Who knows if anything will ever come of it? At any rate, learning Arabic is just part of the plan, and at the very least, her Arabic will come in handy in greeting visitors to our town.

Both girls were actually home at the same time for a total of 13 days! Aliyah just returned from her year in Italy, and is getting used to communicating in English again (her program forbade the use of English, all her papers had to be written in Italian, and her host family spoke virtually no English). Following her academic year, she received a one-month travel fellowship to research the development of early Renaissance vernacular music in Umbria (south of Florence), and also got to visit with some of our friends in Italy who have supported our work in south India, where the two of us went together to help out following the 2004 tsunami. She's enrolled herself for the summer in a course in intensive German four hours day, and is pleased that the instructor, who is Swiss, also speaks Italian, so she doesn't have to go "cold turkey." But this week she is away at a Quaker conference. The 13 days were enough to take some pictures for the grandparents.

WHEN I WAS 17, back in the age when dinosaurs roamed the earth, my parents told me that I could go to college anywhere I wanted, so long as it was within a three-hour radius of New York City. Now I tell my kids they can travel anywhere they want, provided it is within a three-day plane journey of Seattle. Both my wife (who hitchhiked throughout Europe for six months when she was 17) and I agree that the world is a much, much safer place for young travelers than it was 30-40 years ago (yes, there are a few places it is likely wise to avoid). Our own lives have been indelibly changed by our network of friends from around the world, from Burundi to Italy to Japan and all points in-between, and it is hard for me to comprehend how much our lives would be impoverished without them.

I have written elsewhere that the ultimate purpose of education is to learn to treat each other better. In keeping with that theme, I have equipped my kids with five principles that I hope they will continue to take along with them on their travels:

- So much of who we are is an accident of birth – we don't choose our parents, our place of birth, our race, our gender, or our class, and travel is a constant reminder of that.

- We are responsible for the world to the degree that our position in life is a result of the fortune of our births.

- There is a difference between travel and tourism. It is good to travel to many places, but also to understand one other place besides your home really, really well. Learn the language, and plant some other roots.

- Travel is about making human connections – and there is no better way than to spend time in other people's homes, and invite them into yours. Make them part of your life and you will discover that you can travel without leaving home.

Bring your best skills and gifts along on your travels; find ways to develop and use them for the community's and world's good.

The house is kind of quiet. I shouldn't be allowed to grumble. I always hoped to raise world citizens, so I can't complain when they're not home. What I hope for my children is the same thing I hope for myself, to recognize that home has truly become a much larger place.

I'm looking to buy a canary.

THERE ARE MANY wonderful travel opportunities for homeschoolers and homeschooling families. Two of my favorites are:

AFS (http://www.afsusa.org/) – AFS is the oldest and largest international exchange program in the world. They've been at it for 60 years. Each year, some 11,000 young people spend a summer, semester, or year in more than 50 different countries. Almost all the programs involve a home stay with a local family, and either intensive language instruction or a school experience; some provide significant community service opportunities. While the programs can be relatively costly, there are scholarships available, and advice and support for raising funds in one's home community. A strong alumni association of past exchange students is an added benefit.

SERVAS (http://www.usservas.org/) – SERVAS is a cooperative network of "international travelers for peace." There are more than 14,000 members in 135 countries who will open their homes to you, engage you in conversation and fellowship, and show you their town. Travelers and hosts are both screened in advance, and there are lists of members with their interests and ability to accommodate. Individuals or families can travel, and there are opportunities for youth travel and hospitality as well. And for some of you who just can't get away, you can bring the world into your home by becoming a host yourself! Cost is $40/year.

The Plague of Childhood

"In thus taking away all duties, I take away the instruments of their greatest misery—that is, books. Reading is the plague of childhood and almost the only occupation we know how to give it."
      -- Jean-Jacques Rousseau,
      Emile, Book II

IN SOME OF the international commitments I've been involved with for a very long time, I am now working to create new training opportunities for older youth and young adults to equip them with skills and tools for creative partnerships and learning with people all over the world. Recently, I created a new organization – "Friendly Water for the World" (www.friendlywaterfortheworld.com) and, among other ventures, I'm hoping to pair young people with retired folks to go out and work with and learn from communities to ensure clean drinking water for everyone (without having to purchase it from Coca-Cola). Clean drinking water should be a basic human right.

What prompted me to write was a mailer I received from the local school district. They've sent them to me for the past three years. It is likely you have received them, too. Generally speaking, we only get them when the school people are trolling for dollars, which is now apparently an annual affair, and it would be nice if they could get someone different to write them each time, because they can get a bit repetitive. Of course, this only affects the few of us who actually read them, and respond to their requests.

Every year, we are told the kids are doing great, the schools are doing great, and the sports teams are doing great. But budget times are tough, they have to take a lean, hard look at things, and they would like suggestions of what to cut.

Now, the school district folks really don't want or plan to cut anything, but are trying to build a constituency to get us to pay more for their hostage-taking of the kids. No need to remind them that we have voted for every bond issue they've issued for the past 20 years, despite their having run out of schools to build. Never mind that they just constructed a new, six million-dollar football stadium (cheap! there is a new one in Texas that cost $60 million), which is only used by maybe five percent of the students, and which was erected on the last remaining open park land in the neighborhood (where hundreds of residents used to run or walk to keep in shape. In typical fashion, the sports facility makes it less rather than more likely that people, including students, will stay physically fit). Disregard the fact that there are now double the number of assistant and deputy superintendents than there were 15 years ago, despite the reality that there are actually fewer students.

Never mind all that. Each year I take them at their word, and look for a place to cut which will save substantial sums of dough with the least negative impact on those forced to occupy the day jail. And so I write to them, with a copy to the local newspaper.

I tell them to eliminate reading instruction. I'm perfectly serious. Get rid of reading instruction, and all the books, workbooks, manuals, displays, experts, and testing that go with.

Get rid of reading? No! I never said that. Dear reader (!), please don't misread me, or misquote me – I did *not* say get rid of reading. Reading is important in our culture (less imperative than the school fetishists would have us believe, less vital than public speaking and public presentation and the ability to get along with people and to be someone who can be relied upon, but important nonetheless), and now that we have few village bards and historians among us, they are our best way of entering into conversation with the past, much as writing is a way to enter into conversation with the future. Or to be less high-fallutin', how else are we going to read the advertising slogans, or the seven-page warnings which come with our meds these days?

No, I delight in the written word, and I want to share this delight with others. Which is why I want schools to eliminate reading instruction.

The reality is that they muck it up big time. Of course, if you have the ill fortune to have to enroll your kid in kindergarten, among the first questions you'll be asked is whether you've taught your child to read yet. Don't get snippy and tell them you thought that is what school is for. You and your child will likely be in for a hard enough time as it is.

Contrary to what the news media will occasionally claim while it sells commercial time and space, there are very, very few truly illiterate people in the country, which is why it is such a big story when they find a couple. The truth is much more mundane (and disturbing) – with hundreds of millions of dollars expended on school reading instruction and "technology," as a nation we don't read very well, and it doesn't improve as we expend more resources on it.

Actually, it has gotten a bit worse. The reason for that is relatively simple to come by. People, and especially families, have gotten poorer – in money, but also in free time, energy, and, likely, books in the house. Study after study indicates that after income, books in the home, books in local libraries, books in the school library (that the kids are actually allowed to use by themselves) and *free voluntary reading* time (getting less and less of that in schools these days) are by far the strongest predictors of reading ability.

Direct instruction? Not so much. In fact, most of the studies demonstrate at best a neutral, and often *negative*, correlation between school time spent on direct instruction (think fonicks) and reading "performance." Since when did reading become "performance," you might ask? Well, phanix instruction does result in little people pronouncing words out loud with greater facility. They are just a bit less likely to actually understand what they are reading. (Don't believe me? Get a hold of a copy of *The Power of Reading: Insights from the Research* – Second Edition, by my friend University of Southern California Professor Emeritus Stephen D. Krashen, 2004. And there's a whole new raft of studies published in 2009 and 2010 demonstrating the same thing. The President likes "Reading First" (intensive fonix) and thinks it should be used in all schools? The studies indicate the results are that the kids pronounce better in the first grade, and comprehend even less than they would have otherwise in the first, second, and third).

But, look, we've spent tens of millions of dollars every year on what we have been led to believe is reading instruction. It hasn't worked, has it? The more instruction is poured on, and the more money spent on testing (and testing, and retesting), and the more punitive the consequences, the worse it gets. Every test results in still lower self-esteem, poorer morale, frightened children, and frightened teachers. The winners win more, and the losers give up, and with good reason. (And the day jail looks more and more like the Gulag – see "Test, Punish, and Push Out: How Zero Tolerance and High-Stakes Testing Funnel Youth into the School to Prison Pipeline," The Advancement Project: March 2010, http://www.advancementproject.org/digital-library/publications/test-punish-and-push-out-how-zero-tolerance-and-high-stakes-testing-fu)

It's easy to see why. A teacher gives two students 20 words to study that might appear on the next "reading" test. The first, with plenty of books in the home, lots of time for free voluntary reading, a well-used library card, and lots of people around her who read for pleasure and for power, knows 19 of them before they were handed out. The second student, whose first language is not English, with few books in the home, and whose family, each of whose members works two jobs, doesn't even know where the town library is, knows five. At the end of the two weeks, the test comes around. The first student now knows 18 of the words, actually fewer than when she started.

The second student now knows ten. The first student gets an "A." The second student gets a charitable "D", despite having learned, arguably, infinitely more than the first. But she has learned something else as well, and very well indeed: no amount of effort is worth it, and not even a 100% increase in learning is going to help: she is going to flunk, or close to it. Again, and again, and again. Teach this lesson often enough, and she'll get the point. It might be decided to put her on drugs as a way of helping her cope with her failures. Put together an entire school system like this and you can create failing schools, failing teachers, and failing students. Wonderful morale booster. Then the failing schools can be closed and the failing students can be bused around to another location if one chooses (the President apparently does), where they can languish in the *forgotten tenth.*

Maybe that's what is desired: after all, that's the way it is set up. (There is a principle in social science – really just a truism – that social systems are perfectly designed to get the results they achieve). But it could be done much less expensively: instead of the tests, simply assign grades according to parental income, or local real estate values, and pocket the cash. It would work just as well (no joke – again, that's what the research conclusively demonstrates), and while there will be outliers and the occasional exceptions, just as accurately. I've always thought that if one wanted to know whether the kids are actually learning anything in the classroom, the standardized tests should be sprung on them without any advance notice or preparation whatsoever. Instead of preparing for reading tests, just think: the kids could actually be reading.

The reality is that learning to read is just not that difficult if one hasn't been scapegoat-ed, stereotyped, embarrassed, and humiliated, and if one is not hungry or hurting or traumatized or has uncorrected vision problems or an organic brain syndrome. (Which isn't to say that hungry, hurting, traumatized children with uncorrected vision problems or organic brain syndromes don't learn to read; on the contrary, they do so all the time. But there are extra hurdles that have to be overcome). Provided the gift of time, all the methods of learning to decode "work" – fanicks (did you know that "c-a-t" spells "such" – you can work it out for yourself), whole language (ever wonder what *half language* is?), doesn't seem to matter. In fact, method isn't required, and what might be a more serious issue for some is whether one learns to decode indoors or outdoors, whether from books or from the literate environment. (For homeschooling families, *phanichs* versus *hole* language is just a bunch of *school stuff* that can be entirely ignored without any deleterious impact). Give the kids magic decoder rings – they will work about as well as anything else, provided the kids have exposure to the written word, and adults who take delight in, or power from, it.

Ironically, the fear that the kids won't learn to decode is precisely what prevents so many kids (and adults) from actually reading. Our last three Presidents haven't been much help in this regard, with the first insisting that if Johnny doesn't know his vowel sounds at six he is likely to become a drug-addicted, homeless criminal; the second having proven that a Yale education doesn't really amount to much; and the third busy 'racing to the bottom', and appointing an education "czar" whose only "big idea" for public education is to militarize it.

The reality is that children *do* learn to decode – they just don't learn to read, or at least not well. They don't find pleasure or utility in it. As Dr. Frank Smith suggests, we don't first master the reading skill and then put it to use. That's not the way our brains work. When we read about 'things that matter' – *to us* – we become better readers. Writers, too, but we'll save that for another time.

And how does one become a better reader? We know that one only too well. As already noted, lots of books in the home. If in school, well-stocked school libraries, and the chance to use them. Quality community libraries with the most important resources in the library – librarians! Free voluntary reading time – lots of it. A quiet space. Few time restrictions. Fewer subject matter restrictions. Oh, and having people read aloud to you is quite effective as well, provided you're prepared to listen. Maybe a bit of the Internet.

But what would the teachers do if they weren't "teaching reading" (all right, I admit it, I believe that's an oxymoron), after they've paid a visit to each child's home and brought a big box of books with them, set up the reading corner, given the kids passes to go to the school library, gotten all the kids community library cards and introduced them to the librarians, had "free voluntary reading" (in school, really another oxymoron), and finished 'story time'?

How about planting a vegetable garden? I mean a BIG vegetable garden, one that provides almost year round. In Gandhi's *Nai Talim* schools, the children (with the help of their teachers) had to grow virtually all their own food, and if they didn't, the teachers didn't eat. How's that for teacher accountability? They also spun cotton for their own clothes, learned to do upkeep on their buildings, cleaned the grounds, learned useful trades.

Granted, this is not pre-Independence India, but then all the kids need to do is grow the produce for school lunches. And learn as they do it.

Let the future excavators dig, and the perfectionists weed. Let the future scientists research the best seeds, and the economists and financial managers ensure that they don't go over budget. Let the mapmakers lay out the space, and the mathematicians keep track of growth, and weigh the fruits of their collective labor. Let the warehouse managers keep track of the tools, and the hydrologists do the watering. Let the doctors and nurses learn first aid, and the nutritionists figure out how to produce a nutritious meal. Let the astronomers keep track of the sun, the meteorologists the weather, and the entomologists the bugs. Let the pipers entertain the fieldworkers, the shamans work their sacred magic on the living world, and the priests bless the first harvest.

And when testing time comes around, don't give the test meant for the nurse to the piper, or the one for the shaman to the economist. Each has his or her own unique place in the community's ecology, and the fact that they all know and relish different things simply means that, together, as a community, we know one great thing.

And that is what really matters.

(P.S. My gardeners will all read – not "learn to read" but "read" – without teachers and school boards having had the opportunity to make a hash of it).

(Speaking of reading, my friend Sasha Crow from the Collateral Repair Project (www.collateralrepairproject.org) in Amman, Jordan reports that she is giving up her last private space, her small bedroom, to turn it into a lending library for Iraqi refugees, both adults and kids. Most of the refugees are educated, but they can't afford books, either for themselves or for their children, and can't use the libraries reserved for citizens. Sasha is setting up book discussion groups and poetry groups, to go along with dominoes night, children's art classes, and English language socials. (You can read about them on my daughter Meera's blog – meerashanti.blogspot.com) Now they need books. No sense sending them – they need books in Arabic only. Used books are inexpensive in Amman, and they can get what they need. But they require some funds to buy them! A little bit can go a long way. Please help! www.collateralrepairproject.org/Donate.html)

Learning? Bah, Humbug!

"I THINK I'M going to have to homeschool," she says, in a tone approaching glum.

A woman with a very concerned demeanor approaches me after listening to the last of a series of three homeschooling talks I gave on the East Coast in the spring.

"I hope I didn't make it sound so terrible!" I quip.

"It's not that," she replies, indicating by her tenor that my attempt at humor has been misplaced. "It's just not something I planned on."

Rather than jumping in and risking one of my repeated episodes of foot-in-mouth disease, I let her continue.

"You see," she explains, "Both of my third graders (twins) are about to be suspended from school."

"Why's that?" I ask, trying to really focus (and suppressing my inward glee).

"They were caught reading sixth-grade books in the third grade."

Now I'm really holding it in.

"They were called down to the principal's office," she continues, "who made it emphatically clear that *Unauthorized Reading* would not be tolerated."

"Suspended?" I ask, as gingerly as I can (which is not very gingerly).

"Yes, but it was their *second offense*. I had to go down to school to meet with the principal. He said it could not be allowed, because the curriculum called for the students to be *learning* to read during language arts. Besides, what if *all* the students decided not to follow directions? What then?"

All that went through my mind was the trial of Galileo, but I thought the better of referencing it.

"Unauthorized reading. They sound like homeschooling material to me!"

She bought three of my books.

Now, if I allowed myself to be lazy (I do on occasion), I would have allowed this tall, *true* tale to stand on its own, with its tickling of my anarchistic antiauthoritarian sentiments, and called it a day. After all, you, dear reader, could feel smug (as I do), without having to read through an anti-school screed, and knowing that you have indeed, by homeschooling, done the right thing.

Neither you nor I get off that easy.

When I really thought about it, what struck me was the disparagement of reading in favor of "learning to read."

Now it's been a long time since my childhood, but somehow I can't remember ever wanting to "learn to read", and certainly not to be "taught to read." No, I wanted to *read*. I wanted to glean information about the world and in the world like the big people did, I wanted to amuse myself with stories, I wanted to have conversations with the past and distant places, just as writing would later allow me to have conversations with the future, and with distant people.

And the research conclusively backs up what would have otherwise seemed to be simply my personal predilections. What makes for good readers? It turns out neither phonics nor whole language. In fact, it doesn't have anything to do with teaching or method at all. That's just school stuff. Putting aside poverty (and, I have learned, you can *never* put aside poverty – I am a firm believer in "No Child Left Unfed" and "Race to the Table"), the research demonstrates that having kids read well is associated with (in no particular order); a great quantity of books in the home; plenty of good conversation; examples of adults deriving power and/or pleasure from reading, whether from books or in the environment; (if in school, a profusion of books that can be freely accessed in the classroom, and unfettered access to a well-stocked school library); community libraries with an abundance of books and good librarians; reading aloud and storytime; and lots of free voluntary (*unauthorized*) reading. If the kids have access to these, they don't *learn* to read. Most just read, (or, as Maria Montessori asserted, there is "an explosion into reading"), some sooner and some later, and over time, they get better at it.

For me, the same was true with math – I wanted to *do* math. I wanted to help buy the groceries, count my allowance and the stamps in my stamp collection, compute big numbers for fun, multiply everything by 11. I didn't want to "*learn* science" – I wanted to know how leaves turned color and figure out where to find the planets in the sky (quite a trick in New York City). I didn't want to "*learn* to play baseball" (I grew up thinking the Little Leaguers were sissies, though my family couldn't have afforded my joining in any case), I wanted to *play* baseball. I didn't want to "*learn* to play the saxophone", I wanted to *play the saxophone*. I wanted to *know*, to *understand*, to *see*, and to *do*. Learning was just an instrumentality, and I would take every shortcut I could find, which, looking back at it, is what accounted for my personal academic success.

Even in adulthood, I continue to desire to expand my world. I don't want to *practice* my violin; I want to *play* my violin. (John Holt, in my all-time favorite of his books *Never Too Late: My Musical Life*, on his learning to play the cello after age 40, indicated that, for him, thinking of time with his cello as *practice* would have been the kiss of death). I don't want to *learn* to speak Tamil; I want to talk to my Tamil friends. The oil painting is not far off. And if I have to *learn*, I will seek the least painful, most efficient means possible.

What I'm suggesting is that we should no more make a fetish of learning than schools do of teaching. Learning happens. If we allow it to happen, our kids will *learn* to take shortcuts, a good thing, if it makes it possible for them to more easily access worlds into which they wish to enter. When faced with alternatives, finding the easy way *in* is a sign of intelligence. And what will be the easy way in for one will be the more difficult for another.

Now I don't wish to protest too much. For me growing up, learning was inextricably bound up with competition, with rewards and punishments, and with distrusting my natural inclinations and curiosity in favor of pleasing others. And I was a player. It took me much of my adult life to unlearn lessons that I learned all-too-well, and to recognize that true learning is not about competition or pleasing others or even about subject matter, but about discovering the contours of our own interior landscapes, and to be introduced to, and meet up with, ourselves.

Growing Out

OUR CHILDREN HAVE this nasty habit of growing up, while we fight a seemingly losing battle against growing out. Actually, the metaphoric "growing out" is likely more accurate than "growing up" in any case, as many of the kids reach their full physical height at 13 or so, even as they are beginning to reach out and embrace a world of which they still have only the barest inklings.

My older daughter Aliyah, then 17, returned to south India last summer, by way of Cambodia and Thailand. She raised the funds for the trip herself. We had been there together, as many of you remember, following the tsunami, providing what little assistance we could (with the help of many of you), and reporting back through our web log (shantinik.blogspot.com). Aliyah continued the blog this summer, which I believe you will find a good read, as well as completing a short history of the organization with whom we are working [Land for the Tillers Freedom (LAFTI – www.friendsoflafti.org)]. We had initially planned to go to celebrate publication of a book I edited – *The Color of Freedom* – about the life and work of the organization's founders (which you can find on my website – www.skylarksings.com – all proceeds go to support their continuing efforts). Sadly, the fates had other things in store for us.

Also sadly, though on a much smaller scale, as the children grow out, in our case we get to see less and less of them. Honestly, I shouldn't be allowed to complain, though I do anyway. As I tell folks, somewhat wistfully, and trying to hide my little regret, they really are home.

Home is just becoming a bigger place.

> *Mama may have,*
> *Papa may have,*
> *But God bless the child that's got his own.*

MY LITTLE SISTER Meera's voice floats out of the living room, sounding, well, not quite like Billie Holiday, but pretty good anyway. It's certainly a lot better than I sounded at 15, or would ever sound on that particular song. My voice teacher currently has me working on unknown Bellini arias and songs by semi-anonymous 18th-Century English composers.

Last September, when my Dad asked me to guest-write an article for his column, I jumped at the chance. I had just come back from a two-month trip to India, Cambodia and Thailand, and wanted to tell everyone about it. However, I am also a sophomore at Smith College, with Italian quizzes and music theory papers and operas to work on, and this article got lost in the shuffle. Now, however, I'm home for two weeks, and I ought to be able to finish this, even as my Dad demands that I help him with his Italian correspondence.

So what does my trip to Asia have to do with my sister's jazz singing? They are both expressions of a growing independence from our families and from tradition. Meera's music, was, in fact, perhaps her version of adolescent rebellion, coming from a family of serious classical performers and composers. My travels were certainly not rebellion, (I have never been a particularly rebellious woman; stubborn, yes; but I never attempt to cause trouble to anyone else without very good reason). But all the same, they were a literal moving away from the territory which I have lived in and explored all the 17 years of my life.

I spent two months in a country where I didn't know the language, with people who, although I already loved them dearly, I had only met a few times before in my life. I spent a week in Cambodia, in a country which no one else I knew had ever visited, landing in an airport, almost a euphemism, alongside Angkor Wat. I learned numerous things while I was there, including random Tamil words and phrases (*mangalam* means mango), and a bit of Malayalam and Gujarati, various methods of transplanting wild water lilies to the tank behind the building where I was staying, never to drink Vimala's sugared milk, colored brown with tea. if I could help it (I never learned how Veerasamy managed to get his tea, without sugar), and not to use a pressure cooker when making soup.

I met Gandhian activists, the District Collector of Nagapattinam (the town that was the center of the tsunami damage in south India), Sulak Sivaraksa, a famous Thai activist and Nobel Peace Prize nominee, and Beth Goldring, a friend of my Dad's from his graduate school days, now a Buddhist nun running AIDS hospices in Cambodia. I witnessed 50 houses being built (thank you for helping, fellow homsechoolers), from making bricks to plastering walls, by and for some of the poorest people in Tamil villages, in a nearly miraculous display of organization and cooperation.

Although I had been to India three times before, and had been attending Smith College in Northampton, Massachusetts for more than a year, I had never really traveled abroad alone before (though I have been traveling solo within the United States for a very long time). I wasn't really alone, however. Aside from all of the friends and family I already had whom I had met previously, there was Lila, the LAFTI worker and community organizer who arrived from Kanyakumari "to be arrested" (she had been arrested during a protest several years before, but the police had only now decided to press charges, and she didn't want to damage her reputation by being arrested in the district in which she worked); the college student on the train from Chennai to Thiravarur who asked me about my family and shared her jackfruit with me (which I was too polite to refuse, though I find jackfruit almost sickeningly sweet); and my uncle Bhoomi's odd collection of international friends in Phnom Penh.

It was very different traveling without my family. At large gatherings of people, I tend to stick next to my Dad and let him do the talking (he's much better at it, and he likes talking much more than I do) but that wasn't really an option when traveling by myself. I did make mistakes, and I became known as "Aliyah Uh-huh" to some of the people at Kuthur because of a lack of communicativeness (my Tamil never did reach conversational level, though I usually knew what was going on). I did, however, provide some amusement to the hostel boys, especially by proving myself a slower runner than almost any of them, and I quickly and completely exhausted my repertoire of songs, because they kept asking me to sing.

Perhaps the most important thing I learned was that I could build upon the relationships I had inherited from other people and add to them. This forming of my own personal community, separate from that of anyone else, is perhaps my most important task of the past two years. I have learned that I am capable of doing well in challenging situations, and that I can make my own new connections. I went to see my grandparents and found out that I had grown up.

Or grown out.

Who is My Child to Be?

WHEN IT COMES to education, I am a lover of everything "alternative."." For much of my adult life, I've read virtually everything about alternative schools I can get my hands on. I can wax eloquent about the historical importance of Francisco Ferrer's Modern Schools, first in Spain, and then in New York City (the historian Will Durant was the first principal!), and the little spinoffs in Piscataway and Lakewood, New Jersey. I avidly read all about Summerhill as a teenager, and continue to be energized by the successes of the Sudbury Valley Schools. I am inspired by the memory of Maria Montessori's educational work among the waifs of Rome some hundred years ago, and by Rudolf Steiner's school serving the sons and daughters of cigarette factory workers in Stuttgart, as well as his invention of biodynamic agriculture. The Albany Free School remains a beacon to my consciousness. My Gandhian friends in India have developed some extraordinary 'experiments with truth.' And there are so many others before whom I bow.

There have been wonderful experiments in public schools as well, and interesting, exciting charter schools. From the distance at which I sit, the successful innovations seem to have only one thing in common: dedicated, caring, and hard-driven educational crusaders (for lack of a better term) who really care about children, and are often willing to put much of their personal lives on hold to be their advocates. Or perhaps to express it more accurately, caring and advocating for children has become their personal lives, and I honor them for it.

Sadly, because of this common factor, neither the alternative schools nor the public education-oriented innovations often find themselves replicated. They require very special individuals (I have been privileged to know more than my share, and am proud to call many of them friends), and such people seem to be in relatively short supply. I am old enough now to have seen the same special 'innovative' program, recapitulated successfully, in the same school district (and, in one case, even in the same school building!) with 30 years intervening between them, with the latter having no institutional memory of the former, and only to suffer the fate of most 'successful' educational innovations, that is, to vanish without a trace. It would be difficult to argue that, in the global scheme of things, my friends have made much of a difference, even if their charges will remember them forever with gratitude. Perhaps we are all like proverbial drops of water upon the stone.

Of course, in the scope of human history, public education as we now experience is the alternative. No civilization in the history of the world before ours subjected virtually all young people ages 5-18, and who were not convicted of any crime other than being young, to compulsory imprisonment in cellblocks populated by individuals of the same age, denied them basic human rights (even the right to go to the bathroom!), and imposed autocratic rule in the room, and bureaucratic control beyond it in determining what activities and routines they would be compelled to experience in the workhouse. We may have survived the ordeal (and some of us even learned to "like it" –"Rejoice, Rejoice, We have no choice," to quote an old Crosby, Stills, and Nash song – I know I'm dating myself), but we are fooling ourselves if we believe that as individuals or as a society any of us escaped entirely unscathed. This may be a stage in the evolution of human endeavor, but it is surely one I would have been happy to have missed.

Then, here we are – homeschoolers. Yes, we are different. Really! Over the past decade, in contrast with a couple of hundred alternative education visionaries and education reformers, there have been millions of homeschooling parents. We came to homeschooling for a wide variety of reasons, and with an even wider variety of experience. Some of us remember loving school ourselves, and others hating it. Some of us came with strong interests in education and children, well-developed even before we had children of our own. Others of us had given it virtually no thought at all, until circumstances required us to do so. Some of us had planned to homeschool the day we found out our first child was conceived; others found ourselves doing so unexpectedly with our fifth child when she reached adolescence, after the other four had spent 13 years each in public education and managed to get by.

But what we have in common, and what sets homeschooling apart from the other educational alternatives, is that we have *all* become educational crusaders, though few of us attempted to use the PTA as our venue of choice. Our kids just didn't have time to wait. We have all had to learn to become more empathetic, and more assertive in ensuring our children's learning quests are honored and advanced. We are not limited to a few innovators, and we don't have to have thought it all out in advance. We can be experimental, and scientists, free to figure out what works with our children, with our families, in our communities.

Our kids begin with three great educational gifts that kids in the box almost never experience: love, listening, and time. I don't imagine we'll see large, compulsory institutions incorporating these gifts into their book of business anytime soon.

Most of us were not trained as scientists (thank heavens not as educators!), and so much of this is so new to us (at least initially) that this new venture can give us a sense of walking a tight rope without a net, or simply falling free before we have learned to fly. Watching and listening, and then listening and watching some more is just not the way we were trained when we were in fifth grade that education is supposed to happen, and we mistrust our ability to see and hear our own children. So, if you are like most homeschoolers, at some point you grasp for tethers.

YOU'VE BEEN BOMBARDED with curricula. Maybe you've even tried a couple. Some of them worked okay, or so you think, and some made you and your child's homeschooling lives together miserable. Maybe the one you liked best is one she hated most. Or maybe the curriculum your older son just loved gave your daughter stomach aches. Perhaps a classical approach might be the way to go, but then you thought that maybe with all your Hispanic neighbors, Spanish might make more sense than Latin, and Jimmy really wants to learn about auto mechanics. And maybe now you've become convinced that curricula are not a good way to learn, and you've decided to swear off them (at least for now; you reserve the right to change your mind, keeping the spare in your back pocket).

Now you've learned all about learning styles. Maybe Melanie's kinesthetic and tactile, while you've been assuming visual-spatial. Actually, you didn't know about either until two weeks ago. Then someone told you about convergers and assmilators, but you can't seem to keep them straight in your mind. You found out that there are 71 different theories of learning styles! As soon as you've learned one system, there's another, all claiming to be 'neurobiologically based'. Then you realize that you don't enjoy thinking of your child as diseased, and that (maybe) she'll learn everything she needs to learn in time, at her own pace, and maybe, since her brain will change, her learning style will change, too, just about the time you think you've figured it out. You wish she were reading better, and maybe she's dyslexic like her friend in gymnastics, and then you remember reading that the folks at the Sudbury Valley School claim never to have met a true dyslexic in 40 years. And wasn't there some famous brain scientist knighted by the Queen of England (Dr. Susan Greenfield) who said that from a neuroscientific point of view, the learning styles approach to teaching is utter nonsense? But even if it is nonsense, perhaps it is a good thing that schoolteachers might have to pay at least a little more attention to each individual child. However, Melanie isn't in school, and you are really uncomfortable with all the labels, and after awhile they make your head hurt.

Then you came upon all this wonderful material about multiple intelligences, Howard Gardner's revolutionary though all-too-obvious notion that there is more to intelligence than what they measured on all of those tests. Whew! You always knew you were smarter than what they said! And you were always good at art. But what do you actually *do* with this multiple intelligences stuff? For awhile, you thought that maybe you should organize the homeschool day so as to encompass each of the eight-and-a-half intelligences, but then you realized that it began to look like a day at the local middle school. Perhaps you should stress those areas where Stevie isn't particularly adept, but then you heard this great homeschooling speaker who said you should always work with and from a child's strengths. But what exactly are his strengths? All you can come up with for sure is bowling. It's not "kinesthetic intelligence" – he doesn't run really well, isn't particularly agile, doesn't climb trees or hit a baseball or jump – it's just, well, bowling. Someone gave you an article about a homeschooler in Missouri who got a four-year bowling scholarship to college. Maybe bowling intelligence is the key, but how do you teach literature through bowling?

All of this keeps you completely spinning, and feeling inept and maybe even a little frightened. Certainly the school people haven't figured it out. Your little experience of them, through your son Mason, suggests that it has probably gotten worse since you were in school 30 years ago. Perhaps you should unschool, not out of any special commitment to unschooling philosophy (some of the folks you've met who do so seem particularly scary!), but maybe it means fewer decisions to make. But how then do you fill out all the forms?

No one ever said this was going to be easy. I don't know anyone who chose homeschooling because it was easy, but rather because, as the most important people in our children's lives, we choose not to semi-blindly abnegate responsibility for any part of it.

But who is my child to be? Not simply her own individual characteristics or proclivities or "intelligences" or learning style or uniqueness which, above all else, *must* be attended to with the full respect they deserve. But rather, how do you conceive of the real interests of the child you choose to serve so that she will become the resourceful, self-satisfied, life-affirming person you imagine? Who exactly is this person you are educating and how do you conceive of the outcome you are seeking?

Now, please, don't suggest you don't have any preconceptions. I've never met any parent who didn't. What I hope to do here to do is help you unearth them, allow you to hold them up to your own scrutiny, and hence help you clarify your own values as go about your homeschooling journey.

These have all filtered down to you, I suspect, from one place or another. As you hold them to the light, you will now join an entirely new circle of educational philosophers! My experience is that if you can just step back from the day-to-day process to understand what you think you might be doing with your kids, both your insight and your practice will deepen, with great benefit to both parent and child.

With thanks to the holistic educator Ron Miller who first suggested the usefulness of this kind of typology (though not necessarily tied to homeschooling), I want to suggest seven different educational 'lenses' by which you might view your 'child to be,' and the beginnings of "pros and cons" of each especially as they relate to possible applications in the home education setting (to which I am sure you will be able to add).

My Child is to Be:

The Carrier of Cultural Tradition

FOR SOME OF us, the central purpose of education is to convey to our children our cultural, religious, ethical, or other traditions. Indeed, they are to be the carriers of these traditions into a future we ourselves will never know. Of course, times change and there is a great deal of uncertainty, and falsehood in the ways of the world, from which it is best to protect our children. But more than that, it is our belief that real truths are timeless, not subject to change, and must be the center of any education truly worthy of the name, and toward which all efforts should be directed.

For others among us (and the groups may overlap), our cultures and traditions are under threat, and the only hope we may have of sustaining them is through our children. This can even be in the manner in which these traditions – through education – are to be transmitted. Some of us, and I am thinking particularly those of us from Native American traditions, may even find ourselves in a position of recreating a traditional educational culture which had already been eviscerated, if it had not vanished entirely.

Pro:

- There is a subculture of adult community support.

- Desired outcomes are clear.

- There are clear modes of transmission (specific books or sources of authority).

- Recognizes that some truths may be universally true across time and space.

Con:

- Requires obedience which, for the child, is at least semi-blind.

- There may be no real role assigned to childhood.

- It may leave little room for individual or unique proclivities that are not valued within the culture.

- By definition, it is culturally insular.

The Progenitor of a New Future

TO OTHERS OF us, the history of the world is the hard-won story of progress, often tentative but nonetheless relentless, from darkness to light, from oppression to liberty, from superstition to reason. And we see it as our highest duty to educate our children to be part of this march, not only as individuals, but as part of a larger community.

Our children are the agents of social transformation. As such, our job is not to transmit knowledge and preserve cultural traditions, but to help them develop a spirit of inquiry into the conditions of their culture and society – and their own condition – and begin to provide them with the critical tools to transform them. Although the world has experienced progress, we still see it beset by violence and oppression, exploitation, and the devastating ecological and societal impacts of corporatization and globalization. Academic skills are not neutral; they are to be taught in order that our children can become morally aware, socially responsible, engaged and active citizens ready to take their place on the platform of history.

Pro:

- Begins from the premise that the future will not be the same as the present.

- Roots education in the reality of the child's daily existence as the center of inquiry.

- Encourages social engagement from the youngest possible age.

Con:

- Requires a community of learners similarly engaged, and a ready field for action, both of which may be difficult to find.

- Requires teachers and facilitators very well versed in social, economic, political, and cultural affairs.

The Bearer of Society's Laws and Norms, and a Builder Upon a Bedrock of Knowledge

CHANGE IN THE world is slow, and hard-won, and the reality is our children are born to fit into it. And it is a good world! There is an authoritative objective body of facts that is outside our children's direct experience, and certainly beyond their personal preferences. In addition, there are preferred ways for such knowledge to be acquired, to be transmitted from those who know to those who don't yet know. Our children are born *tabula rasa* ("blank slates", the concept was conceived by the philosopher John Locke who, it should be noted, didn't have any children), and it is our job to ensure that only the proper information and understandings are written upon the slates, and in the best possible handwriting!

There is a specific body of knowledge that our children need to acquire, from the alphabet to Shakespeare. (For Locke, the idea that a child could truly be said to be educated without proper Latin and Greek was an absurdity). In order to participate effectively in society, individuals require a background of cultural (and scientific) literacy so as to be able to engage fully with the world round them. It should be noted that what is necessary for that cultural literacy is a matter of intense debate. To engage fully with your neighbors across the street or across the globe, do you need familiarity, for example, with Plato, Chaucer, Thomas Aquinas, Keats, and T.S. Eliot, or with Advaita Vedanta, the *Dhammapada*, and the *Koran*, or the writings of Lao Tzu, Hafez, Chinua Achebe, and Pablo Neruda? Should our children learn Greek so they can eventually read Aristotle, Sophocles, and the New Testament in the original, Russian so they can take part in the national effort to defeat the Soviets in the arms and space races (that's what happened to me), or Chinese in order to be able to engage the most populous (and perhaps, in the future, most productive) nation on the planet? Or maybe Spanish so they can talk to the next-door neighbor?

The transmission of knowledge is the role that education is to play, and to do so efficiently requires a mode of transmission that is also not a matter of personal preferences. In order to participate in the world as we know it, and join the march, our children need to be able to acquire knowledge in standardized ways, regardless of their own particular proclivities or idiosyncrasies, because that's just the way the world works. And when they are themselves ready to transmit knowledge, they will be prepared in how to do so.

Pro:

- Generally recognizable and understandable by society as a whole.

- The mode of transmission is clear, with information transmitted from teacher to student.

- The knowledge to be transmitted is defined by the past and by tradition, and *may* be easily determined.

Cons

- There is little room for a child's individual choice regarding what to learn, or when to learn it, or for the expression of individual proclivities.

- Emphasis is on teaching, not necessarily upon learning.

- The specific body of knowledge that children need to acquire in a changing world is neither fixed nor obvious, and is a matter of intense debate.

The Fullest Possible Expression of Freedom

OUR CHILDREN ARE born with everything they need to know and an unquenchable desire to make sense of and master their world. Left unfettered to the fullest possible extent, this desire and the ability to fulfill it will unfold in the fullness of time. Our job is to (minimally) protect our children from that which would do them harm, provide them with the maximum space for their autonomy to find expression, and then to get out of the way! Left to their own devices, they will explore what they need to know, what is relevant to their lives, and such experience of free exploration will drive them to further learning. The only way to educate for freedom is to allow people to live and learn freely, and to trust that they will find their own way. And this must start with our children.

Children are individual and unique, and so are their families, and so are their circumstances. Our individual differences are to be acknowledged and, more than tolerated, they are to be celebrated. For, as we learn in science, individual diversity is nature's way of caring for the species.

Pro:

- Education is child-centered.

- Allows the child to decide what to learn, and when to learn it, and hence learning will simply be a part of living, taking advantage of the child's own interests and inner resources.

- Enables the expression of individuality and uniqueness.

- Does not disrupt the natural relationship between parent and child by interposing the role of educator.

Con:

- May confine a child's interests to her immediate surroundings, or those of people immediately around her.

- While respectful of a child's individuality, may not take advantage of what is known more universally about child development.

- Requires much more trust than most parents are accustomed to giving children, or that they may have experienced themselves; it therefore may require some special discipline among adults to resist "teaching."

An Unfolding

YOU CRAWL BEFORE you walk, you walk before you run, and the biological requirements for each are different, as is what you are able to see while engaging in any of these forms of locomotion. The butterfly develops through its four stages, each of which requires different food and a different environment in order to flourish.

Children, like butterflies, develop from the inside out. And so while the child requires the freedom necessary for her inner spring to uncoil and for new energies to find their necessary objects, we know enough about this development (together with our listening to each individual child) to provide the necessary framework, structure, environment, and materials for this to happen effectively. To ignore the truths of this unfolding, either in the name of freedom, the transmission of knowledge, or a higher historical or cultural purpose, is to undercut the needs and potentials of the child, and ultimately to sabotage the ends for which education is designed.

And what shall be the end? We have faith, as all of the truly great educators have had, that it will itself be known through unfolding in the fullness of time.

Pro:

- Education is child-centered.

- Recognizes that children (as well as adults) experience stages of development, and that learning opportunities/challenges can be attuned to this development.

- Makes use of best available research.

Con:

- May inhibit recognition of, and working to feed, any individual child's specific and unique gifts and proclivities.

- Requires a substantial commitment to understanding and implementing the findings of contemporary research.

- Requires a high degree of sophistication in teasing out the interrelations between biology and culture.

A Meaning-Maker Who Joins the Community and World around Her in Meaning-Making

THE WORLD AROUND us is socially constructed. Our children are born into a world where they take part in the dynamic construction of knowledge through collective inquiry, collaboration, and creative problem-solving. Really, when you come right down to it, there is no such thing as 'individual intelligence,' only community intelligence. While our children may have some innate abilities, those abilities can only find their truest expression in the context of a supportive and cooperative learning environment. It makes no real sense to talk about cultural traditions, expressions of freedom, societal laws and norms and the transmission of knowledge outside of the context of the child's ever-expanding sense of community, from family outward as far as she is able to go.

In this conception, the singular emphasis in education is to assist our children in finding their place in the world. There is no absolutely essential core of knowledge outside of a community context and one's role within it, and there is no standard way for obtaining the knowledge necessary to construct meaning for oneself. Even stages of development are culturally based, with expectations and understanding of children mostly a function of the roles children are assigned in the context of their own particular community or culture. Every child must be assisted to help find her own way, and to understand that this way will be valued so long as she gives back to the community as much or more than she takes.

Pro:

- Focuses on the goal of community, as opposed to individual, intelligence.

- Does not assume that all individuals need to learn the same things, nor is it advantageous that they do so.

- Fosters a deep appreciation of the contributions of others, of group problem-solving, and collaboration.

- Brings forth a sophisticated view of what makes for a good family, good community, and good society.

Con:

- There is a heavy emphasis on group learning and group activity.

- Poorly applied, may encourage 'group think' rather than individual difference or initiative.

- Can be culturally insular.

- There is no standard for 'truth.'

A Vessel of Compassion

THERE IS ANOTHER possibility, perhaps only ancillary to the others, or perhaps the only one that really matters.

I am reminded of the 3rd Century philosopher Plotinus who, searching for the source of human happiness, finally concluded that happiness consists of "aligning oneself with the highest good." And hence the purpose of life (and of education) is to find that highest good for ourselves, and to hold true to it.

After my own long consideration, my still-tentative conclusion is that the only true purpose of education is to learn to treat each other better. For while as individuals we may only have a cloudy notion of what constitutes "the highest good," our best hope of getting there is to seek out the highest good in others, and to learn to serve it, and to educate our children as the vessels of compassion they could turn out to be. Imagine what the curriculum would look like! Imagine how we would rewrite the history books! Imagine the examples we would use in the application of mathematics! Imagine how we would seek to harness the spirit of scientific inquiry!

Pro:

- Focuses on 'highest good,' rather than viewing education as simply instrumental.

- Provides for outward orientation, yet encouraging of individual difference and initiative.

- Family context is critical.

- Learning has immediate application.

Con:

- It may not account sufficiently for the 'stages of moral development' in children.

- Difficult to be accomplished without continuous preaching, in families, without significant community support.

- A curriculum – for history, scientific inquiry, mathematics, etc. – is only in its infancy, and thus may require unusual and sustained levels of parental creativity

WELL, HERE ARE seven possible conceptualizations. I'm sure there are others. Which ones rock your world? It is likely that you uneasily carry around in your subconscious more than one – and until you were homeschooling, you may never have given it much thought.

So my invitation to you all is to become philosophers. The world *needs* more philosophers. But as I do so, I will enjoin you to consider the words of Janusz Korczak – doctor, director of orphanages, educational innovator, lover of children, who ended up running an orphanage inside the Warsaw Ghetto, and who finally led 200 children to the trains to be taken to Treblinka, never to be heard from again:

"Know yourself before you attempt to get to know children… First and foremost you must realize that you too are a child, whom you must first get to know, to bring up, and to educate."

Training

FOR THE PAST 20 years, I've been employed professionally in day jobs for which I have had none of the listed qualifications, neither academic nor experiential. I manage to get these positions because I am well-spoken, write well, and have turned what might be perceived as the weaknesses of my resumé into a strength. I have a track record as a "quick study," can digest large amounts of new information very quickly, and use it in the development of policy. I pick up new tools easily – I use quantitative analysis and epidemiological statistics in my work…and I haven't taken a math course since high school. I am collegial, a team player, and since I don't derive my identity from my work, am perceived as non-threatening (if personally unambitious). Over the years, I've gone to more than my share of conferences, where I listen to the presentations, but often gain more through a shrewd exchange of business cards, lunches, and follow-up phone calls and e-mails.

A requirement of being a state employee, and a manager, is that I am also obliged to attend "training." I can say with some certainty that, in terms of assisting me in doing my work better, the taxpayers are not getting their money's worth.

This isn't to say that I never learn anything. Occasionally I do. But the transfer of skills and information is tremendously inefficient. Some of this has to do with the training itself; most of it has to do with me. The training, prepared and packaged in advance, is based on the initial assumption that I don't know what it is that is to be delivered. When I do, well, I end up drinking a lot of coffee, now and then I write a letter or two; my notepad is full of doodles; sometimes I make shopping lists. I can get very bored, and try to control my more sarcastic instincts.

The second assumption is that I am ready to learn that which is being taught. There are infrequent occasions where there is basic knowledge that is assumed which I simply don't have. When this happens, knowing that I could take up too much of other people's time (as well as being unwilling to appear *too* ignorant), I simply wait it out.

More commonly, there are other influences on whether I learn much. Did I have time to eat breakfast? Am I sleepy after lunch? Are the chairs comfortable (or too comfortable)? Are there other things happening in the office or in other parts of my life that require my attention?

Finally, will I have a near-immediate use for any of this, or is most of it remote from my day-to-day responsibilities? If the latter, the only vestige of my day will be the training notebook, which is likely to be lost quickly in the crush of paper on my desk.

From years of experience, I have learned that the teacher doesn't matter much. I've had instructors who were kind, engaging, amusing, and entertaining, and I will long remember the jokes they tell or their training techniques, but the content will be quickly wiped cleaned from my poor brain. In contrast, I can learn from teachers who speak in monotones, who are disorganized, or easily rattled or short-tempered, provided I am already interested and know how I will make use of the information being transferred, and there aren't other personal factors (mine, not the instructor's) that get in the way. The number of people at the training is similarly unimportant, and the use of advanced training technologies (even when they don't break down in the middle), doesn't seem to matter all that much in the long run either.

Frankly, I doubt that my experience differs significantly from that of every government school administrator who ever walked the earth. So why, when it comes to kids, do we as a society choose to saddle ourselves with an educational paradigm and structure that, in terms of learning, has such a proven track record of downright stupendous inefficiency, and we all know it?

LEFT TO THEIR own devices, children are like me – or more accurately, for reasons of which yet I am not entirely cognizant, I am like a child. If you spend enough time around children who aren't as yet browbeaten into conforming to the education enterprise, you know that they have a style of learning that both fits their condition and meets their individual developmental needs. Children work to make sense of their world, to see patterns and consistency within the limits of their own development, and are constantly growing out of the patterns they've previously perceived as out of old shoes. They organize, correct, self-check, all in an unending upward spiral that allows them to make increasing sense of, and to navigate in, what is for them an ever-expanding material and mental environment. That which works today doesn't work tomorrow, and it only requires their inborn 'inner teacher' and her exquisite timing to tell them so.

In other words, they know how to think, and no one ever had to teach them how. What we do in school, in contrast, is, to quote John Holt, "teach them to think badly, to give up a natural and powerful way of thinking in favor a method that does not work well for them and that we rarely use ourselves."

We don't have to motivate them either. Children strive to make sense of their world, through increasing competence expand their realm of freedom, to do those things which they see the adults around them doing. They are building neural pathways, booting and rebooting the hardwiring of the brain, and pruning those dendrites that atrophy through disuse.

But the obverse is true as well. When the world presented is limited, when children's strivings are constrained, narrowed, or discouraged, when the realm of freedom becomes more circumscribed rather than increasingly expanded, and when the roles played by significant adults with whom they spend most of their day are limited to teaching, it is not surprising when we grow into more limited versions of the human beings we might otherwise have become.

In listening to thousands of homeschoolers over the past decade, I've come to the conclusion that the vast majority of problems that come my way with are a result of far too much attention being given to "schooling" and not enough being given to "learning." We search for answers in the perfect curriculum, in a facsimile of what might occur inside a classroom, in scope and sequence, in organizing the content in some way vaguely familiar enough that it might please our "inner schoolteacher" even when it leaves the kids flat.

The reality is that none of the content schoolers are confronted with inside the boxes is rocket science except rocket science, and there are desperately few institutions teaching rocket science these days. As in the case of my training, whether it is learned or not often has very little to do with the content or its delivery and everything to do with whether it "speaks to our condition."

My success on the job, such as it is, is due to my flexibility, adaptability, curiosity, and drive to learn new things. I am rewarded not so much for what I know, or even what I know how to do, but how I behave when confronted with that which I *don't* know. And since the realm of that which I don't know is so vast (and continues to be so interesting to me), somehow I've managed to make a career of exploring little pieces of it.

As for schools? The one concession I am willing to make these days is a grateful acknowledgment that they often provide breakfast.

Acts of Enclosure

"There was a time when every meadow, grove, and stream,
The earth, and every common sight,
*   To me did seem*
*   Apparelled in celestial light,*
The glory and the freshness of a dream.
It is not now as it hath been of yore; --
*   Turn wheresoe'er I may,*
*   By night or day.*
The things which I have seen I now can see no more."
*   – William Wordsworth,*
*   "Intimations of Immortality"*

I DIMLY REMEMBER learning about British enclosure laws. I believe it was during my last year at junior high school (all right, it was a pretty advanced class). It had something to do with putting up fences to keep cows inside the farm, and prevent sheep (or was it goats?) from roaming over the "village commons." I think I may still have that confused – was it that the lords of the manor wanted to graze their own sheep on the commons so they could make money off the wool?

But what did I know? There I was in New York City, and I'd never really been up-close-and-personal with sheep, goats, or bovines. A village commons? You mean there were parcels of land that were shared collectively, that made it possible for poor folks to keep a few animals for milk and meat without having them all fenced in? Did they once exist in my neighborhood? Who were the lords of our manor who had taken it away?

There was some kind of truth behind all of this stuff, but it wasn't apparent to me. Rather like the "Triangle Trade" where (as I wrote about in *Homeschooling and the Voyage of Self-Discovery)* the point was that the real business of the African slave trade was almost entirely an affair of the *northern* colonies. (To be as fair as I can to my teachers, I'm pretty certain it never clicked for them either). Somehow, although there must have been something important going on with these enclosure laws (or they wouldn't be teaching it, right?) I seemed to be missing the fact that poor people with their goats were getting shafted, the goats would soon be gone, and the people would be off to work like sheep only worse in airless, soulless factories, and their kids would (a-hem) be going to school.

My old friend John Taylor Gatto has analyzed what I might call a new set of "enclosure" acts that have taken place in the United States in the past half century or so. Basically, he argues, the expansion of schools into the suburban reaches was a great boon promoted by real estate developers, and remains so to this day, while increased school taxes – a 600% increase in less than three decades –and real estate taxes born of the school boom, drove a million small-farm families off their land. These families now joined the landless (and goatless) army of office workers and their ilk. Agricultural properties were dumped on the market to be broken up into tens of millions of housing plots, with individuals representing real estate interests sitting on thousands of school boards across the nation. Meanwhile, the goats, cows, sheep, pigs, and barnyard fowl of all varieties vanished, green space was swallowed up, tomatoes at the supermarket turned plastic, and whatever did happen to the village commons? (or sandlots, or park ponds, or even vacant lots?)

Gatto's main point is that the impact of the new enclosure acts (really much like the old ones) is that they took a class of independent-minded, self-reliant, creative, family-oriented folks, who did not define their self-worth by the size of their bank accounts, and who relied on neither government nor big business interests for very much but who worked for themselves, and sent them (and the kids) off to the "workhouses." I concur with this view, but I would add what seems almost too obvious: millions and millions of people who lived much of our lives outdoors now find ourselves enclosed inside as well.

We really weren't bred for it. Like French Angora rabbits, it will probably take a hundred generations or so, or maybe a little extra genetic fine-tuning, before we are fully acclimatized. Until then, survival of the fittest has us attuned to the greens and yellows of trees and fields, our eyes and our body chemistry adapting to changes in the slant of light and fluctuating temperatures and the blue, black, gray, and azure of the expanse above our heads.

And until we adapt, it won't be surprising if we suffer. In case anyone hasn't noticed, as a culture we are getting noticeably larger. You recognize it most readily on airplanes, where the seats haven't shrunk (though since you, dear reader, have probably expanded as well, your picture of what that trip to Pittsburgh was like 20 years ago is likely to be somewhat distorted). Our eating habits have changed radically – there is corn syrup and corn starch and corn fructose in most everything, and we don't grow much of what we eat, and most of what we do eat is barely within six degrees of separation. (In 1970, the average American ate half a pound of high-fructose corn syrup a year; by 1997, it was up to 62 1/2 pounds and rising. A 2009 study indicates that high levels of fructose in the diet may greatly increase risk of Type 2 diabetes and heart disease, independent of weight gain). A walk around the neighborhood is for many a big event, if we walk at all, and we live somewhere that resembles a neighborhood. Our blood pressures are going up. Alzheimer's seems to be making its appearance at earlier and earlier ages (though, in the past, it may well have been well under-diagnosed). We wake up a lot sorer than we used to, and, if psychological surveys and the radical increase in prescriptions for anti-depressants are any indication, our relative wealth betrays a distinctly acrid air of unhappiness.

Our kids, too. They are, to be polite, becoming *wider* than is thought to be healthy. More sedentary. Suffer from more allergies. Prone to childhood diabetes and vitamin D deficiency. Much more likely to suffer from depression than children virtually anywhere else in the world. And as the government steps up its invasion into our collective homes in the form of "homework" (wish it were covered by Department of Labor standards), they are less likely to be found playing ball in sandlots, fishing in local ponds, picking blackberries, or just messing around in "vacant" spaces, if they are lucky enough to be able to find any. The kids are just plain stressed out.

A set of recent studies conducted at the Human-Environment Research Laboratory at the University of Illinois-Urbana/Champaign suggests that that even small amounts of "green activities" – those that take place outdoors in at least semi-natural settings – substantially reduces ADHD symptoms (no, this is not going to be an ADHD rant, though I often think our children are "canaries in the coal mines," so we shouldn't be surprised when sometimes their behavior does not meet with general approval, like the canary who doesn't sing. If a greener environment can play a role in putting ADHD into remission, what about the converse: could ADHD be a set of symptoms initiated or aggravated by lack of nature exposure?) Green activities increase concentration, impulse inhibition, and self-discipline. Another study suggests that symptoms may even disappear entirely for boys who take a 40-minute walk with their fathers in a wooded setting before school (would this mean the disease is in remission, or didn't exist to begin with? Whoops, didn't I just say I wouldn't go there?) This all assumes of course that there is a wooded setting, or a dad, to be found. Maybe we can find a way to put "green" into pill form?

Several other studies demonstrated that school performance improved when children were placed next to windows and allowed to look at the green outside. Now that's quite a trick if you are in a school where there are no windows, or the windows are frosted (as they are in Hawaii), or you have one of those teachers who believes that staring out the window means you are not paying attention. (Maybe not paying attention improves performance?)

Wait: it gets better. In a follow-up experiment, it was found that children who spent 20 minutes on a guided outdoor walk saw the greatest benefits when they sauntered in smaller groups or one-on-one, compared with those who walked in larger groups. The main author of the study, Dr. Frances Kuo, suggests this is because, within a smaller group, children are less likely to be competing for a teacher's attention, awaiting their turn, or resisting the distraction of other kids, and hence are more "relaxed." Why is it that I'm not surprised?

There is a disheartening aspect to the way all the research is reported, though. It all seems to boil down to whether a child can pay attention in school. But isn't what the research actually suggesting is that children shouldn't be in school at all? Duh! Might there be more value, more "to be learned," from a daily amble in the woods with dad? (Let's hear it for dads!) Or just a small group of children doing what it is children do, with no teacher competing for *their* attention? Why must children be forced to "burn off pent-up energy" rather than reveling in it? Has anyone bothered to compare the "marginal educational utility" of the new, local neighborhood school, and the great associated sucking impact on community resources, against that of the wooded area cut down to make way for it? Are we simply condemning the kids (as other research suggests), to a lifetime of higher levels of aggression, domestic violence, crime, mental fatigue, anger, frustration, and poor health? Is being allowed to look out the window at the last remaining tree going to be enough?

Rather than looking backward, can't we look forward to a time when a walk in the woods can just be a walk in the woods?

WE USED TO say about our older daughter Aliyah that, for every hour of time with other people, she required two hours of time by herself, and that her favorite space for such time was in the woods near our home. When I look back at it, I think we were being overly glib. It was (and still remains) true that substantial amounts of time alone make Aliyah a happier camper. My wife and I, both having been brought up as urbanites, perhaps overly naïvely chalked this up purely to an interesting personality trait (which we would still think it likely is), but without much regard to (or particular understanding of) the physical environment where that character trait found its happiest manifestation.

The thing about the woods (and even how it differs from a park or other outdoor setting) is that it is an open, non-directed field. There is nothing external in the field itself that directs attention over and above anything else. Physically, one can just as easily examine the play of sunlight on leaves, explore the roughness of tree bark, observe the wings of a beetle, watch the slithering of a snake or meanderings of a slug, monitor the activity of the honeybee as it collects pollen, survey the progress of a twig as it floats downstream, study the eddies in a puddle. There is no requirement as to which of the five senses is to be engaged: one may find oneself scrutinizing the movement of ants hurrying up and down a tree trunk, feeling the wave of wind upon high grasses or the close rush of owl wings, tasting the bitterness of miners lettuce or the sourness of salmonberries, smelling the slightly sweet decomposition of oak leaves underfoot, listening to the cackling of crows at twilight or the mumbling of a midsummer brook.

Aliyah taught us that the woods provide a locus for the unfettered operations of virtually all of the multiple intelligences, at whatever level a child can make use of them, with, in time, perhaps the heaviest stress upon the intrapersonal one. The woods is a psychophysical space where a child can escape from scripts, important but limiting building blocks in the processes of development, to a place where she finds emerging opportunities to create her own; an escape from a world wholly created by others to one co-created by the child with Nature Herself. Regardless of how richly we can populate the child's room with the cornucopia of contemporary educational possibility, it still remains an expression of poverty compared with the bounty that the natural world offers freely (or not, as it becomes more and more difficult to find).

I am insisting on the unscripted, non-directed field that the natural environment offers as perhaps what makes it so inviting to children, provided (and Aliyah says this is key) we allow them to experience it alone and unmediated. But perhaps my claims for it are too modest, for the offering may, at its most profound, be that of the hidden scripts of Nature herself, both in the world and as she plays upon the heart. I am reminded of another poem of William Wordsworth, "Lines Composed a Few Miles Above Tintern Abbey," a nature poem which contains almost no images of nature after the first paragraph. Wordsworth first makes what he considers to be a lesser claim for the workings of the natural world,

> .... *feelings too*
> *Of unremembered pleasure: such, perhaps,*
> *As have no slight or trivial influence*
> *On that best portion of a good man's life,*
> *His little, nameless, unremembered, acts*
> *Of kindness and of love.*

Only to make a greater claim in the climax of the poem:

> .... *And I have felt*
> *A presence that disturbs me with the joy*
> *Of elevated thoughts; a sense sublime*
> *Of something far more deeply interfused,*
> *Whose dwelling is the light of setting suns,*
> *And the round ocean and the live air,*
> *And the blue sky, and in the mind of man;*
> *A motion and a spirit, that impels*
> *All thinking things, all objects of all thought,*
> *And rolls through all things. Therefore am I still*
> *A lover of the meadows and the woods,*
> *And mountains;*

And so I ask again: is being allowed to look out the window at the last remaining tree going to be enough?

SOME OF US respond to scientific evidence about learning environments; others of us respond to poetry. If neither of these yank your chain, how about *morphological computing*?

For years now, physiologists have become increasingly aware that the capacities of the brain and nervous system, taken by themselves, are not sufficient to process the sheer volume of information human beings are confronted with in daily living. To fully make sense of the world around us, our bodies themselves take up some of the slack. At the simplest level, we all know that, as our hands move away from flames or from water that is too hot even before our minds have had the opportunity to recognize the danger. The same is true as we taste with our sense of smell.

But there is more to it than this. Researchers have found evidence of synesthesia, the conflation and cross-referencing of sensory modalities, among infants. It is a natural characteristic, though one we lose (though perhaps only partially) over time. The whorls and ridges of fingerprints are designed to sense vibrations, and to interpret them independent of brain activity. People "hear" with their skin, interpreting certain consonants according to whether they feel a puff of air accompanying the sound. If we do, "ba" becomes "pa"; "da" becomes "ta." We also hear language with our eyes as well, as we are far more accurate in interpreting what is said when we can actually see the speakers.

In short, morphological computing suggests we can hear with our eyes, see with our skin, taste the wind, feel the earth in our joints and muscles. This idea is not at all uncommon in non-industrial societies, even if within our own, it has until recently been confined to the realm of poetry. And there is so much more waiting to be rediscovered!

But it is also suggestive of something darker. Compulsory confinement of children to the day jail (followed by hours of home confinement through homework) may deprive them of the necessary experience of the psychophysical space where both their sensory awareness and capacities may grow. Alternatively, they may be deprived of the opportunity to maintain some of that synesthetic capacity with which they are born, so that it atrophies, and is no longer available to them to feed their creativity as they develop. In other words, children's growth may be stunted and misshapen, leaving them both mental and physically (and perhaps emotionally, too) retarded specifically as a result of their "education." (So what else is new?)

There has to be a better way. (Thank heavens, there is).

> *Up! up! my Friend, and quit your books;*
> *Or surely you'll grow double:*
> *Up! up! my Friend, and clear your looks;*
> *Why all this toil and trouble?*
> *The sun, above the mountain's head,*
> *A freshening lustre mellow*
> *Through all the long green fields has spread,*
> *His first sweet evening yellow.*
> *Books! 'tis a dull and endless strife:*
> *Come, hear the woodland linnet,*

How sweet his music! on my life,
There's more of wisdom in it.
And hark! how blithe the throstle sings!
He, too, is no mean preacher:
Come forth into the light of things,
Let Nature be your teacher.
She has a world of ready wealth,
Our minds and hearts to bless—
Spontaneous wisdom breathed by health,
Truth breathed by cheerfulness.
One impulse from a vernal wood
May teach you more of man,
Of moral evil and of good,
Than all the sages can.
Sweet is the lore which Nature brings;
Our meddling intellect
Mis-shapes the beauteous forms of things:—
We murder to dissect.
Enough of Science and of Art;
Close up those barren leaves;
Come forth, and bring with you a heart
That watches and receives.
                    - William Wordsworth
                       The Tables Turned

My Chair (New American Family Style)

I WAS CONTACTED by the memoirist Rebecca Walker, author of *Black, White & Jewish* and the more recent *Baby Love*. I have long admired her work, and so when she invited me to contribute a chapter to an anthology on "The New American Family," I jumped at the opportunity.

But we made an unusual agreement. I was to write about anything but homeschooling. She thought she had someone else who was going to do that. Sounded good to me. As I writer and storyteller, I inhabit more than a few different personae (bet you haven't seen that one very often), and this was a welcome chance to flex my authorial muscles in a different way. Besides, I thought it would be fun! (which counts for a lot for me these days).

So then I sat down to write. Out came something about…well, homeschooling? At least the way I think about homeschooling. I can't separate homeschooling from my family life, and as I learn about myself, I expect (actually, by this time I *know*) that the kids (hardly kids anymore, but they'll always be kids to me…) are learning as well.

In some very profound ways, just as we are embodied in the relationships we have with others so that sometimes it is hard to know where our own consciousness ends and another's begins (as every mother with an infant can well attest), so we are also embodied in our relationships with objects in our physical world. We change together, and it is consciousness of that change, and how we choose to take charge and structure that change, both in our minds and in the world, is what constitutes learning.

I am *in* my chair.

WE MOVED INTO our current 1970s tract home (post-avocado and mustard periods) when the kids were still small. I brought my chair with me.

It was a recliner, purchased at the local Salvation Army store for $10. It was probably 15 years old when we first acquired it, and would last us some 15 more.

It was brown in color. Not brown as in chocolate. More like beef stew, in something resembling corduroy. It absorbed coffee stains and coffee spills well, and other than a little bit of café aroma, after a day or two, one couldn't even tell that something untoward had taken place.

The kids used to like to cuddle up on the chair. Occasionally dog number one, too, until she (Gracie being half-Airedale/half-German Shepherd, and winner of the Westminster Dog Show in the Resting Group) became too large and too old to lift herself up. Lots of articles, and more than a few stories were written from that chair, usually in black pen on a long yellow legal pad. And there were occasional dreams as well. It was my well-worn brown perch from which I came to widely peer out over the growing life of my family.

But after a decade and a half of bearing my weight (which I am more than willing to admit has increased over the years) in sleep and in wakefulness, the recliner was coming to the end of its natural life. The cushions were crushed, the now-yellowed and crumbly polyurethane peeking out through the seams, the footrest worn through, the reclining mechanism giving out, the arms long ago having reached a maximum caffeine saturation point. It was time for a new chair.

My wife Ellen went back to school to become a nurse at the same time my older daughter Aliyah went off to college. We decided that as Ellen's graduation present – actually, for both of us, this being the final occasion either of us was likely to be able to celebrate earning a degree – we would purchase a new chair.

Graduation came and went. Ellen went to work at her new job. Aliyah prepared for her junior year in Italy. Meera, my younger one and serious gymnast since the age of five, was now back in the gym after finally having her knee heal. I ran around the country lecturing. We never managed to cross the threshold of a furniture store. (In fact, I can't even remember visiting one since the early 1990s, and performing a quick mental survey of our home, I can't find a single item purchased – by us – at a *real* furniture emporium). A friend calls our odd assortment "New American Family Style."

Meanwhile, Meera needed a car so she could commute between the community college and the gym, so we began shopping. We went to visit a 1990 Honda in a parking lot that turned out to be a clunker, but it was next door to a large furniture store. Ellen and I shrugged our shoulders, took a deep breath, and went in.

We were directed to the second floor – recliners. Oh, my! There was a room full of 'em, bigger than our entire house! There were blue ones and green ones, topaz and mauve, prints and stripes, leatherette and microfiber. There were chairs with rounded arms and square, curlicued and plain, arms accented in wood, or with cup holders on the end. There were wide ones and narrow, taller and squat, those that leaned back fully horizontal, and others meant to abut walls. There were child-proof and fire-proof (no dog-proof from what I could see), ScotchGarded and Wipe-Aways, electronic and spring loaded, track-sliders and knob turners and vibrating.

We sat in a few. They all seemed fine to us. Most cost around $500, give or take, about the same amount necessary to feed two entire families involved in projects in India my family supports for a whole year (for more information, visit www.friendsoflafti.org) No guilt, though – we could afford it, and this chair was going to last most if not all of the rest of our lives. But which one?

On the way out, there was another room, this one filled with sofas. We had a perfectly fine $50 sofa that both dogs seemed to like. (The dogs don't seem to know the difference between a sofa –a word which comes from Turkish and smacks of the orientalism of 18ᵗʰ Century Paris and seat cushions encased in transparent slipcovers in my grandmother's parlor – and a plain old-fashioned Middle English couch. Neither do I). We got to sit on it, too. But here were sofas in their various and sundry sizes, colors, fabrics, and mechanical incarnations – with recliners on each end!

What a vision! In my reverie, I could sit in the left hand recliner, coffee cup on the left arm, computer on my lap, papers and books and telephone (and dog – this one at least nominally Meera's, an unkempt little West Highland White Terrier named Duncan) on my right side, Ellen seated, feet up, fantasy novel in hand, on the recliner at the other end. Familial bliss! How could we ever have lived without one?! Thousand bucks – food for four families; but food is hand-to-mouth while furniture can last a lifetime!

We left the store. Single recliner or couch? What size? Would a sofa fit in our small family room? What would we do with the old one? Would the dogs be offended? It all made our heads hurt.

Ellen went to work that evening. Aliyah and I decided to see *The Merchant of Venice* at a little semi-professional playhouse near our home. On the lawn in front of a house two blocks from ours, there it is. "Take Me," it reads, "$20." Aliyah sits in the chair. Seems fine to her. I sit in the chair, and put my feet up. It doesn't smell of cigarette smoke. Nothing torn. The reclining mechanism works. It even rocks!

By eight o'clock the next morning, the recliner is in our family room. Only then do I realize it doesn't match anything and, I suspect, it didn't match anything in the home of the previous owners either. Is that why they got rid of it? The fabric is some sort of nubbed tweedy (worsted?), rather roughish to the touch, in fading wedgewood and aged dijon, a little brown, taupe, and yellow thrown in. Factory leftovers, or was it actually planned this way? The reclining mechanism handle is oak. In the family room, the walls are bright yellow, with a green leafy wallpaper border. The curtains are maroon, with leaves in orange-gold and emerald. The linoleum somewhere between aqua and slate; the aforementioned couch is gray with embroidered flowers, though Ellen suggests that at one time it might have been off-white or cream. There is a cherrywood chest with a snake aquarium on top, Tassel and Silk the mutated cornsnakes – one cream, the other rust-colored – inside. (Aliyah used to breed snakes; now that she is off to college, we seem to have inherited them, and we still keep microwaveable mice in the freezer for their fine dining pleasure). The bookcases are white pine. Echo the bunny is busy at work within his wired cage, scattering hay beyond his confines. The black treadmill stands upright in the corner. There is a 19-inch "Konka" TV (I kid you not) in cheesy silver plastic, with a DVD player and the cable box below, on white shelves. Posters of wolves and owls grace the walls, reflecting the naturalist interests of the kids now mostly dormant. Boris and Sylvie, the Dino-pillows on the couch in green and gold (Boris long missing an ear until Ellen sewed it back on) date from the year Aliyah was born.

Then I realize that *nothing* here matches anything else. A domestic archaeologist could have a field day. An appalled interior decorator would probably throw it all out, and start over.

Ellen had a dream last night that we somehow had acquired all new furniture, and it all matched. There was even a corner sectional, especially amusing as there is no corner in our current family room in which it could be placed. "Very bizarre," she said.

Anyhow, my new perch sits in exactly the same place as my old one once did. Its color, as noted, is still a bit indeterminate, and a lot more difficult to describe. The same could be said of my hair, relative to the black of my younger days, and my mustache gets scruffier every year. The chair doesn't fit with anything else in the room.

But it fits me just fine. New American Family Style.

Matzoh Ball Math and More!

A JEWISH HOMESCHOOLING friend of mind – the psychologist and writer Dr. Jeffrey Fine (Jeffrey specifically asked me to identify him and his family by name, and he is the author of the excellent new book *The Art of Conscious Parenting*) just went through a life-threatening disease episode. He was in a coma, and the doctors said he was within hours of death, but through something akin to a miracle, coupled with spectacular advances in medical science, Jeffrey's own extraordinary willpower, and perhaps a little prayer thrown into the mix, he is well on the road to recovery.

During this episode, which lasted for a period of almost half a year, his wife Dalit enrolled their eight-year-old son Kessem in Kumon math. They both felt Kessem needed to be doing *something* at least vaguely academic, and perhaps add a little bit of regularity to a situation that was totally out of his control. They asked for my blessing, as if they really needed it (well, to be fair, having someone outside the family do so provided at least a little peace of mind), and I readily gave it. I wasn't so concerned about what Kessem was actually going to learn, if anything, but rather that there be a bare semblance of normality in his life, and that his parents didn't feel any extra burden of guilt on top of what was already an extraordinarily trying situation.

Kumon math does a pretty good job, for what it is. Most families find their way there when the kids are doing "poorly" in school, not "keeping up," or "falling behind" (all those quotation marks are deliberate), and are being stereotyped, picked on, scapegoated, humiliated, embarrassed, or ignored accordingly (by teachers, fellow students, or the institution itself). Needless to say, many of the kids lose self-esteem in the process, feel stupid, and often either lash out or withdraw as a coping mechanism to deal with the injuries being dealt to them in the process of their "education."

So what Kumon does, first and foremost, is work to raise children's self-esteem. And they do so by requiring only "work that is easily completed." The idea is never to give a child work at which she won't be successful. So instead of, as is usual in most educational theory, providing assignments at the proximal level of a child's development so that she may learn either through teaching or through a process of error and correction, the only work required is that at which the child is sure to succeed. "Success from the start" is Kumon's motto, and ensuring there is no frustration is the key. In other words, if a child is ready for "two plus two," the "self-motivated learning model" will have the child "working on" "one plus one." All material must be completed with a perfect score within a prescribed period of time before the child is allowed to progress on to anything more difficult. Daily worksheets are provided that must be completed until they are mastered in the required amount of time before moving on. If it works, self-esteem is restored, and the child will be able to transfer the self-knowledge that success is possible back to the location of the original insult and humiliation.

It didn't take long, however, for Kumon to chafe on poor Kessem. He couldn't see any reason to work on worksheets containing information he already knew for 20 minutes when he could do it in ten, especially as no new learning was taking place. His mother asked me for ways to get him to "concentrate," and all I could find myself doing was trying to assure her that Kessem had already proven that concentration wasn't the problem.

The point being of course that if you get all the answers right, powers of concentration aren't at issue. Your self-esteem might increase for awhile (until you figure out you are being patronized, and look for ways to non-cooperate), but you probably wouldn't be learning anything, except that no one ever really cared about the worksheets once you had completed them, perfect and all. Kessem wasn't suffering from lack of concentration; he was suffering from a growing lack of interest.

This morsel being hard to stomach raw, I reached for my trusty "that reminds me of a story" approach, which I borrowed some quarter of a century ago from the great anthropologist and systems thinker Gregory Bateson.

Bateson used to tell a story about a learning experiment with a dolphin he conducted and observed in Hawaii. The experimental protocol involved a number of repetitions with a hoop that any experienced dolphin trainer would have warned would be boring, so the animal would break the sequence by tossing the hoop off to the side. "Funny," said Gregory's assistant, "every time he does that he gives a little chuckle." Gregory asked her if she wrote the chuckle down, but there was no place to record it. All that was recorded was that the dolphin had failed to demonstrate successful learning. Hmm.

This seemed to hit the spot, if not so much with Dalit, at least with Jeffrey, who recognized this other form of frustration from his own school days. "What do we do now?" he asked.

"Hold a graduation ceremony for Kumon, and move on to something that is now a big part of your and Kessem's world. I suggested. What's up for you?"

Jeffrey thought a minute. "Well, I never thought I'd live to see another Passover. And the Angel of Death seems to have passed over our house, at least for now. (The word "Passover" refers to the Biblical story that the Angel of Death passed over the houses of the Israelites and killed all firstborn males among the Egyptians, resulting in the expeditious exit of the Israelites from Egypt). So we are doing it up big. Grandma is coming from Israel for several weeks to help out, and we expect around 20 people for the *Seder* (the ritual Passover meal)."

"All right. And Kessem knows the Four Questions?" [The youngest participant at a *Seder* gets to ask four ritualized questions, preferably in

Hebrew, which the rest of meal (that can take up to six hours or longer, depending on how thorough one is), is set up to answer.]

"He's got those down," Jeffrey said proudly.

"Well, then I've got just the thing, but grandma will have to get in on the action. Matzoh Ball Math."

Back up. *Matzoh* is a kind of unleavened cracker, eaten during the eight days of Passover (there are folks who eat it all year round) in remembrance of the haste with which the Israelites left Egypt, so quickly that they didn't have time to allow the bread to rise in the oven. For some folks, one of the great treats of Passover is matzoh ball soup, chicken soup (vegetable soup for vegetarians is of course acceptable) eaten with a kind of round dumpling made with matzoh meal, eggs (unless cholesterol free), and various and sundry kinds of extras. There are matzoh ball connoisseurs, and there are various factions prepared to do battle for seasoned or unseasoned, with *schmaltz* (chicken fat) or not, onions/no onion, firm or feathery, traditional or light textured, gluten-free or cajunfusion. (You can find a terrific selection of recipes at Ellen's Kitchen – www.ellenskitchen.com/resource/matzoballstrad.html – I've posted a simple, traditional one at the end of this chapter). In my extended family, we have members of both the *sinker* (prefer the matzoh balls on the bottom of the soup) and *floater* persuasions. [My wife and I are both floaters. It is said that flotation can be ensured by not peeking into the covered pot during cooking – this could be a subject of scientific inquiry (it may be folklore, simply an old wives' tale designed to keep nosey husbands out of the kitchen;) I prefer simply adding a little seltzer to the recipe.]

Matzoh Ball Math is something that can be done over a period of years, to match a child's interest and mathematical readiness. There's no need to do it all at once (and certainly not in order, even if the name for the Passover meal – *Seder* – means "order"), and for those who celebrate the holiday, it can be incorporated a bit more at a time each year, a new "ritual" grafted onto the old.

The first lesson, of course, is simply in the making of the matzoh balls themselves. (I suggest that children be provided with separate materials for their own pot of matzoh balls. That way one is sure to have enough for consumption, without having to be concerned about the ultimate fate of the objects of mathematical inquiry. Of course, you'll want your children to be able to make good ones so that even if they don't turn out to be math whizzes, they'll have a sense of what it is to be a good cook!

Equipment (besides the basic food stuffs needed for the recipe, normal cooking utensils, and a good pot with a tight lid) consists of: two scales (one which can weigh an entire pot full of stuff, one that can weigh small amounts of ingredients, or an entire cooked matzoh ball); teaspoon and tablespoon measures; marked measuring cups and pitcher; a small ruler; string; butcher paper; eight small colorfast buttons (two each of four different colors); and a set of calipers. Oh, and of course, a handy white board with erasable colored markers.

Ready? The first thing for a child to learn is measurement, and in doing so, about bases. (I am presuming that she has already learned the basics behind base 10). So start playing with matzoh meal. How many teaspoons in a tablespoon? Make sure to put the results on the board. Write equations: draw three small spoons = 1 tablespoon. Write it out in words – words are in fact a form of algebraic expression, where the words substitute for the thing itself. Then turn it into more formal algebra. (I am convinced, by the way, that most kids are prepared to handle basic algebra by age 7 or so). Let Teaspoon = A; let Tablespoon = B. $3A=B$. $6A=?$ Show her the symbols for greater than ($>$) and less than ($<$). $4A>B$. Some kids are going to like the writing part best; others, playing with the spoons – you'll quickly find out whether yours is a writer or a spooner.

She gets to do this with all kinds of measurement. How many ounces in a cup? (If you have an ounce measure, actually have her perform the operation to find out rather than simply reading the side of the liquid measure). How many cups in a pint? Pints in a quart? Quarts in a gallon? How many ounces does the four-gallon pot hold? Write out all the equations: in pictures, in words, in algebraic symbols. (This will all pay off later when you start reading recipes together).

Same with grams, ounces, and pounds. Ah-oh. There are two kinds of ounces – how are we going to write the symbols so we don't get confused? Do liquid ounces of various different substances weigh the same amount? Try it out – with water, oil, and flour. Write the results on the whiteboard, and use the less than/greater than symbols.

IF SHE DOES this all backwards, working from the largest measures to the smallest, you will have learned fractions. The rest is just a writing exercise (which you should do, in the equation format).

Now one needs to know how to read the ruler. All of sudden we have fallen into a world of fractions, and base 12! The calipers, too. With the ruler, start measuring the kitchen world. The diameter of the pot; the radius of the pot (show how you can get the same result using the ruler or the calipers); the height of the scale and the measuring cup. Length, width, and height. Make a couple of "LWH" charts, and begin to examine the relationships of the measures.

Wow – that made me all hungry. Time for some *gefilte* fish. en.wikipedia.org/wiki/Gefilte_fish. Those of you who like to fish can go in quest of the giant Gefilte. Do I have stories for you! (you can look up many of them online).

TWO THOUSAND WORDS, and we haven't cooked anything yet! Time to roll the matzoh balls. Make them about an inch across. About 15 of them should do.

What are different ways you can measure the diameter? One way is simply to leave them on a flat surface of butcher paper, and use a ruler to measure them end-to-end. Another way is use the calipers. A third way is to cut one in half, and measure the diameter on the open face. See if you come up with the same answer all three ways. write it on the board – D = 1. What about "r"?

Now let's make things interesting. Let's name four of the matzoh balls: "Abraham", also known as "Matzoh Ball A", "Benjamin – B", "Chaim – C", and "Daniel – D." Let them represent the four brothers who traditionally are said to ask questions at the *seder* – the wise son, the simple son, the wicked son, and the one who is too young to ask. Figure out together how you might determine how "long they are around." In other words, the circumference. Use a string or thread, and take a measure of the girth. Take the amount of string required to go around the middle, and measure it with the ruler. Now do it to three or four more. Write down the results in a little chart for A, B, C, D. Let's see: 3 1/2, 3 1/8, 3 1/4, 3. (Abraham was a little lumpy; Daniel was kind of small). On the white board, write out their relative sizes using the "<" and ">" symbols, and scramble the order. Now on another line on the chart, list the diameters of each. What is the ratio between the diameter and the circumference?

Sooner or later, you'll be singing the Pi Day Song, which will make the exercise truly ecumenical. (We sing it in my office, as the price of a slice of pie, every March 14th). It's to the tune of "Oh Christmas Tree":

Oh, Number Pi
Oh, number Pi
Oh, number Pi
Your digits are unending,
Oh, number Pi
Oh, number Pi
No pattern are you sending.
You're three point one four one five nine,
And even more if we had time,
Oh, number Pi
Oh, number Pi
For circle lengths unbending.
Oh, number Pi
Oh, number Pi
You are a number very sweet,
Oh, number Pi
Oh, number Pi
Your uses are so very neat.
There's 2 Pi r and Pi r squared,
A half a circle and you're there,

Oh, number Pi
Oh, number Pi
We know that Pi's a tasty treat.
        - (Words by LaVern Christenson, Windom, Minnesota)

Now it's time to weigh each of the four matzoh balls (in grams), and put their uncooked weights on the chart.

Then we are going to cook them in a covered pot for 40 minutes or so (40 is a very important Biblical number, as in "It rained for 40 days and 40 nights," Moses went up to Mount Sinai for 40 days, or the Israelites spent 40 years in the desert. Forty years is another way of saying "a very long time," as is 40 minutes for many seven– or eight-year-olds). Follow the recipe. A vexing question arises: how are we going to distinguish Abraham, Benjamin, Chaim, and Daniel from each other when we take them out of the pot? This question vexed me, too, so I consulted two Quaker experts, neither of whom had ever made matzoh balls, but one had made plum pudding, and the other was a preschool teacher. We all agreed that we could try to dye them each a different color, but most of the color might likely wash out, leaving all the matzoh balls an unappetizing gray. Not a good move. So we came up with another method, though you and your child might come up with a better one. (Write me). Get eight small colorfast buttons, two each of four different colors, and assign a color to each matzoh ball. Make sure to put the assigned colors on the chart. Tie the two similarly colored buttons together with a string, with about a one-inch space between them. Stick one button in the middle of the matzoh ball, and let the other dangle on the outside. (We also thought of fancy-colored toothpicks that are blunt on one end, but we feared they might stick to another matzoh ball).

Carefully measure the amount of water being placed in the pot. Then, when the water comes to a boil, carefully drop all the matzoh balls in the water, including the four brothers. Cover the pot, weigh the whole thing, *and don't look!* (As already noted, there are people who believe that uncovering the pot turns floaters into sinkers – this, as noted, could be the subject of some more advanced experimentation. I haven't had the time).

When cooked, carefully remove the matzoh balls with a slotted spoon. Weigh the total for the matzoh balls, and the water that remains in the pot. Add the two weights together. Has any weight been lost? Where did it go? Measure out how much water is left in the pot, and compare with the amount put in. You could use this as the beginning of an exercise in understanding percentages.

Now separate out the four brothers. Weigh them individually. Measure their girth. Find the diameter and radius. Expand the chart: now there is a "Before" and "After."

There is so much more than can be done. The volume of the spheres. The volume of cylinders. The ratio between weight and volume (density). Exercises to calculate the rate of change at various temperatures (in other words, a matzoh ball curriculum in calculus and organic chemistry). All of this can wait for future years.

And there will be questions! Plenty of them, more than could possibly be generated by just the four sons – and we have daughters, too! You will have become matzoh ball scientists.

But you can't do any of this without a recipe! Here's a relatively simple one:

Ingredients:

> 3 eggs
> 3 tablespoons chicken fat (vegetable oil will work)
> ½ teaspoon salt
> 3 tablespoons hot water or chicken soup (I also believe in a spritz of seltzer water)
> ¾ cup matzoh meal

Separate the eggs (that is, the whites from the yolks!)

Beat the yolks until they are thick

Add the salt, fat/oil, water/soup/seltzer.

Beat the whites until stiff but not too dry, and fold in.

Fold in the matzoh meal. Put in refrigerator for an hour.

Roll into balls.

Carefully drop the balls into two quarts boiling salted water or soup.

Cover and cook for 25 minutes. DON'T LOOK!

If cooked in water thus far, transfer to soup for another 15 minutes.

Eat!

Well, I think I gave Jeffrey, Dalit, Kessem, and grandma more than they were likely to handle this Passover. That's fine, as it will give them plenty to chew on (though matzoh balls should melt in the mouth), and there will be plenty more Passovers to follow. In the meantime, I suggested that they not save one of the traditional Jewish blessings exclusively for the lighting of Passover candles, but they could use it to inform every day of their homeschooling lives:

"Blessed are You, Ruler of the Universe, who has given us life, sustained us, and brought us to this very special occasion."

Simon Sez

"The mere habit of obedience is not preparation for life in a democracy."
– Maria Montessori (1915)

I DON'T THINK I've played Simon Sez in more than 35 years. I can't honestly say that I've missed it. I don't have any especial expectation that I'll walk into work on a particular Monday morning, and there will be my boss waiting to have a go at us. Or least I hope not, and I'd have even less desire for it to happen on a daily basis.

I remember Simon Sez pretty well, though, as I expect does most everyone who's ever played. Folks line up and take orders from "Simon," which can either be in the form of copying his physical action or, alternatively, obeying a specific verbal command. If, however, a command is given which is not prefaced by Simon's signature mark of authority – the words "Simon Sez" – the command is not to be obeyed.

The whole idea is to catch one out while, in the course of complying with all the correct commands, inadvertently acting upon the one which contravenes Simon's authority. When folks "disobey," they are progressively banished from the game until, finally, there is a single person left standing, the "winner."

Usually, those unfamiliar with Simon Sez, or who are hard of hearing, or slow to convert verbal commands into accurate, near-instantaneous responses, find themselves relegated to the sidelines almost immediately. As a rule, the commands begin simply, and then get more complex and farfetched and, in a utilitarian sort of way, less useful. "Simon Sez scratch behind your left ear with your right index finger" or a speedy "Do this" following on a chain of "Simon Sez's" grasping one's belly with alternating hands will usually knock out at least a few of the contestants.

The thing is, Simon has to manage to keep all the remaining participants engaged and involved. If all the contestants continue to move on command after command, they will soon weary of the game. So they must be kept in a state of active alert, engulfed by fear (of the game variety) that if they do not remain in a condition of vigilant expectation, they will be among the next to be eliminated. This diversion rewards the quick-witted and agile, wily and acute, a neo-Darwinian representation of the 'survival of the fittest.'

Perhaps I grew up just a spoilsport, but though I was actually quite adept at Simon Sez –being simultaneously, if I might toot my own horn, quick-witted, agile, wily, and acute – I do not remember either myself or any of my friends requesting to play once we'd been taught the rules. This was some adult's idea of a good time, and though I can remember some vague enjoyment in finding yet something else I was good at, and an occasional laugh, I can't imagine ever thinking that this would be a fun thing to suggest to my friends that we do on our own.

The games adults choose for children and those kids choose for themselves often vary considerably. Adults tend to teach "culling sports," from Simon Sez to dodge ball, that quickly turn large numbers of participants into sitters, but at the same time requiring that the group be kept intact. Can anyone ever remember the early dodge ball or Simon Sez culls being invited by adults to go off and play something else (or even read a book!) while the rest of the game was going on? It is as if adults conceive of it as being really fun to cheer on the remaining participants, when, in fact, the sitters have long ago become resentful, or, if always an early spectator, simply resigned.

In contrast, watch what kids do to culling sports when left to themselves. In most neighborhoods, Tag rapidly evolves to Freeze Tag – no participant is ever totally "out" unless all are, simultaneously, and, once unfrozen, all participants are expected to assist in the liberation of others, even those more agile or athletic than themselves. Hide 'n' Seek mutates to the point that when you are found, you simply become one of the seekers, the idea being to keep *everyone* in the game, with no one relegated to the sidelines.

The little amusement engendered by Simon Sez, other than for those of us who got an adrenalin rush out of competitively complying with increasingly complex (and ultimately meaningless and quickly forgotten) commands, stems from the degree to which it serves as metaphor for the rest of a child's existence, especially that of school. Consider that every day, for six hours a day, 200 or so days a year, you were told where and when to sit, when and where to stand, when and about what to talk and when to be quiet, when to read and when to close the book, when to be inquisitive and when to be a cipher, when to write, add, subtract, paint, sing, eat, listen, defecate, or put your head down. Failure to respond to Simon's commands is punishable, one quickly learns, and as children, malleable as we are, we learn to conform to the ground rules. Some of us even "enjoy" it. And if you are "culled," you are not likely to be invited to do something else, but simply required to do more of the same, but with progressively lowered expectations. If you or anyone else you know today ever feels at a loss of what to do with yourself, consider that it is because you have been trained not to know. Manufacturing this state of unknowing is called "socialization," and it breeds ignorance of one's own needs, thoughts, desires, hopes, and aspirations. If you really want to know what you should be feeling or thinking (or consuming!), you should go ask Simon.

An extended 12-year exercise in Simon Sez is not a particularly effective way for a child to learn, no less a necessary one. I have seen no evidence – anywhere – that it is. Industrial education was and is from day one education on the cheap, with its primary goal not to be found in the content of any of Simon's commands, but in obedience to the commands themselves. The objective is the production of a docile, compliant workforce, who will not rebel, and who will seek our life satisfactions solely through the production and consumption of material goods. And the first and foremost requirement of such an education, now and when it was conceived more than a hundred years ago, is that one becomes habituated to obedience. Let's not dress it up: doing things which are just plain dumb because you are ordered to "builds character" and "prepares you for life."

Is the nation worried about literacy? Look a little more closely. Almost a century ago, Maria Montessori found a way to take children, even those we today would consider "learning disabled", from the most harrowing home and social conditions, dens of vice and human degradation far worse than can be found virtually anywhere in North America today, even children from multiple cultures, with illiterate parents or none at all, and possessing no shared language whatsoever – and have them writing and reading by ages three, four, or five[35]. But there were requirements. Teachers had to provide the right tools in the right environments, and then get out of the way. No Simon Sez permitted; teachers were to observe carefully, and make sure their charges were individually presented with the appropriate materials, but were strictly forbidden from teaching. The child simply learned to become an autodidact and a self-disciplined human being, and acquired the skills independent of adult-inflicted punishment or

---

[35]   Note: this was never one of Montessori's goals, nor, I dare say, one of mine. It was just a goal sought out by the kids themselves. Today, of course, many Montessori schools, serving middle-class families, have made a fetish of early academic skill acquisition, about which the inventor would be ashamed.

rewards or words of praise or public shaming. As a society we could do that today if we chose, and the fact that we don't make such a choice (or are never even presented with it as an option) is extremely telling.

The great game of Simon Sez that is public education is fundamentally anti-democratic. I recognize that this is a pretty shocking thing to say in a nation in which, for a very long time, school has been viewed as the great leveler. But I call it as I see it. It is not only anti-democratic because from the first day of kindergarten, the culling machine is busy chewing up those unfamiliar with the language of the game, or who are hard of hearing, or who are slow to convert verbal commands into accurate, near-instantaneous responses, and remain capable of doing so, on book and on schedule, for the next 12 years. It is not only anti-democratic because it stacks the game by pouring resources, both human and economic, into those born with enough privilege to be least in need of them, and withholding those resources from those with the greatest need. It is not only undemocratic because of the forced association of individuals solely by chronological age, without any regard to their individual and particular interests, abilities, hopes, dreams, or aspirations, and because it denies any and all principles of democratic free association.

No, it is fundamentally undemocratic because it perverts the elemental need of the young, and the fundamental need to be served by education, and that is to acquire independence, and as much independence as one's individual developmental proclivities demand. A free society is only free to the extent that its members are able to find and develop those inner resources that facilitate the expression of their own individual and unique humanity.

No one ever put this better than the psychologist-philosopher Erich Fromm:

The right to express our thoughts, however, means something only if we are able to have thoughts of our own; freedom from external authority is a lasting gain only if the inner psychological conditions are such that we able to establish our own individuality.

When democracy is perverted to mean simply that we are occasionally allowed the opportunity to choose a new Simon, we know that somewhere things have gone off track. As the German theologian Dietrich Bonhoeffer once noted, the Second World War was the inevitable result of good schooling. Perhaps the best thing that can be said of public schooling today is that, as a society, thankfully we aren't very good at it.

Imagine what might happen if the paradigm for education was no longer Simon Sez, but Freeze Tag, where the purpose of learning is to help liberate each other, from our ignorance and misperceptions, our preconceptions regarding our own limitations, to a world of possibilities? What would it be like if the objective was no longer to "find people out" for purposes of exclusion from the game, but rather to invite them into an inclusive and democratic community of seekers, and provide an ever-expanding zone of freedom so that they could invent their own?

THE REALITY IS that I don't see much in the way of groups of kids playing anything in the neighborhood anymore. The increasingly invasive intrusion of government schooling into their lives and that of their families, coupled with parental management of the minutiae of their children's remaining extra-school existence, has turned many a neighborhood, when it comes to significant gatherings of children, into an empty wasteland.

There is a game that I now remember from my childhood that perhaps provides a counter narrative to that implied in the Simon Sez one. It is a game called "Ring-a-Levio," and from the little research I've been able to do, it seems to have originated in New York City, probably in Brooklyn, in the late 19th/early 20th Centuries – alongside the institutionalization of mass government schooling – and, also from what I can tell simply by asking lots of people, doesn't seem to have traveled very widely.

Ring-a-Levio is a sophisticated cross between Tag and Hide-and-Seek. There are variations to the game, but here's the version I grew up with. Two teams gather, and a marked area is set aside as the "jail," complete with a limited number of "guards." One team goes to hide. As each hider is found, s/he is brought back to the jail. However, if at any time a member or members of the hiding team can "attack" the jail without getting caught by the guards, get inside the marked area and yell "Ring-a-Levio One-Two-Three," all the prisoners can run free until caught again.

There you have it. Ring-a-Levio. A liberation tale. I can barely tell you how much I would have relished someone rushing past the guards and getting into my fourth-grade classroom to shout "Ring-a-Levio One-

Two-Three" so we could all run out. There was a great world out there.

Still is.

My New Exercise Regimen

I WAS WAITING for the service elevator in a wheelchair, ready and eager to leave the hospital, when I spotted a sign on the wall. "Did You Know?" read the headliner. "Using the stairs burns up to five times as many calories as taking the elevator." A stick figure climbed stairs at the bottom of the poster.

"Hmm," I thought, and nodded to my wife. "That could be my new exercise regimen."

"How's that?" she asked.

"Well, I could ride up and down on the elevator five times and lose as many calories as taking the stairs. Do it often enough, and I'll be a lean-mean-fighting machine." Since I am temporarily relegated to the elevator, this was a heartening thought.

When I arrived home, I e-mailed a homeschooling friend to see if her kids could figure out whether I was likely to lose more calories going up or coming down. Perhaps there is a sports physiologist out there who can tell me whether I am better off having the energy drink before or after.

All right. I was in the hospital because, having just returned from speaking at a homeschooling conference in Winnipeg (or 'WinterPeg,' as the locals endearingly call their hometown) and while playing in one of my thrice-weekly squash games, I experienced a major heart attack. Would have won, too. We called 9-1-1 at 7:15, and I was in the emergency room at 7:30, and in emergency surgery at 7:45. Assuming I am still around by the time this gets published (there is no reason to believe I won't be, as, *pace* Mark Twain, reports of my demise are greatly exaggerated), this is a living tribute to a community that has worked together to make it possible for modern medicine to do its magic, and for which I am extremely grateful.

But the next day in the acute cardio-telemetry wing at the hospital gave me much pause for reflection. The weather being unusually balmy and dry (I'm not sure if there was a connection but…), not a single doctor, according to the nurses, had set foot on the floor, for any of the patients, the entire day. From what I could tell, the ward had become a revolutionary feminist commune, and, my wife being a nurse herself, I guess that's not too shabby (though I think the contestants on Project Runway could have a field day with hospital garb, for nurses and patients alike).

Around eight-o-clock, the cardiologist who helped save my life in the emergency room rolled into my room like a great ball of fire, and announced that he was going to treat my case "very aggressively," and he already had a treatment plan. The off-the-shelf treatment scheme assumed I was an overweight, nicotine-addicted, alcohol-swilling couch-potato with high blood pressure, diabetes or at least high blood sugar, out-of-control cholesterol, a weakness for nachos, potato chips, and an uncontrollable penchant for fast food.

There was only one problem: I have low blood pressure, normal blood sugar, moderate and controlled cholesterol, a hankering after sashimi and Greek salad, lost 10-12 pounds in the past year, don't smoke or drink, and had my moment of excitement while burning 800 calories an hour playing a game against competitors barely half my age (and some older and in better shape than I am as well). Have swallowed an aspirin a day for more than a decade, along with the fish oil. The reason he didn't know any of this is because, in his smug omniscience, he hadn't even bothered to ask. (The drug companies don't seem particularly interested in folks like me either – there isn't a single cholesterol drug on the market designed or even tested for individuals with my profile).

Needless to say, I will not be availing myself of my former cardiologist's services any longer. But what this reminded me of immediately was the school combine, where educational strategies are prescribed by national and state committees, curricula designed by immensely profitable publishing companies and purchased by school boards, and educational approaches implemented by well-meaning teachers without knowledge of, nor even the barest acquaintance with, any single child. To paraphrase the philosopher and mystic G.I. Gurdjieff (totally out of context!), "Out of the vacuum and into the void." We could all have a field day ruminating about the "side effects." Fortunately, there are at least two million of us who have discovered we no longer require their services as well, and we've learned that it is in our children's best interests to pull them out of the way of the onrushing public education steamroller.

Kat, my personal doctor and perfectionist, came in with a hangdog look. She felt like a failure in not preventing my death (and subsequent resurrection). I, on the other hand, felt that the two of us were extraordinarily successful. I am the first male on my father's side of the family not to suffer a major heart attack by age 39, or to live past age 55. From my point of view, this was going to happen sooner or later, it is better that it was later, and, as my good friend the homeschooling author Jean Reed (*The Home School Source Book*) quips, I can now take something off my To-Do list. As far as I'm concerned, we are both overachievers, imperfect to be sure, and when I see her next week we'll have plenty to talk about, and perhaps I'll bring a box of chocolates.

So next time you see me at a homeschooling event in your community, (and I plan to get around to you soon!), you'll have to forgive me if I ask you to do the heavy lifting. My wife's doctor, a friend with a great sense of humor and a limited color selection of v-neck sweaters, told me to "be careful."

I promised that I wouldn't overdo the elevator thing anytime soon.

P.S. WITH THANKS to my homeschooling friend and fellow bird fancier Shell McCoy, I bought a canary! He has a haircut like one of the Beatles. (Okay, I know birds don't have hair, but you can take a look – www.avianweb.com/glostercanaries.html . As you'll see if you visit the site, Gloster canaries make for a great lesson in genetics). Turns out that he isn't a John, Paul, or Ringo, not even a Herman. He informed me in no uncertain terms that his name is Barnaby. Go figure.

P.P.S. I just received the results of my nuclear (No Nukes!) stress test from my *new* cardiologist. "Absolutely, completely, and unusually normal," he says. Little does he know.

P.P.P.S. Barnaby died, too, and hasn't come back, at least to me. I now have an American Singer canary named Ugo. After shedding, Ugo forgets how to sing, and so to get him started again, we got a recording of the Luciano Pavarotti of canaries, and after three days, Ugo is singing away again.

A Tether Between Our Teeth

LAST NIGHT, I took my daughter Aliyah, home from college, to a gospel music worship service – actually a history of gospel music – at our local (mostly) African-American Baptist Church. I emphasize 'mostly' because in reality New Life Baptist is the most racially integrated house of worship in our town. Years ago, we helped Aliyah reorganize an entire homeschooling week so that she could attend and perform in a "women of praise" gospel music workshop there.

When I arrived, I was certain that I didn't want to be there. It had nothing to do with religion, even though my own is very different – brought up Jewish, and a convinced Friend (Quaker) for more than 30 years. We usually worship in silent expectation, waiting upon that which will call us to ourselves that very day. Sometime it is profound; sometimes I make "to do" lists in my head; I learned long ago that profundity and shopping lists are both part – and probably necessary parts – of God's continuing soap opera for me. Others will feel differently. I have friends at New Life Baptist, and since I don't get there very often, I expected it to be a real treat, and had been looking forward to it for several weeks.

But now I was certain I didn't want to be there. I have been sick for the previous ten days – sore throat, cough, fever, chills, running nose, difficulty swallowing, ears ringing, you know the drill – and haven't yet been able to shake it. I sat down feeling sorry for myself, and all the things I had hoped to accomplish in the past ten days which were now down the tube. Mucus ran down the back of my throat, and I'd forgotten the throat lozenges, and my handkerchief was disgusting. And then I began to reflect upon the fact that I wasn't likely to get better for four or five days more, imagined all the things I now wasn't likely to accomplish, and felt even sorrier. I just wanted to go lie down, even though I was quick to acknowledge to myself that lying down simply made me feel worse!

I was in a sorry state. I was caught between past regrets and future intimations of suffering (I did promise my wife that I wasn't going to die soon, if I could help it). And then they started to sing. It took me awhile to be cleansed in the reverberation. I didn't want to surrender my misery. Slowly but surely, or maybe not so surely at least at first, I was swallowed by song. Took a little while longer for forgetfulness to kick in, and for me to be surrounded in the bubble. I began to keep time on the side of my pew with my right hand (I purposefully sat on the end, in case I needed to run out for a drink of water), and then decided I could clap, and then decided I could stand up, like everyone else, and then I couldn't remember what the last song was as soon as the next one began, and then I couldn't even remember the last verse, and the way the call-and-response broke up the lines into single words, I couldn't remember the line that came before.

And then there was only the present. Past regrets had melted away. Future doubts were yet to be known. I was right here, finding a place of stillness awash in sound. No ears ringing. Present. Just a beating heart. Or as my favorite religious poet Gerard Manley Hopkins put it ("God's Grandeur"), "World broods with warm breast and with ah! bright wings."

I slept very well that night, perhaps for the first time in ten days. Awoke still with the sniffles.

MY ONLY NEXT-DOOR neighbor Evalyn Poff died this morning, after a long and compelling life. She was 86. Her memorial service is likely to be attended by the Governor if she is in town, various members of the state legislature, the Mayor, virtually everyone who knows anyone in the political life of our fair city. She was never elected to public office, but was county chair of one of the political parties, and one of our town's most respected denizens.

However, that is not how Evalyn will be remembered in our family. Evalyn was Meera's first piano teacher (at age 2), though the relationship was never formalized. It was simply the place where she and, it turns out, half a dozen other children in the neighborhood learned to play, between snacks, snatches of conversation, and hitting up her husband Dick for pennies and nickels, and occasional dollar bills (most of which we made her return).

Evalyn's career pathway was wide-ranging, from shoe saleswoman, to international clothing buyer, to university accountant, to legislative aide, at which she worked until only six months before her death. But I think what made the largest impression, and which she said had kept her young all these years was her first job, working her way through college (and out of South Dakota, where she was one of 10 children) as a circus trapeze artist and acrobat. "There," she'd say, pointing out the old photograph of the 20-year-old in a leotard, "I used to swing out over the circus ring by holding onto a tether between my teeth."

Evalyn was a godsend for Meera. Both my wife and I are rather sedentary sorts, not just in our levels of physical activity, but in the depths of who we are. We try, occasionally, we get up on the treadmill, I haul myself down to jazzercise, but the truth is we are, like Aliyah, nouns, not verbs. Meera is most assuredly a verb. So was Evalyn. We have two favorite photographs. The first shows Meera at four (and Evalyn in her mid-70s), on rollerblades, Meera dressed in red sweatpants, red shirt, protective helmet, and a mink stole pillaged from a neighborhood yard sale. The second is the two of them on bikes, Meera decked out in pink tutu – I don't think Evalyn could find hers that day.

And so from Evalyn, we learned about verbs, not only how to deal with ours, but what they can look like as active, engaged, extraordinary adults. We knew none of this when we moved in 15 years ago, and for reasons unclear, the value of having the right neighbors is not usually included in real estate prices. Good thing, too, for, with Evalyn being priceless, we never could have afforded the house!

It is unlikely that many of you reading this would have come to know me, or I you, were it not for Evalyn. In late December 1996, we experienced an ice storm that left us without electricity for 11 days. As it turned out, our gas range still worked, but we had no heat. Evalyn's house had a wood stove for heating, but no way to cook. So for 11 days, we ferried back and forth. I sat in a rocking chair next to the wood stove with a yellow legal pad, and wrote what I thought at the time would simply be a keepsake for the kids. Those scribblings became my first homeschooling book *And the Skylark Sings with Me*.

So much of what makes a difference in our homeschooling lives is the degree to which we allow the best that our communities and neighbors have to offer to enter into them. This would be true for non-homeschoolers as well, but what homeschooling does is to allow us to open ourselves to such opportunities with intention. We allow our children to become rooted in a series of concentric streams of experience: within our families, neighborhoods, communities, ecosystem, nation, and world. And once we start thinking about rooting our kids this way within these interpenetrating streams of experience, somehow some of it is likely to wash over us as well. Unbound from the factory mentality that public education has come to embody, and free from "the dreary shower," our children and, if we can gather up the courage, we ourselves, are ready to joyously swing out over the circus ring of this strange and wondrous world, the tether held firmly between our teeth.

Thank you, Evalyn!

Bontshe Shvayg

I'VE SPENT A substantial amount of energy mining my memory of my own school experiences. As one who was a school "success story," but at the same time both lacking in self-awareness, and crippled in my understanding of what the institution was actually trying to do to me and my classmates, my pick-and-shovel approach allows me to come to grips with who and what, for better or for worse, shaped me into whom I am today.

Doing so makes it easy to illustrate that the emperor of public education has no clothes, and I plead guilty to having taken more than my share of cheap shots, especially as the target is so difficult to miss!

But I have also discovered that working to understand my school experiences gives me power. Environment does not have to be all-determining. By coming to terms with how institutional education shaped me and the way I view the world – and my capacity to learn about it – I gain the freedom to make other, more empowering decisions, both for myself, and with my children.

My poor brain is still cluttered with detritus gathered up in those 12 years, and I've never managed a spring cleaning. There are snatches of Russian-language dialogue tapes (I was a "Sputnik baby" with an IQ over 90, which means I was to be nuclear physicist who would invent the magic weapon that would destroy the Soviet Union forever). I can wax poetic about the mating habits of the three-spined stickleback fish (as distinguished from the Chinese Communist eight-spined variety), bore you with bits of a poem about a calliope, and I think I can still manage square roots on a slide rule.

But as I mine, I notice that there is almost a complete blank when it comes to how I learned any of this stuff. Oh, I can remember the books, and the blackboard, and the names of virtually all of my teachers, but the method by which I was expected to acquire knowledge now seems largely opaque to me.

What I do remember are the culling sports, from reading to dodge ball. I remember vividly when I learned that cooperation was really a sham, and how and when I learned to cheat. I learned the seven lessons of John Taylor Gatto's "Seven-Lesson School Teacher" (hometown.aol.com/tma68/7lesson.htm) profoundly well: confusion; class position; indifference; emotional dependency; intellectual dependency; provisional self-esteem; and inability to hide. I was well-rewarded for the effort. I learned that no work is really worth finishing (becoming a writer required significant retraining), that there is no past and no future outside of the class period, and that I could be saved by the bell! And while I know they made me sit through dozens of them, and read several dozen more, other than a few novels I have reread as an adult, I can't remember a single story!

And then, as I reflected back, a story returned. It wasn't from school at all. No, it was from a TV show, one that I thought I must have seen when I was eight or nine, and it came back to me fully clothed in words and pictures, and I wrote it down as I remembered it.

Ah, the wonders of the Internet. Within 24 hours of having written down the tale in a white heat, I found out that the dramatization of the magnificent Yiddish story "Bontshe Shvayg" had aired precisely once (on December 14th, 1959 – I was indeed nine at the time), and that most of the original tapes from this series (but not this one, titled "The World of Sholom Aleichem") were destroyed in a fire. By the end of the week, I had a videotape, featuring some of the finest Yiddish actors of the 20th Century, including Zero Mostel, many of whom had been blacklisted during the McCarthy Era.

I didn't remember any of this, though. What I did remember was the story of a man whose expectations had been diminished, and who, offered the entire world, could no longer even imagine what it was to desire. And something inside me, even at age nine, responded to this tale of thwarted aspirations, and of a man who wasn't allowed to have any, and this tale has stayed with me for more than 50 years. My school education had failed me, and for this I am forever grateful.

Desire more for your children, and allow them to have desires of their own. Feed their aspirations (and allow them to change). Take the seven lessons of the "Seven-Lesson Schoolteacher" seriously, and play them out in reverse. And fill your children's lives with stories, and your own as well.

HERE'S THE TALE:

Bontshe Shvayg

by I. L. Peretz, as retold by David H. Albert

On the day Bontshe Shvayg died, people almost didn't notice. They knew something was slightly amiss when they came to the synagogue for morning prayers and didn't find him curled up on the front stairs. So they looked around the side of the building, and there he was, stretched out straight and narrow on the snow, eyes closed, as if already perfectly prepared for his pauper's pine coffin. He didn't want to cause the undertaker any extra trouble. Two crows hopped about nearby, oblivious to the fact that the Angel of Death had visited close at hand.

Bontshe arrived, dazed and bedraggled at the gates of heaven. The angels were singing, intoning his name in astonishment and wonder, as if a great guest had just arrived. "He's here, he's here, Bontshe Shvayg, Bontshe Shvayg!" they chanted, and more gathered, eight and ten deep, just to see if they could get a peek at him through the beating of wings. "Bontshe Shvayg, Bontshe Shvayg," they whispered to their angelic children, who spread celestial rose petals before him. Bontshe didn't look up, but shuffled slowly, confusedly toward the open court that stood before the great gates.

You see, it is custom in heaven that before one is allowed to enter, a trial is held to ascertain if one is worthy. Seated in the center on His great throne, two steps above everyone else, was Lord God Himself, the Judge of all, lines on His forehead furrowed from all His cares for the world, and pulling on the ends of His cloudy white beard, frayed from worry. And there, on His right, a step down, a flaming sword on his large desk together with mountains of books, papers, and scrolls, and a permanently frozen half-frown/half smirk barely concealed behind a pencil-thin mustache, was the prosecuting angel. On the left, behind a smaller desk, swept clean except for one small piece of paper, was the angel prepared to speak for the defense.

The angel for the defense rose (for in the courts of heaven, it is the custom for the defense to say its piece first).

"This is Bontshe Shvayg," he began, as the angels leaned in to hear. "He has had a long and difficult life."

"On the day he was born, his mother cursed him as just another mouth to feed. His father deserted them all, ran off with the chimney sweep's wife. His mother was a drunkard, and beat him every morning before breakfast, when there was any and what there was of it, and, one day, she too ran off with the village rag peddler, leaving the children to fend for themselves. And Bontshe Shvayg never complained. His brothers left what little gristle they gave him in the dog's bowl, so he and the dog could fight over it, though Bontshe never

fought. But the dog grew to hate him nonetheless and finally ran off, food bowl and all. And Bontshe Shvayg never complained.

"At the synagogue, in exchange for his lessons, he followed the sweeper on his hands and knees, picking up the little wafts of dust and grit left behind by the broom. His teachers covered his knuckles and shoulders with bruises from their switches and yardsticks. And Bontshe Shvayg never complained. They married him off to the miller's wife (she had already gone through six husbands), and they had two daughters, who used to kick him and belittle him, until all three – his wife and two daughters – ran off to America, never to be heard from again. And Bontshe Shvayg never complained.

"He slept in ditches and in goats' pens, and shared the leavings of meals with the pigs. And Bontshe Shvayg never complained. He ran odd jobs for the beadle and the beadle's wife, and half the time they forgot to pay him, and he never complained. And even at his death, he saw to it that he didn't cause anyone any extra trouble.

"My Lord," he concluded, "This is Bontshe Shvayg, let him be judged according to Your Will."

And the defending angel sat down. The prosecutor rose to make his statement, and the angels shivered, for the prosecuting angel knew all, and his eyes were unforgiving. He looked down among his papers and books and scrolls, glanced over at the burning sword, and then at Bontshe Shvayg, and, in an uncustomarily weak voice, said, "I have nothing to say against this defendant," and sat back down.

A great murmur rose among the angels; nothing like this had ever been seen in the courts of heaven. All around, one could hear the whispers, "Bontshe Shvayg, Bontshe Shvayg," knowing that he soon would be admitted to their company.

And the Holy One, Blessed Be He, gave off feeling through His beard for the woes of the world, and rose from His Seat of Judgment, came down the two steps, and lifted Bontshe Shvayg from the floor before the throne by his elbow.

"Bontshe Shvayg," He said, in His Godly weariness, "The courts of heaven cannot judge you, for, with your life as it was, what is there left to judge? Now the gates are opening to receive you. And what's more, because you have borne a life hardly worth bearing, and have never even once complained, I hereby stand ready to grant your every wish, every boon. My Kingdom and all that is within My Dominions are yours. Ask and you shall receive it."

And, stunned, Bontshe Shvag looked up into the tired eyes of the Most High. The angels were hushed. The prosecuting angel looked down at his scrolls, and the defending angel folded his hands in front of him And Bontshe Shvayg said, still unsure of himself, "If it isn't too much trouble, perhaps, if it could be arranged without it being a problem, and please don't go out of Your way for me, maybe I could have a warm roll with a little bit of butter every morning?"

THE BEST AVAILABLE adult edition of some of Peretz, a giant of world literature, is *The I.L. Peretz Reader*, edited by Ruth Wisse (2002). A nice illustrated edition suitable for adults and children is *Seven Good Years: And Other Good Stories of I.L. Peretz*, translated by Esther Hautzig (2004). The video

"The World of Sholom Aleichem" contains three short plays. The first one, "A Tale of Chelm", is guaranteed to please children of all ages, and the second one obviously held me for almost 50 years.

The Middle

BEING THE NOTORIOUS homeschooling author I am, I get to speak at lots of conferences. Many of them are held in hotels, which, especially if they are located near airports, seem to be almost wholly interchangeable. Often, I will not get outside for three or even four days, and by the third day, except for the predominant accents of the homeschoolers I meet, I would have no idea what city I'm in.

I pick up my program and a little map of the hotel, and discover whether my next talk is in the Tulip Room or Ballroom A. It really doesn't seem to matter, because even before I get there, I know that they will look pretty much alike. Commonly, the room will lack any windows. The chairs will be laid out in long rows, usually much deeper than wide, which means I am really going to have to project if I plan to reach the back benchers.

The podium will be set up at the front, facing the middle of the room. But, and now here's the thing, most commonly there will be a rather wide aisle down the middle, with seats to the left and to the right. If I speak from the podium, to the middle of the room, I will be addressing absolutely no one.

Of course, I can have fun with this. To my left is the "Oooh" section; to the right the "Aaah" section. I can play upon this arrangement to loosen up my listeners. Divide them up into Robins and Bluebirds (reminding me of my first grade class back in the Dark Ages, which you'll learn about later in this book). The talk is to be delivered in living stereo. But the fact remains that if I direct my attention to the middle of the room, there is no one there.

Okay. You're waiting for the punch line, the meaningful analogy that will have made it worthwhile for you to have been so indulgent with me thus far. Well, don't let me put you off any longer. Last time I looked, there were no middle aisles in our nation's classrooms. But when school officials and teachers make the claim that they are required to "teach to the middle," the reality is that such teaching addresses virtually no one.

On its face, the reason for this is rather obvious. Whether or not one subscribes to Howard Gardner's notion that they are (at least) eight "natural intelligences" of which all human beings partake, or simply that each and every person is a unique concatenation of needs, proclivities, capabilities, instincts, intuitions, passions, and desires all wedded to an equally unique developmental pattern, the possibility of successfully addressing "the middle" with any reasonably sized group of human beings over time is virtually nil. This is especially true when the only reasons they are there at all is barely concealed compulsion and societal habits over which they have had absolutely no control. Even when I speak to homeschooling groups of parents who (I hope) are there purely voluntarily, I know enough to promise only fun. Whether anyone actually learns anything, or what it is exactly that she learns, is totally up to the individual, and might just as well have had something to do with what is eaten for dinner as with what it is precisely that I say.

This *scientistic* idea (as opposed to scientific – scientistic being the notion that modes of investigation in the natural sciences should be applied in all fields of inquiry, however inappropriate) of a "middle," when it comes to human beings is a thoroughly modern creation, no more than 170 or so years old. One simply fails to find it in any educational discourse in any culture in the world at any time before then. The scientistic creation of the middle was "proven" by the same leading educational psychologists who also demonstrated beyond reasonable doubt that 88% of Jewish immigrants to the U.S. in the 1910s and 1920s were "mental defectives" and three-quarters of African-American males were mentally unqualified to serve as targets for cannon and poison gas in World War I. We know where this kind of thinking led.

Our similarly scientistic approaches to instruction – whether it be reading, writing, or 'rithmetic – are highly suspect, and I strongly caution homeschoolers against being hooked into any of these approaches "based on the evidence." Over the course of the last decade, I have read scores if not hundreds of studies, and summaries of hundreds, if not thousands of others, regarding the "best way to teach," well, you name it. Every single one of the studies, without a single exception that I can remember, began with a simple, unstated assumption: "scientific" best practices for teaching are being evaluated *in an institutional school environment*, where it is the responsibility of the instructor to "teach to the middle." The so-called "rigorous scientific research" conducted by our doctors of education have all been carried out inside or in the context of anti-human, anti-social, anti-natural school environments, often with bad air, where students, sometimes 35 to a classroom, are (and learn to expect to be) systematically sorted, stigmatized, scapegoated, or punished for "lack of (tangible, meaning testable) progress," and which they are compelled or inured into accepting. None of the studies ever measures these so-called "best practices" against no practice at all or, more specifically, against the practice of freedom outside the cell walls. It is rather like trying to figure out how young lions in a pride on the savannah learn what they need to know by experimenting on detoothed and declawed lions in a very sad circus whose tent hasn't changed in a hundred years. (In my state, the leading thinker behind the new so-called educational reforms, a much discredited psychotherapist, has taken to calling students – *children*! – "learner-products.")

Once you surrender the strange, quasi-religious notion of average children, you open up your family to an entirely new world of creative possibilities. That's pretty scary, of course, which is why I urge homeschoolers to latch on to each other rather than to the curriculum developers (whose products you should feel free to use; just treat their claims with two heaping handfuls of sodium chloride). Hold each other close. When you enter the world of homeschooling, you've gained admission to a realm of experts, each of us knowing our own children (and, in time, ourselves) better than any of the good doctors of the sad circus. And you are going to be one, too. If you must measure at all, measure what you do, not against the realm of the non-existent middle, but against your children's budding hopes, dreams, and aspirations.

And next time you see me at a homeschooling conference, feel free to pull your chair into the center aisle and I'll know we're already acquainted.

The Cult of Right Answers

Ring the bells that still can ring.
Forget your perfect offering.
There is a crack in everything.
That's how the light gets in.
  - "Anthem"
    Leonard Cohen

I GREW UP in the cult of right answers. To this day, I'm sure I don't know quite why my schools thought it all that important to initiate me into the cult. My wife in her antiquarian pursuits balances the family checkbook. She says the bank is virtually always right, so if things are more than a few cents off, she assumes she got something wrong, and adjusts accordingly to make things conform. Meera, my future-accountant daughter, would likely do the same, though she'd bother about the pennies as well.

In my quantitative work in my day job, when my hunch is that things are "off," I've learned over time that it is almost never the result of a math error, but because of a problem at the data entry point, a computer shut-down, or any number of exigencies having virtually nothing to do with arithmetic. I have learned to look for results that are consistent; unless I have alarm bells set off elsewhere, I almost never examine them to see whether they are right.

When I go to the grocery store to buy a jar of spaghetti sauce ($1.89 on sale) and a package of spaghetti ($.99), if I want to know whether I've got enough money, I always add from left to right (just how I was taught not to do when I was in school), I estimate well enough, and I pay absolutely no attention to the fact that the final digit in the addition is "8." Since I am likely to pay for it with my debit card, I am not going to count the change either.

I do the same with estimating the time the bread is baking in the oven (have any of you actually checked the accuracy of the electronic timer?), how long it will take to defrost the chicken in the microwave, my gas mileage or the distance to my destination, or the amount of salt to put into the dish when the recipe calls for "a pinch."

And so, looking back at my school experiences, it is difficult to see what purpose the cult of right answers, which extended far beyond the world of mathematics, served, other than as an odd kind of social sorting mechanism. The successful competitors (including me) sat on the edges of our seats, ready to perform our next trick and obtain a herring from our trainers, the less successful got hungrier in the back until many forgot what food was. But the actual purpose for my initiation was, I believe to this day, to indicate that they thought they "owned" me, and that, deep down, I was one of them. Am I? In more than 30 years of deschooling, this is something that I am still trying to figure out.

There is nothing wrong with right answers of course. When I drive over a bridge, I am depending on the architect and builder having calculated the load capacity correctly. I need to be sure that the loan calculator used to figure out my mortgage payment is accurate, and I want to feel certain when I read that someone other than Ichiro has won the American League batting championship.

That's all well and good, but I think it can't be emphasized enough how the cult of right answers can be damaging to one's capacity to learn, and can stymie both creativity and curiosity. And this is true whether one turns out to be good at it or not.

I was most definitely a science and math nerd in school, and was well-rewarded and advanced in the cult for my right answers. I also had some very concrete experience of what happened when the "right" answer (you'll see the reason for quotations marks in a minute) wasn't forthcoming. This is a tale not even my mother knows. I was nominated for an all-expense-paid, two-week trip to a newly established (soon to be prestigious) math camp, for which we had to take a competitive exam. There were six scholarships awarded. There were 50 questions, each worth two points. Six of the competitors scored 100 points on the exam. I scored a 99. Why? In a geometric proof, I left out A=A. Well, duh! This is more Gertrude Stein ("A rose is a rose is a rose") than Isaac Newton. I can't imagine there is a mathematician in the entire universe who would have cared (though I never really met a mathematician until I was in my mid-20s), but I learned my lesson well. I never took a single math course after high school; now I use quantitative analysis in my daily work. Go figure.

I often recommend the wonderful book *The Number Devil: A Mathematical Adventure* by Hans Magnus Enzensberger to homeschoolers. The book is engaging and very well written, nicely illustrated, and opens up a world of mathematics to children and youth that they might otherwise never know was even there. It was originally written for 10-11 year olds, I think, but I have actually discovered that children as young as seven (some of whom having had it read to them) find great pleasure in it.

And, yet, I have a confession to make. I recently retrieved my copy down from the shelf and read it for the third time. Each time, I experience the same response, a falling feeling in the pit of my stomach. I want to put it down, but I fight through the queasiness. The number devil poses conundrums that cannot be solved, provides answers that are clearly correct but cannot be explained, and are intended to excite a general sense of wonderment at the wide, beautiful world of mathematics. But the feeling of wonderment when it comes to mathematics was confiscated from me when I joined the cult's inner circle. And like my permanent record, it seems to have disappeared into the ether long ago, and it is awfully difficult to cultivate it anew.

The cult of right answers is based at bottom on the fear of wrong answers, fear of failure, fear of error, fear of disappointing those upon whose favor one has come to depend on for one's self-esteem and self-worth. It may work short-term, but in the longer run, fear is a very poor motivator for learning, and a prime cause of apathy. For while a continuous string of right answers might assuage fear for a while, an equally effective way of coping with fear is to cultivate a feeling that learning really doesn't matter, or to deliberately (even if sometimes unconsciously) respond with wrong answers so that external expectations are lowered, or to simply attempt to absent oneself from the entire enterprise. After one experiences failure enough times and sees that the short-term consequences are really not so devastating, apathy born of failure becomes an acceptable response. Once having become discouraged, humiliated, baffled, or fearful, an apathetic silence can become a welcome refuge.

This silence can easily be reinforced, of course. Most of the days I passed in school I spent with the 'know-it-alls.' They expended most of the day talking at me. It might have been the case that they were there to answer our questions, but it quickly became evident, as virtually every school child knows, that the know-it-alls (the teachers, of course) asked 95% of the questions, and 98% of the time already knew the answers. Sometimes there were "discussions," which never really resembled anything like discussions in the real world; they were just manipulative tools for soliciting right answers. How many times I can remember the leading questions being answered by a classmate in a way already predetermined to being just not quite right, and the teacher calling on someone else to remedy the 'ignorance' displayed by the first responder. Shame and learning cannot occupy the same psychological space at the same time, for when they are forced into the same box, the only likely result is loss of self-respect.

It is better to duck and keep one's head down, for silence, of course, is relatively safe. Outside of illness – real or feigned – it really is the only reliably effective way for a child to retain the autonomy of her own thoughts and feelings when being pelted by what the poet William Blake called "the dreary shower" (from "The Schoolboy" in his *Songs of Innocence and Experience* – it apparently wasn't much different back then). It should be emphasized that "the people who are paid to know" have their own uses for silence. Eliminate recess, and time in the schoolyard, and the possibilities of conspiracies hatching, or at least of kids comparing notes, are lowered. If that doesn't work, the new trend – "Silent Lunches" – should work, and can be promoted as a way to increase standardized test scores. (One school in Rhode Island, I kid you not, uses the excuse that silent lunch helps staff members hear if a child is choking. Now *I* want to choke…) Good preparation for life.

In a healthy learning environment, individuals store up lessons learned from errors and mistakes for future use. As the philosopher Friedrich Nietzsche once said, what doesn't kill us makes us stronger. We collect data from our slip-ups, and they inform our hunches, which, in a healthy learning environment, simply get better over time.

I had a homeschooling mom ask me recently about helping her 11-year-old learn to spell better. My first question, of course, was whether *he* wanted to spell better, but, as I suspected, the answer was indeed yes, ("Finally!" she exhaled), which I found not at all surprising, as it is usually 10-12 year olds who want to make sure they are able to follow conventions of all kinds (especially those of their peers). Anyway, while Kevin is a voracious reader, his visual recall doesn't help him when it gets to writing. He learned phonetics years ago, and he is mainly unconscious of them at this point. So my suggestions surprised Mom quite a bit. He needs to know how to spell words *incorrectly* (he's got that down) and know that they are incorrect (that's the challenge), in order to sharpen up both his hunches and his recall. She remembered my Unspelling™ game (it can be found in *Have Fun. Learn Stuff. Grow*). I also suggested finding workbooks or computer programs with *incorrect* spellings that have to be fixed – where words were spelled what would have been correctly based on phonics, or irregular plurals, or strange past tenses (isn't English wonderful?) – and had to be changed to something "incorrect" in order to be "right" (if you catch my drift). Finally, writing on the computer using the manual spellchecker will display both incorrect spellings and correct ones, providing the knowledge base to sharpen up the spelling center in his brain. All without flash cards, remedial (and unrelentingly boring) phonics, or memorizing the dictionary!

SO WHAT ABOUT math? My distant friend Suma Vivekanandan, a primary school teacher in Gujarat, India (and contributor to the holistic India Learning Network) notes what virtually everyone always knows. The kids get bored with drills, problem sets that are stand-alone and decontextualized, and this boredom sets in whether they are learning anything or not. So, in the spirit of *The Number Devil*, she has taken to providing her charges, to their delight, with problems that are open-ended, or do not have only one correct solution (there goes the cult of right answers), or which simply don't have any explanation. There are books of these, of course, but I'll just share three that she has used.

Choose any whole number from 1 to 100. If it is even, then divide it by two. If it is odd, then multiply it by 3 and add 1. Repeat the process endlessly:

For example: 6 -> 3 -> 10 -> 5 -> 16 -> 8 ->...

The surprise is that whatever number you start with, it always ends in one particular number. Suma writes that there is no mathematical proof for this result. The entire process can be captured graphically as a river with many tributaries joining it at different points as the river ultimately reaches the sea. Like the Ganges!

USE NUMBERS 1, 2, 3, and 4 in the same sequence along with any acceptable mathematical operator and get all numbers from 1 to 100. There are literally hundreds of possibilities. Some examples:

1+2+3+4=10   12+34= 46

12 divided by 3+4=8   12-3x4=36

12-3-4=5

Draw a chart from 1 to 100 and place a solution in each box, and see how many you can come up. Or expand beyond 100, and, when learned, use more sophisticated operators such as square roots, logs, factorials, etc.

TAKE ANY TWO-DIGIT number, say – 24. Write below it a number that describes the number above, as follows: 24 consists of two digits – 2 and 4. The quantity of 2 is one and the quantity of 4 is one.

So the number that describes 24 is written as 1214 (one of 2 and one of 4).

Repeat the process, now describe 1214. It consists of three numbers – 1, 2 and 4. The quantity of 1 is two; the quantity of 2 is one; the quantity of 4 is one. So the number that describes 1214 is written as 21-12-14 – 211414.

Repeat the process: 211214 is described by 31-22-14

312214 is described by 21-22-13-14.

Continue the process for between 8 and 12 steps and you'll meet up with a surprise! Then try another two-digit number and repeat.

Find more ways to do this, and all of a sudden you and your children may indeed find yourselves members of a cult, one far more beautiful, and with far wider vistas than the cult of right answers might ever have allowed you to imagine. You'll know that you've joined a new band when you find yourself, when nobody else is around, asking at least once a day, "I wonder if…."

IF YOU'D LIKE to know more about the India Learning Network, visit www.learningnet-india.org; Suma Vivekanandan's problems appeared in the March 2007 edition of their newsletter *Chiguru*.

Emotional Equations (Part I)

I ♥ U.

The graffiti on the wall downtown was easy enough for me to "read." Or maybe I should say "to *translate*."

I KNEW FROM experience that I had to work it out from left to right. There is nothing obvious about that, and I know from experience that had I read it from right to left that, except for the grammatical incongruity which I figured out when I was three, the meaning would be rather different. I am reminded how "unnatural" and intensely learned these grammatical operations are by my memory of my older daughter's sentences at age two, which seemed to have had a grammatical structure somewhere between German and Pashto.

The capitalization of the sign "I" could signify two different ideas. The first is that "I" was the beginning of a sentence, hence confirming the left-to-right orientation. The second is that this isn't just any letter, to be pronounced like the organ of sight on my face, but refers to the first person singular. Not "I", either the one reading the scribbles on the wall or the strange mustached person sitting here at my computer, but some unidentified "I" who wishes to proclaim his or her message to the world.

♥ is an icon for the heart. Anyone who has seen an actual heart or the picture of a heart knows that ♥ doesn't look anything like one. But one doesn't need to have seen the bloody pumping muscle in order to read ♥ as "heart." [In fact, as a matter of history, the icon '♥' may have originated as the depiction of the seeds of the now-extinct *silphium*, a plant from ancient Cyrenaica (in present-day Libya) used as an herbal contraceptive.]

Except that ♥ is really neither an icon nor a symbol for heart, but through an act of substitution that we make almost instantaneously in our minds, for love. There is history attached to this as well. The Greeks, including Aristotle, thought of the heart as the seat of thought, reason, and emotions. The Stoics taught that the heart was the seat of the soul. However, the Roman physician Galen believed that while the heart was the seat of emotions, passions came from the liver. It seems to me unlikely that anyone has ever mistaken a ♥ for a liver.

And what is love? Don't get me started – we could do a tour of the world. I remember an anthropology professor of mine who, after having studied the matter cross-culturally for a very long time, determined that the best that could be said about love in all its varieties is that it is shorthand for "enduring diffuse solidarity." I doubt that the graffiti artist had this in mind.

"u" is a sign for the sound of a letter from the alphabet. It is not the usual sound associated with the letter "u", which is more commonly "oo" or "uh" (though there is "use"). The "u" stands for the sound "yew," then spelled "you" (as in Tony Soprano's "Yous guys"), referring to the second person pronoun, either singular or plural, unidentified (where art "thou" now that we need thee?) Is the graffiti scribbler speaking to us, or are we overhearing an intimate conversation?

So what does it all translate to? Best I can make out is, "The first person unidentified desires to express enduring diffuse solidarity with the second person (singular or plural) unidentified."

I have had a few four-year-old acquaintances and friends who could translate "I ♥ u," though never making use of the terms above! Some more five-year-olds. Even more six-year-olds, and I suspect the majority of seven– and eight-year-olds (who might take to writing similar little notes on the white board in the kitchen, or on scraps of paper to place on mom's pillow). They've got the sign, symbol, icon, 'stand for' equivalence, 'sign for sound for word for meaning including grammatical usage' or 'symbol for word for concept for word for meaning' thing entirely under control, mostly with very little instruction under their belts.

Perhaps we could call the ability to read "I ♥ u" "Pre-Algebra" (in much the same way that I am "pre-retired"), or "Algebra Readiness." Frankly, I think this misses the point – I am convinced that because the concept of equivalences is an everyday reality for children from the time the first "momma" out of their mouths results in a confirming and positive response, the best time to introduce children to the wonders of algebra is between the ages of four and seven. That's going to have to await another demonstration. Once they've launched their little boat into the ocean of equivalences, provided some adult doesn't come along and poke a hole in the bottom, there are all kinds of wonderful islands and archipelagos to go and visit.

Maybe even some to live on. I know a really interesting one with a sleeping volcano of bent time and space….

Emotional Equations (Part II)

MICKEY'S MOM WAS fuming. She was tired of the puddles on the floor. She had lectured, cajoled, begged, growled, screamed, groaned, and acted reasonable. All to no satisfactory conclusion. Mickey just wouldn't dry himself thoroughly after he had gotten out of the bath, and Mom thought he was old enough to be doing this by himself.

"Sigh. I've just got to try something else," she thought.

"Mickey, when you're done, let's have some fun on the whiteboard."

Mickey paddled into the kitchen in his bathrobe, still dripping.

Mom wrote on the board, making sure she was using the blue dry erase marker (there had been a mistake in the past, the shadowy red remnant of which was still visible, even after much scrubbing).

"M = ☹"

"The 'M' is for me, Your Mother!" said Mom officiously.

"Oh," said Mickey, grabbing another marker.

"Y", he scribbled.

"M ≠ ☺"

"m ≠ D"

"Is the little 'm' for me?" asked Mickey. And what's the 'D' for, and why is there a slanty thing through the equals sign?"

Mom wrote:

"D = Dry

≠ = Not equal to."

"Oh, it's true, I guess," said Mickey, gazing down at the little puddle by his toes.

"Now look at this," said Mom.

$$D = 3TH + 3TB + 3TA + 3TL + 3TF"$$

Then she pointed at various parts of Mickey's body.

"Oh, I get it." Mickey got excited. "H is for Head, B is for Body, A is for Arms, L is for Legs, and the F is for Feet! But what is the 'T'?"

"T is for vigorous Toweling!" replied Mom.

"Oh, that's too cool!" exclaimed Mickey. "And you want me to vigorously Towel each part three times."

"But, just look at you now," said Mom, stepping over the little puddle and back to the whiteboard.

"$m = D - 3TF$."

"Yeah, maybe I didn't," Mickey mumbled sheepishly.

Mom continued. "$D - 3TF = 3TH + 3TB + 3TA + 3TL$"

"All right, all right, I get it. Most of me is dry. I didn't do my feet. But, you know, if I'm using only one towel, and each part gets toweled three times, couldn't we write it differently?"

"Oh, you're so smart, Mickey. You're right."

"$D = 3T(H + B + A + L + F)$."

"I think I understand," said Mickey thoughtfully, "but what if each part of the body needs a different amount of, what did you say? "vigorous Toweling"?"

"Well, maybe, something like this."

"$D = 3TH + 4TB + 2TA + 5TL + 6TF$."

"Hmm," puzzled Mickey, "But, but, but what if you don't know how much Toweling is gonna be needed for my arms or my legs?"

"Now, we're getting into some serious algebra," laughed Mom. "Tell you what. After you take a bath tomorrow, and if you are really dry, we'll do that then."

"Deal!" shouted Mickey. "Mom?"

"Yes, Mickey?"

Mickey went to the board with his green marker.

"M, m = ☺.

m ♥ u."

Mom went to the board with her blue marker.

"m, M ≠ ☹. M = ☺

M ♥ u $2^{1,000,000}$."

"Now it's time to go to bed."

"What are those little numbers, Mom?"

"Tomorrow, Mickey, tomorrow."

ONE OF MY kids liked Henry Borenson's Hands-on Equations –
www.borenson.com. One of the things I especially appreciate about it is that
it allows students to move away from the "real life" demonstration (which I
think is, for some kids, always a good place to start) and into a purely game-
like mathematical world. And having concrete manipulatives for that process
provides an excellent bridge.

Goat Sunday

"The purpose of education is to learn to treat each other better."
  - (I said that).

I WROTE THIS description of "Goat Sunday" for the Quaker Homeschooling Circle, which I moderate (you are welcome to join us – just go to Google Groups and look for the Quaker-Homeschooling-Circle), but thought many of you might find it relevant in your own homeschooling adventures, and maybe, just maybe, there will be an explosion of Goat Sundays around the country.

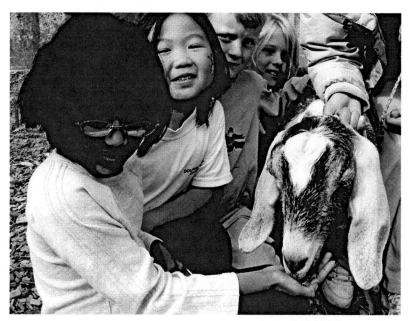

AT FRIENDS GENERAL Conference (a national meeting of liberal Quakers which just met for the first time in 100 years on the West Coast), there were no fewer than 15 homeschooling families represented, one from as far away as Perth, Australia. Since virtually none were already part of the 150-member Quaker Homeschooling Circle, I suspect there are far, far more of us than any of us have previously imagined. We spent time sharing about the connection between our homeschooling lives and our lives as Friends.

While I was there, I was asked to write an article for the bulletin of the African Great Lakes Initiative (AGLI – aglifpt.org). AGLI arose in the aftermath of the Rwanda-Burundi genocide, where the world stood by as more than a million people were slaughtered. AGLI, which is associated with Quakers, has been organizing Trauma Healing and Reconciliation programs. As those from the two previously warring communities, including those who are leaving the refugee camps, have to return to their homes and live with each other, their former enemies, AGLI has been running three-day programs, with 10 men and women from each community, 20 in all, to speak their truths and begin the long process of rebuilding trust. The results thus far have been nothing short of breathtaking. (There are opportunities for older teens and adults from North America to be trained in assisting in this work, or in Alternatives to Violence Projects in the U.S.; contact AGLI for details). Here, the lion will lie down with the lamb, although it is soon discovered that, when it comes to people, it is not always clear which is lamb and which lion.

Our homeschooling family became very familiar with the work of AGLI as a result of our friendship with Adrien Niyongabo, a Quaker, and one of the program's chief organizers in Burundi. He has visited our Friends Meeting twice at our request, and our younger daughter Meera, who especially befriended Adrien, played two piano benefit recitals, one in Olympia, Washington, and one in Philadelphia, to raise funds for the program. In addition, our Meeting has a fund called "Right Sharing of World Resources," whereby 1% of all contributions to the Meeting are disbursed to small micro-economic projects worldwide. The Meeting contribution are very small (typically three $100 grants per year), but the expectation is that members will more than match them. Often the children in the Meeting get involved in fundraisers for the projects. Most important of all, it keeps us aware of our connection with people around the world.

At any rate, when I returned home, a request was relayed to me through Adrien from the Mutaho Widows' Cooperative (by way of the AGLI office in St. Louis). The Widows' Cooperative, made up of 54 former wives of genocide victims and their children who were now leaving the refugee camps, was trying to rebuild some form of subsistence agriculture. But they returned home with virtually nothing. So they wanted money for 12 goats. The main purpose of the goats is not milk (though much appreciated) nor the occasional meat. Rather, applying goat manure to their bean plants – beans being the major food staple – triples the yield. Each goat costs $30, plus $13 for de-worming and medicine, for a total of $43. (Heifer International goats cost $120 each; they do wonderful work, but it is amazing how many more you can get when there isn't any overhead).

I wrote back to the St. Louis office, asking why only 12 goats for a cooperative of 54 families? They responded that the request was probably too modest, but the women thought it would be unfair for the entire cooperative to have goats when there were so many people who didn't have anything. Hmm. Anyhow, we settled on raising funds for 27 ($1,161), with an understanding that the women receiving goats will give the first-born female offspring to other families until they all have one. Goats and goat manure for all!

Our Meeting Children's Committee and Right Sharing program co-sponsored a "Goat Sunday." We had goat art projects and songs for the children's program. We downloaded maps and pictures of Burundi, so that everyone would know where the goats are going. We had "goat hospitality" – the Meeting bakers made goat cheese cannoli and spanakopita and other goat cheese specialties for sale (and distributed recipes). Then there were goat storytelling sessions for both children and adults – virtually every culture has goat stories to share; I told several from the Yiddish and Asian Indian traditions. And a special four-legged guest (a Nubian goat named Freya) made a "guest appearance." By the end of the day, we had raised the funds for the 27 goats, with a little left over for agricultural implements.

The "Goat Sunday" idea is now spreading through the Quaker Homeschooling Circle, and I would like to see it spread among other homeschoolers as well. This could be a terrific project for a church for the holiday season, or for local homeschooling groups. I am sure the AGLI office can put you in touch with other communities where goats are needed.   I just gave two goats as a wedding present to friends who, in the global scheme of things, already have absolutely everything else.

AFTER HEARING OF our efforts, Adrien wrote us from Burundi:

"When I was a child we had goats at home. While we were at school, we tied them to a tree so they could not destroy the fields. Upon getting back from school, we usually untied them so that they could find grasses wherever they might. But most of the time, the goats would remain standing at the same place although they were no longer tied to the tree.

"Sometimes I think that something similar happens in people's minds. It is not so easy that we come to realize that the storm is over and that, after having ourselves been pulled up by someone, we can help others to stand up as well."

ONE IDEA THAT, looking back on it, I wish we had instituted in our family when the children were smaller, is a 1% Fund for Families. We would take 1% of our income (I know many of you already tithe), and work as a family to figure out together where we thought it might do good work, paying particular attention to where we could make direct contact with the recipients. It would be a joint exercise in global responsibility and world geography and economics ("micro" – within the family – and global) and, hopefully, set a pattern for personal accountability for the world that the kids would carry forth with them into adulthood.

I first drafted this article in far south India, with several children of migrant laborers who we have taken into a hostel literally hanging over my shoulder. If you want to read more about what I have been doing here, check out my blog at shantinik.blogspot.com.

Shantiniketan

"I was fortunate enough in extricating myself before insensibility set in."
- Rabindranath Tagore

WHEN MY KIDS were young, we named our house "Shantiniketan." It fit for many reasons. My wife and I both decided to discard our last names – mine being made up and hers being unpronounceable – and had given both children the last name "Shanti", meaning "peace" in Sanskrit, and "niketan" can mean "house, abode, garden, or school." "Abode of Peace" seemed fine to us, as did "Garden of Shantis." Giving the house, and hence our homeschool a name, complete with sign painted by the children, was a signal that we viewed our commitment to learning and to peace as something for everyone, not just for the kids, and that we saw ourselves as a learning (and, we hoped, peaceful) community.

We both knew of course that "Shantiniketan" was the name of the famous school in West Bengal, India, founded by the Nobel Prize-winning poet, dramatist, storyteller, and painter Rabindranath Tagore more than a hundred years ago. The school (also known as 'Vishva Bharati' – "Nurturing the World") became a famous place, not so much for its formal pedagogy, but for its relative lack of it. A commitment to learning in and from nature, opportunities for exploring the arts in a living way, and the presence of interesting people to experience and learn from and with pretty much sums it up. Its lack of pretentiousness didn't prevent Shantiniketan from producing its share of extraordinary people – the world's foremost humanist economist Amartya Sen and the great Bengali film-maker Satyajit Ray, just to name two.

As Tagore himself might have foretold, the freewheeling and open-ended nature of his school did not long outlive him. It was slowly crushed by waves of visitors and devotees, and government bureaucrats who have successfully turned it into a third-rate Indian university, or so I am told, surrounded by condos, apartments, and tract houses for the wealthy.

Still there are those of us who continue to carry the spirit of Shantiniketan inside us, or, as we live with our children, on our backs like turtles. My children are grown now (even if they will always remain 14 to me), but the sign is still hanging on the house, next to the front door.

Here's the notion behind the sign, as Tagore explains it himself:

My School

I STARTED A school in Bengal when I was nearing forty. Certainly this was never expected of me, who had spent the greater portion of my life in writing, chiefly verses. Therefore people naturally thought that as a school it might not be one of the best of its kind, but it was sure to be something outrageously new, being the product of daring inexperience.

This is one the reasons I am often asked what is the idea upon which my school is based. The question is a very embarrassing one for me, because to satisfy the expectation of my questioners, I cannot afford to be commonplace in my answer. However, I shall resist the temptation to be original and shall be content with being merely truthful.

In the first place, I must confess it is difficult for me to say what is the idea which underlies my institution. For the idea is not like a fixed foundation upon which a building is erected. It is more like a seed which cannot be separated and pointed out directly – it begins to grow into a plant.

And I know what it was to which this school owes its origin. It was not any new theory of education, but the memory of my schooldays.

That those days were unhappy ones for me I cannot altogether subscribe to my peculiar temperament or to any special demerit of the schools to which I was sent. It may be that if I had been a little less sensitive, I could gradually have accommodated myself to the pressure and survived long enough to earn my university degrees. But all the same, schools are schools, though some are better and some worse, according to their own standard.

The provision has been made for infants to be fed upon their mother's milk. They find their food and their mother at the same time. It is complete nourishment for them, body and soul. It is their first introduction to the great truth that man's true relationship with the world is that of personal love and not that of the mechanical law of causation. Therefore our childhood should be given its full measure of life's draught, for which it has an endless thirst. The young mind should be saturated with the idea that it has been born in a human world which is in harmony with the world around it.

And this is what our regular type of school ignores with an air of superior wisdom, severe and disdainful. It forcibly snatches away children from a world full of the mystery of God's own handiwork, full of the suggestiveness of personality. It is a mere method of discipline which refuses to take into account the individual. It is a manufactory specially designed for grinding out uniform results. It follows an imaginary straight line of the average in digging its channel of education. But life's line is not the straight line, for it is fond of playing the see-saw with the line of the average, bringing upon its head the rebuke of the school. And this was the cause of my suffering when I was sent to school. For all of a sudden I found my world vanishing from around me, giving place to wooden benches and straight walls staring at me with the blank stare of the blind.

The legend is that eating of the fruit of knowledge is not consonant with dwelling in paradise. Therefore men's children have to be banished into a realm of death, dominated by the decency of a tailoring department. So my mind had to accept the tight-fitting encasement of the school which, being like the shoes of a mandarin woman, pinched and bruised my nature on all sides and at every movement. I was fortunate enough in extricating myself before insensibility set in.

Though I did not have to serve the full penal term which men of my position have to undergo to find their entrance into cultured society, I am glad that I did not altogether escape from its molestation. It has given me knowledge of the wrong from which the children of men suffer.

The cause of this is this: that man's intention is going against God's intention as to how children should grow into knowledge. How we should conduct our business is our own affair, and therefore in our offices we are free to create in the measure of our special purposes. But such office arrangement does not suit God's creation. And children are God's own creation.

We have come to this world to accept it, not merely to know it. We may become powerful by knowledge, but we attain fullness by sympathy. The highest education is that which does not merely give us information but makes our life in harmony with all existence. But we find this education of sympathy is not only systematically ignored in schools, but it is severely repressed. From our very childhood, habits are formed and knowledge is imparted in such a manner that our life is weaned away from nature, and our mind and the world are set in opposition from the beginning of our days. Thus the greatest of education for which we came prepared is neglected, and we are made to lose our world to find a bagful of information instead. We rob the child of his earth to teach him geography, of language to teach him grammar. He was born in the human world, but is banished into the world of living gramophones, to expiate for the original sin of being born in ignorance, Child-nature protests against such calamity with all its power of suffering, subdued at last into silence by punishment.

We all know children are lovers of the dust; their whole body and mind thirst for sunlight and air as flowers do. They are never in a mood to refuse the constant invitation to establish direct communication which comes to their senses from the universe. But unfortunately for children their parents, in the pursuit of their profession, in conformity to their social traditions, live in their own peculiar world of habits. Much of this cannot be helped. For men have to specialize, driven by circumstances and by need of social uniformity.

But our childhood is the period when we have or ought to have more freedom – freedom from the necessity of specialization into the narrow bounds of social and professional conventionalism.

I well remember the surprise and annoyance of an experienced headmaster, reputed to be a successful disciplinarian, when he saw one of the boys of my school climbing a tree and choosing a fork of the branches for settling down to his studies. I had to say to him in explanation that "childhood is the only period of life when a civilized man can exercise his choice between the branches of a tree and his drawing-room chair, and should I deprive this boy of that privilege because I, as a grown-up man, am barred from it?" What is surprising is to notice the same headmaster's approbation of the boys' studying botany. He believes in an impersonal knowledge of the tree because that is science, but not in a personal experience of it. This growth of experience leads to forming instinct, which is the result of nature's own method of instruction. The boys of my school have acquired instinctive knowledge of the physiognomy of the tree. By the least touch they know where they can find a foothold upon an apparently inhospitable trunk; they know how far they can take liberty with the branches, how to distribute their bodies' weight so as to make themselves least burdensome to

*branchlets. My boys are able to make the best possible use of the tree in the matter of
gathering fruits, taking rest and hiding from undesirable pursuers. I myself was brought up
in cultured home in a town, and as far as my personal behavior goes, I have been obliged to
act all through my life as if I were born in a world where there are not trees. Therefore I
consider it as a part of education for my boys to let them fully realize that they are in a
scheme of existence where trees are a substantial fact, not merely as generating chlorophyll
and taking carbon from the air, but as living trees.*

*Naturally the soles of our feet are so made that they become the best instruments for us to
stand upon the earth and to walk with. From the day we commenced to wear shoes we
minimized the purpose of our feet. For us it amounts to a grievance against God for not
giving us hooves instead of beautifully sensitive soles. I am not for banishing footgear
altogether from men's use. But I have no hesitation in asserting that the soles of children's
feet should not be deprived of their education, provided for them by nature, free of cost. Of all
the limbs we have they are the best adapted for intimately knowing the earth by their touch.
For the earth has her subtle modulations of contour which she only offers for the kiss of her
true lovers – the feet....*

*There are men who think that by the simplicity of living, introduced in my school, I preach
the idealization of poverty which prevailed in the mediaeval age. From the point of view of
education, should we not admit that poverty is the school in which man had his first lessons
and his best training? Poverty brings us into complete touch with life and the world, for
living richly is living mostly be proxy, and thus living in a world of a less reality. This may
be good for one's pleasure and pride, but not for one's education. Wealth is a golden cage for
children. Therefore in my school, much to the disgust of the people of expensive habits, I had
to provide for this great teacher – this bareness of furniture and materials – not because it is
poverty, but because it leads to personal experience of the world.*

*What tortured me in my school days was the fact that the school had not the completeness of
the world. It was a special arrangement for giving lessons. It could be suitable for grown-up
people who were conscious of the special need of such places and therefore ready to accept their
teaching at the cost of dissociation from life. But children are in love with life, and it is their
first love. All its color and movement attract their eager attention. And are we quite sure of
our wisdom in stifling this love? Children are not born ascetics, fit to enter at once into the
monastic discipline of acquiring knowledge. At first they must gather knowledge through
their life, and then they will renounce their lives to gain knowledge, and then again they will
come back to their fuller lives with ripened wisdom.*

*But society has made its own arrangements for manipulating men's minds to fit its special
patterns. These arrangements are so closely organized that it is difficult find gaps through
which to bring in nature. There is a serial adjustment of penalties which follows to the end
one who ventures to take liberty with some part of the arrangements, even to save his soul.
Therefore it is one thing to realize truth and another to bring it into practice where the whole
current of the prevailing system goes against you. This is why, when I had to face the
problem of my own son's education, I was at a loss to give it a practical solution. The first
thing that I did was to take him away from the town surroundings into a village and allow
him the freedom of primeval nature as far as it is available in modern days. He had a river,
noted for its danger, where he swam and rowed without check from the anxiety of his elders.
He spent his time in the fields and on the trackless sand-banks, coming late for his meals*

without being questioned. He had none of those luxuries that are not only customary but are held as proper for boys of his circumstance. For which privations, I am sure, he was pitied and his parents blamed by the people for whom society has blotted out the whole world. But I was certain that luxuries are burdens to boys. They are the burdens of other people's habits, the burdens of the vicarious pride and pleasure which parents enjoy through their children.

Yes, being an individual of limited resources, I could do very little for my son in the way of educating him according to my plan. But he had freedom of movement; he had few of the screens of wealth and respectability between himself and the world of nature. Thus he had a better opportunity for a real experience of this universe than I ever had. But one thing exercised my mind as more important than anything else.

The object of education is to give man the unity of truth. Formerly, when life was simple, all the different elements of man were in complete harmony. But when there came the separation of the intellect from the spiritual and the physical, the school education put entire emphasis on the intellect and the physical side of man. We devote our sole attention to giving children information, not know that by this emphasis we are accentuating a break between the intellectual, physical and the spiritual life.

I believe in a spiritual world, not as anything separate from this world, but in its innermost truth. Born in this great world, full of the mystery of the infinite, we cannot accept our existence as a momentary outburst of chance, drifting on the current of matter towards an eternal nowhere. We cannot look upon our lives as dreams of a dreamer who has no awakening in all time. We have a personality to which matter and force are unmeaning unless related to something infinitely personal, whose nature we have discovered, in some measure, in human love, in the greatness of in the martyrdom of heroic souls, in the ineffable beauty of nature, which can never be a mere physical fact, nor anything but an expression of personality.

Experience of this spiritual world, whose reality we miss by our incessant habit of ignoring it from childhood, has to be gained by children by fully living in it and not through the medium of theological instruction. But how this is to be done is a problem difficult of solution tin he present age. For nowadays men have managed so fully to occupy their time that they do not find leisure to know that their activities have only movement but very little truth, that their soul has not found its world. . . .

I had been immersed in literary activities when this thought struck my mind with painful intensity. I suddenly felt like one groaning under the suffocation of nightmare. It was not only my own soul, but the soul of my country that seemed to be struggling for its breath through me. I felt clearly that what was needed was not any particular material object, not wealth or comfort or power, but our awakening to full consciousness in soul freedom, the freedom of the life in God, where we have no enmity with those who must fight, no competition with those who must make money, where we are beyond all attacks and above all insults. . . .

I for my part believe in the principle of life, in the soul of man, more than in methods. I believe that the object of education is the freedom of mind which can only be achieved through the path of freedom — though freedom has its risk and responsibility as life itself has. I know it for certain, though most people seem to have forgotten it, that children are living beings – more living than grown-up people, who have built their shells of habit around them. Therefore it is absolutely necessary for their mental health and development that they should not have mere schools for their lessons, but a world whose guiding spirit is personal love. It must be an ashram where men have gathered for the highest end of life, in the peace of nature; where life is not merely meditative, but fully awake in its activities; where boys' minds are not being perpetually drilled into believing that the ideal of the self-idolatry of the nation is the truest idea for them to accept; where they are bidden to realize man's world as God's Kingdom, to whose citizenship they have to aspire; where the sunrise and sunset and the silent glory of stars are not daily ignored; where nature's festivities of flowers and fruit have their joyous recognition from man; and where the young and the old, the teacher and the students, sit at the same table to partake of their daily food and the food of their eternal life.

Lecture delivered in America: published in Personality London, Macmillan, 1933. This article has been obtained from the compilation on VidyaOnline. More information and articles can be found at www.vidyaonline.net. *Tagore's short story "The Parrot's Training" is appendixed to this book.*

Chemistry

I CALLED HOME during one of many trips visiting with homeschoolers, and asked to speak to my daughter Meera. My wife indicated that, as usual, she wasn't at home. But what was surprising is that my wife reported Meera was going with some of her friends to a local creek to see the salmon spawning.

Now *that* was unusual. Many years ago, we moved from inner-city Philadelphia to the West Coast, among other reasons so that the kids could grow up with some experience of, and appreciation for, the natural world. Our older daughter became quite the naturalist, and even walking in the woods with her becomes, for me – New Yorker that I am – an adventure.

But it didn't work out quite that way with Meera. Even when she was small, it seemed she would only be comfortable touching the earth while wearing two pair of rubber gloves. She would complain mightily about any family outing that might be considered too "naturey." And, to be fair, to this day she is the favorite attraction for every biting insect known to humankind. A walk in the woods with Meera was an opportunity for her to monopolize conversation; when we would plead for a moment of peace, she would proclaim, "I am a no-talking bug, I am a no-talking bug. See, I am a no-talking bug." Her idea of nature is Central Park in New York City, and science (or at least science as we think of it in the context of school) just isn't a part of her vocabulary.

So I was certain that her excursion did not reflect any kind of conversion experience, but a chance to spend time with good friends, despite having to get her shoes a little muddy. It was a trade-off, the kind that adults make all the time. She has indeed grown up.

Meera discovered that two of the colleges to which she wished to apply required that she take chemistry. Ugh. Taking it at the local high school was out of the question. "Five days a week, all year, and a lab besides? No way!" she insisted.

"I'm going to take college chemistry," she declared, "and I'm going to get an A."

"Uh, okay," I agreed.

Meera found an on-line college chemistry course offered by a community college to the south of us. Through our state's Running Start program, tuition was free, though the textbook and workbook took a nice bite out of the family jewels. And through one of the vagaries of our state's high school credit system, just one term of a college course is considered the equivalent of an entire year's high school one.

In theory, a student was expected to learn chemistry by reading the textbook, doing pages from the workbook, performing various kitchen experiments, and then taking a weekly quiz. But, as Meera duly reminded us, the purpose was not to *learn* chemistry, but to *take* chemistry, and to get an "A."

The rules of the course were that one could take each quiz and the final exam as many times as one wished until the desired grade was achieved. So Meera quickly got the idea to start the week with the quiz, answering all questions she could without any additional research. She'd take the remaining mathematical questions and find the required formulas online or in the textbook and apply them. With the final few questions, she'd try to look up the answers online or ask her friends who were taking high school chemistry.

In three months, she had her "A" in college chemistry. But don't get the impression that she actually *knows* any chemistry. "Dad, you've been trying to cleanse your brain of that chemistry clutter you've never used for 30 years. With me, it will be gone in two weeks!" We sold both the textbook and workbook on Amazon in "Like New" condition for slightly more than we paid for them.

Now I know what some of you are thinking. What's the point? The learning activity was a charade, like so many of the others that one finds in what passes for education in this country. Would you hire a doctor who 'learned' chemistry this way? What happens when an entire education is made of a series of mindless hoops through which to jump?

If I had similar prejudices, or was a lover of chemistry, or thought there was any chance that Meera planned on becoming a physician, or that her entire education consisted of hoop-jumping, I might be similarly nonplussed. But the reality is otherwise.

What I see are clear, self-chosen goals, a strategic framework to pursue them, and clear-eyed implementation of the plan. I see efficient budgeting and effective use of time and resources, utilization of research skills when appropriate, and an ability to network with others who can provide the information needed to accomplish a task.

No, she really doesn't *know* anything about chemistry. But she has *taken* chemistry (and she got an "A"!). And if you ask what she would do if she comes upon a problem in her future international development work or business career that requires a knowledge of chemistry, she'll tell you that she'd hire the very best chemist she could find.

It has indeed been a good learning exercise, and she has learned a lot, just none of it having anything to do with chemistry. And I believe that is quite worthy of respect.

But I wouldn't fool myself or anyone else into thinking that this is really the best way to expend intellectual time and energy. When many of us look back at our school-based education, much of it looks like a grand exercise in government waste. I spent four years "learning" a foreign language I was never able to use, took advanced placement physics and I still haven't figured out how to change the oil on my car, and then there are the various bits and snippets of bad poetry taking up space on my neuronic hard drive, all placed there at tremendous government expense.

There has to be a better way. And you, dear homeschooling readers, are proving that there is.

Mohammed and Me

IT'S A WEEKEND to take stock. Meera and Ellen are in Spokane, at what is likely Meera's last meet as a competitive gymnast. I've got time on my hands to reflect, and give thanks for the great gifts my wife and children have provided (and continue to provide) to me.

So for a quick report: Aliyah is graduating from Smith College with a double major in music and Italian studies. She is now best fitted (in my judgment) for a career as an absent-minded professor with impossible handwriting. But it looks like the universe has plans for her to fulfill her *dharma*, for she has received a handsome five-year fellowship to the playpen at Princeton to study musicology and Italian Renaissance Studies, in other words, to prepare for a career as an absent-minded professor with impossible handwriting. I'm jealous, though my handwriting really isn't nearly as bad as hers. But it does mean that now we can take her off our payroll. Together we have formed the "Sophie Chotek Memorial Society for Useless Knowledge." (Those of you who immediately scrambled to find out who Sophie Chotek was, and followed it up with a second websearch about the Second Defenestration of Prague are likely candidates for membership. If you already knew who Sophie Chotek is and the date of the Second Defenestration, you're a charter member!) Her mind remains, as she wrote four years ago, "an archaeological dig", and it looks like she will continue to have the luxury of being paid to explore it. (She misplaced her official offer letter to Princeton in the minefield of her room; she remembered where it was while inside a church dedicated to Saint Anthony of Padua – the patron saint of lost things – in Sicily. It was in an organizer, absolutely the last place she would have looked!)

If Aliyah's mind is a rich archaeological dig, Meera's is a laser pointer, trained on a single target. She s headed off to American University in Washington, DC in the fall as a step toward fulfilling her plan with a joint degree in international business/accounting and international service, with more than a little Arabic thrown in. (see plan below). Her high school years were this unusual combination of homeschooling, high school, and community college designed to meet the requirements of the National Collegiate Athletic Association to pursue a college gymnastics career, now clearly not going to happen.

Having returned from seven weeks in Cairo last summer with a surprising amount of spoken Arabic now part of her repertoire, she immediately began putting it to use through regular videoconferencing with youth and staff involved with the Rachel Corrie Youth and Cultural Center in Rafah, Palestine. And then, after a more than two-year hiatus, she announced she was performing another benefit piano recital. "They really need the money," she said. Ellen and I tried to appear nonchalant about the whole thing. (NOT!) But she got "her people" to organize the hall, take on the publicity, deal with money, and do just about everything but her hair (that was our contribution).

Sigh. In three months they'll both be gone. But I'm not ready to reflect upon being an emptynester. Not yet. I'm still basking in the glow. Maybe always will – we'll just have to see.

In the meantime, Meera agreed that I could share her college essay with you:

Mohammed and Me

This is my friend, Mohammed Abu Asaker, from Rafah, Palestine. He is my future business partner. Together we will rebuild Gaza and the West Bank.

I have been preparing myself for this partnership for a long time, although I didn't always know it. Following the events of September 11th, (although I am neither Muslim nor Jewish), I began attending a Muslim-Jewish dialogue group in order to connect with my community (Olympia, Washington) and to educate myself about the Israeli-Palestinian conflict.

In spring 2003, a young peace activist and college student from my hometown, Rachel Corrie, whom I had met several times at my local Friends (Quaker) Meeting, was tragically killed while protesting the demolition of a Palestinian home in Rafah. Immediately after this incident, I began working with the newly-founded Rachel Corrie Foundation for Peace and Justice, and this is how I later came to meet Mohammed. It took Mohammed three years to get out of Rafah to come and study in the United States. He was deeply moved by Rachel's death, and felt that he needed to acquire skills in the field of economic development to bring back to his home to continue Rachel's legacy.

At a very young age, I began playing the piano and later became a concert pianist. In late 2003, I offered to perform a recital as a benefit for the Israeli-Palestinian Families of the Bereaved Forum for Peace. This is a group of Israelis and Palestinians who have lost a family member to the conflict. They are coming together to try and solve their common problems so that people on either side do not feel they have to resort to violence. Following their three days of presentations in Olympia, I had the privilege to travel with two members of the group on the rest of their speaking tour in Washington State. Rami Elhanan is an Israeli father who had lost his daughter, Smadar, who would have been my age, but was killed by a suicide bombing while she was walking home on her first day of middle school. Ghazi Briegeith is a Palestinian whose two younger brothers were killed by the Israeli Defense Forces. After spending time with these two men, I felt (and still feel) called to help end the suffering caused by the Israeli-Palestinian conflict.

While Mohammed was attending graduate school, he came to Olympia as a guest speaker at a memorial dinner honoring Rachel's life. He spoke about the work that he hoped would create a more stable economy in Rafah. Later that evening, Mohammed and I had a conversation in which he told me that he needed all the help he could get, and that any skills I had to assist his cause would be a tremendous gift to him and his community. While I knew that I was passionate about this issue, I wasn't really sure in what way I could directly help. That has since changed. I now see using the skills I have previously developed, and those skills I will develop in the future as directed toward this end.

Developing financial skills is a necessary part of realizing my dream. In addition to performing benefit recitals, I have been the treasurer's intern for two non-profit organizations in my town. Interning has been a rewarding experience as I am able to utilize the accounting skills I have been acquiring, as well as being able to observe how finance works in the real world. As dull as it may sound to some, accounting is a subject I enjoy very much. It is the language of business, as it communicates the wants and needs of people and creates a financial structure to measure an organization's performance in fulfilling them.

I am working hard to increase my intercultural communication skills. I have become my community and high school's acknowledged, though unofficial, ambassador to exchange students from around the world – from Italy and Switzerland to Chile and Thailand. In acknowledgement of my efforts, I was recently awarded my County's "Youth Diversity and Human Rights Award." This past summer, I received a "Youth Ambassador" scholarship from the U.S. State Department Bureau of Educational and Cultural Affairs to travel to Cairo for six weeks to participate in a summer intensive Arabic language institute with 24 other students from across the country. I learned Arabic, experienced Egyptian society, and most importantly, built bridges between their culture and my own. On the way to Cairo, we stopped in Washington, DC. Since I already had extensive lobbying experience acquired as part of my work with the Corrie Foundation, I was chosen to help lead a group in lobbying Congressional representatives on increasing funding for intercultural exchange programs.

In my third year of working with the Corrie Foundation, I helped organize and then attended a major international peace conference focused on the Israeli-Palestinian conflict.

The conference brought in speakers from both Israel and Palestine: politicians, journalists, teachers, activists, students, and others. Taking part in the conference and its evaluation made me realize that peace is possible if we learn to really listen to one another and seek common ground.

Thus far in my preparation for working with Mohammed, I have developed the rudiments of fundraising, accounting, intercultural communications, negotiation, organizational, and governmental relations skills, and have discovered an aptitude for languages. I have a long way to go, and Mohammed and I both understand that in order for our work to bear fruit, the world must cooperate. It will take time, but Mohammed and I are not naïve, and are in it for the long haul. There must be peace in the Middle East, and I, or shall I say, we, intend to be part of it.

Olympic Epigenetics

SO…I'M SITTING in my recliner (yes, *again*; I really could use a bit more exercise, I remind myself). Favorite pastime – I'm channel surfing between the two stations televising the Olympics. Look! There is the Greco-Roman wrestler from Kyrgyzstan! Hope he wins – at least on the Canadian station, I might get to hear the Kyrgyzstan national anthem. Oh, well, better luck in four years. But, computer in my lap as always, I take a break from a piece of writing and look up the Kyrgyzstan anthem on the Web, and within 15 seconds, it is blaring out of my speakers. Isn't technology wonderful? But I was disappointed – I can't find the lyrics. (The flag of Kyrgyzstan is pretty cool, though). Then I decide that, although the Tuva Republic isn't in the Olympics this year, I can look up their national anthem, too. Here it is, no audio but there is sheet music (gotta get out the violin), and there's a translation of the lyrics (*Tooruktug Dolgaï Tangdym* – "The Forest is Full of Cedar Nuts"):

> *When I walk in my forest*
> *I will always be satisfied*
> *Because my forest is rich with*
> *　　　animals and everything I need.*
> *There in the mountains, the*
> *　　　cliffs, the taiga, I was born.*
> *Because of that I am strong.*
> *I will raise my livestock*
> *　　　and be rich.*
> *Nine different animals – if I herd*
> *　　　them and feed them*
> *And take care of them as my own,*
> *　　　I'll be rich.*

In my family room, there is a bunny, two dogs, and two corn snakes. (I couldn't get Aliyah to take them away to graduate school). The canary is in the kitchen. We used to have nine animals. Two children at home, too. Sigh. I am rich too, but in a different way.

There's only so much beach volleyball and BMX crashes I can take. So between the channels I stopped in on PBS. (Someday, maybe, they'll be Olympic channel surfing!) It is a NOVA show on epigenetics! www.pbs.org/wgbh/nova/sciencenow/3411/02.html, and, non-scientist that I am, I expect it will keep me pondering for weeks and months.

Epigenetics is a pretty simple idea really, though outrageous to those of us who took high school biology 30 or 40 years ago, and took notes. Our lifestyles and environment can change the way our genes are expressed, and there is a biochemical basis for these changes. This is on the cutting edge of biological research.

We know that there are chemical tags that control our genes, turning their expression on and off. Scientists can identify how even identical twins become distinct as they age. Twin mice, with exactly the same genetic makeup, will have different propensities for obesity. Twin adults with the same genetic makeup will exhibit different propensities for cancer or diabetes. We become, quite literally, to a great extent the biochemical offspring of our experience. We 'instruct our cells' in ways we are only just now beginning to understand.

It appears that epigenetic effects are transgenerational as well. Rats exposed to certain environmental pollutants have a higher incidence of diabetes later in life. More than that, their descendants do as well. Studies of records in an isolated town in Sweden indicate that the presence or absence of food at certain stages in an ancestor's life impact rates of cardiovascular disease, diabetes, as well as longevity two generations down the road. Guess I have to rewrite that earlier sentence: we become the biochemical offspring of our experience, *and the experience of those who came before!*

At the same time that this is going on, over in neuroscience we are learning more and more about the impact of early childhood experience (and especially childhood trauma) on neurological development and brain chemistry. (For a great read, get a copy of Bruce Perry and Maia Szalavitz's book *The Boy Who was Raised as a Dog*). What about the potential epigenetic impacts? Will growing up in an alcoholic household affect whether we are prone to diabetes later in life, and whether our children are as well? How about sitting in a little chair behind a little desk six hours a day for 12 years, and never being in control of one's experience?

What does this all have to do with homeschooling? May I suggest absolutely everything?

For many years, I have been writing about how, from a scientific perspective, the "nature v. nurture" debate had long been superseded, and how science has been discovering what many of the great spiritual traditions have always taught, that nature and nurture give rise to each other. Much of what we do as parent educators is to enable genetic potential and predispositions to unfold and flower, and that while schools may not necessary damage children (although they tragically do that all-to-often), they limit us from becoming the people we are truly meant to be.

What the epigenetic research, still in its infancy, suggests is that nurture – and that means YOU, dear friends – may actual *enhance* genetic potential and its expression. You already knew that you provided more for your children than a gene pool. Now we are just in the beginning stages of knowing how much more.

And, or so it seems, we are on the cusp of learning the degree to which what we do with our children in the here and now impacts the very genes of our great-grandkiddies! It's an awesome responsibility but also the most stirring of opportunities. Much too important to be left to strangers, however well-meaning. The love you express for your children today is your hand stretched out to a future you will never know.

Or, in your heart of hearts, maybe you do.

Average

THE EXPLORER HAD been preparing for this journey for a decade. At his prestigious college, he learned all he could about the region he would be visiting, and studied the only existent grammar of the language of the people.

It took him three months in his off-white pith hat to get through the jungle to his destination. And now, finally, he was there!

And here was his first contact with the tribe. He had been practicing what to say (in the local language, of course) for years.

"Take me to your average person," he requested.

The tribesman looked at him quizzically. "What's an average person?" he asked.

"Oh, you know," replied the explorer, "The one who represents the mean, the middle."

"I don't know what you mean," said the tribesman. "But I can take you to our chief. He is a great man. We have had peace ever since he became our leader. You know, he was born with a crippled right arm. Could never throw a spear. I think that led him to be a peaceful man."

"Well, I really want to learn about the people."

"I can take you to meet the woman who takes care of the children when the other women are working in the field. She lost two of her children to disease. And now she loves all of our children even more than she loved her own."

"We also have a great cook. She is a bit elderly now, but she remembers all the recipes of what our ancestors ate, and can prepare them well. Funny, because she has trouble sometimes remembering who each of us is."

"Don't you have anyone who is average?" inquired the explorer, a bit disconcerted.

"There is our medicine man. He knows all the plants in the jungle and their uses. And he is in direct communication with the spirits. Did you know that he's blind?"

And so it went. Each member of the tribe had his or her own unique story, skills, talents, disabilities, challenges, histories. No two the same. Fishwives, weavers, messengers, dancers; athletes, archers, hunters, skin painters, and tenders of the fire pits – each of them different, each with his or her own song, each their own thread in the warp and woof of the community's tapestry.

And, after months with the tribe, slowly the explorer came to realize something else, something which he never learned in his books: a community of average people (even if they had existed) would not be a community at all.

AND SO IT is with our children. There's not an average one in the bunch. Each one unique, no two (even identical twins, we are now learning) the same on the face of the earth, now, or ever. None the same ever came before, or will come after. That's the way Great Nature, in Her wisdom, created us. Or it's the way we've evolved. Or God Himself ordained. The lesson is the same, whatever your predilection. And we ignore this wisdom at our peril, and the peril of our children.

Now, I know what some of you might be thinking. How could schools, with 20, 30, 40, or now 60 (in Detroit) kids in each class attend to the individuality of every child? It would seem merely a matter of administrative necessity. Education on the cheap, one imagines a classroom filled with non-existent average children, and teach them as best one can. Throw in a little special education and an occasional gifted program into the mix, add some testing so there is a ceiling representing what one might be expected to reach inside the system, and you've got what passes for contemporary education.

This is the most benign view. But it is not an historical one. The shape of modern schooling was designed (beginning with Horace Mann's radical embrace of Prussian schooling – which he had never seen, and later expanded upon by the captains of industry who funded the first graduate schools of education in the 1890s) to ensure that children (later, adults) could be manipulated as interchangeable parts in the production process. If human beings are not alike, it is imperative for the education process to treat them that way, not so they can be taught in mass fashion, but to produce men and women who can be depended upon to act as if they are.

In a post-industrial context, instead of products being manufactured, *human beings* – beginning with childhood – *must be manufactured*. They must have the same likes and dislikes, the same moral or political opinions, same moods, same reactions, so they can all be made, at the whims of our consumer culture makers, to twitch all at the same time. There is no use for experience, except of the manufactured variety.

Somewhere along the line, the gods of education took the democratic maxim that "All men are created equal" and transformed it into their own dictum that "We create all men and women the same." Luckily, some of us still have the good sense to know better. And our kids, not an average one in the bunch, count on us to act upon what we know.

Glad we're homeschooling!

Dear Mom

Dear Mom,

I am writing you a letter. I know you might find that surprising, as I can't write my letters yet, but I'm only five and I will. But it doesn't mean I can't write letters in my mind. I write both kinds – why do they call letters that are like ABC and letters that are messages the same thing? I know how to do lots of things in my head, and one day I really will! Write letters, I mean.

Sometimes when I talk, the words don't come out right and so I don't say them. I have to organize them in my mind. I do that a lot when I'm playing with my train set by myself. When I figure them out, I am quite happy, and then I don't think I have to say them at all, and I usually forget, even when it is important. But they go away. And sometimes, Mom, I never told you this, I like to keep secrets, too. There are some things that make me happy that I like to keep to myself, as my own special thoughts, and they help me when I'm not feeling so happy.

Mom, I want to tell you that I love it when you read to me. We always do it before I go to bed, and I think about what we read a lot as I fall asleep. It's the best! And, Mom? You know that what comes out of your mouth is like magic, because the rest of the day, you almost never tell me any stories, and you don't say anything that is too funny very often. Maybe you are just busy. But when you read books, I love being next to you, and I finally found out last year that you didn't just make up the stories to go with the pictures, like I used to do in my head. Somehow there are stories and stuff in the letters! You never really told me that – I figured it out all by myself. I tried to ask you who put them in there, but I got frustrated in figuring out even how to ask. At first, I was a little disappointed when I found out you didn't make up a new story each time you read to me. I only discovered that when we pulled out the same book twice, and the story came out exactly the same. It's kind of nice to be able to learn stories by heart, though that's really little kids' stuff.

Your stories, and the books too, are filled with talking elephants and dancing trees, and funny cars and silly dinosaurs and hippopotamuses, and princes and princesses (dad used to call me 'the prince,' but he doesn't anymore), and poems – I especially like poems! – and all sorts of amazing people and places and buildings that we never see in our town. I sometimes wonder whether they exist where grandma lives, or maybe on the other side of the world? I don't understand why you think it is important that we read the same books again and again. I always like new ones. Oh, and Mom? I like books with facts in them. Lots of facts. When I know facts, it makes me feel really good, and (this might surprise you), I never forget any.

But lately, and this is what I wanted to tell you, it is becoming less fun. First of all, you sometimes want to do it in the daytime, when I have other stuff I need to do. And you make it seem like we have to, like when you make me go brush my teeth, though that's only at night. And then, sometimes, right in the middle of the story, you have started putting your finger under words. And so I push it away, but you don't seem to like that. And now you sometimes point at a place on the page and ask "what's this word?" I HATE THAT! How am I supposed to concentrate and enjoy the story and remember what happened before if you keep interrupting? It's very terrible, and when you do that, I don't want to read anymore. And then I can see you get a little upset, and I'm trying to figure out if I did anything wrong. I mean I know my letters, and lots of other stuff, too.

Sometimes you stop your reading on a particular word, put your finger under it, and make funny shapes and sounds with your mouth. I understand that these sounds are supposed to add up to words or something, but they seem to have nothing to do with the stories at all, so I really wish you would stop.

You know, you sort of do the same thing with the piano. What a miracle the piano is! Dad once picked me up so I could see what happens inside when you play. There are all those metal strings inside a funny-shaped box, with hammer things, and pedals. Dad says the white keys come from elephant tusks (but I don't believe him), and the black keys come from wood from India, where there are also elephants. (You told that to me from a book, about the elephants, I mean). And out of the piano, when you play, comes magical sounds! I love to watch and listen, and sometimes I take my train set right under it when you are playing. Did you know that it sounds completely different from under there? Scruffy (Editor's note: the family dog) likes it there, too.

But then you make me sit on the piano bench and play. Only it really isn't playing. You always tell me where to put my fingers, which are too small anyway, and hit one note at a time, which is boring, and then you tell me to count, only I don't know what it is I am counting because there really is nothing there. It ruins it totally, and then for some reason you get sort of, I don't know, angry?

I know a secret. This one I can share, and it is completely true. I am going to play the piano better than you do. Really! I know this because I have better music pictures in my head, and I am going to play them. And, you know what? I'm also going to read better than you. I'm going to read books without any pictures in them, and with lots of FACTS. Then – you wait – I'm going to be the smartest person in the whole world! And then everyone will know I have the best mom ever.

Well, that's all I have to say right now. Someday I will be able to write my letters down, and I can send them in the mail, and then you can get them and send me letters back. That will be so much fun. But until then, we will just have to wait. Ooo, and I discovered that growing up means there is a lot of waiting. Sometimes this is annoying, and makes me mad, like when you told me I'm too little to cook things on the stove. But other times it's just fun, because I never know exactly what is going to happen next.

I don't know how you are supposed to end a letter. So I guess I'll just say, "Good bye."

>*Your friend,*
>
>*Michael*

For Dads

AS I TRAVEL around talking to homeschoolers and would-be homeschoolers, it would be impossible to miss the fact that my audiences are somewhat lacking in Y chromosomes. I've tried everything – well, not *everything* – but special discounts for 'significant others,' and 'two-for-one' opportunities. Hosts have offered door prizes for fathers who attend. For the most part, they don't work. (I haven't yet taken to paying them). And the same is pretty much true among the e-mails I receive asking for advice. The women outnumber the men maybe 20 or 30 to one. That might also be true for readers of this column.

Now let me let you in on a little secret: this is not as big a problem as it might initially seem. You see, fellow dads, I learned something of critical importance in my family's very first years of homeschooling more than 20 years ago. It eliminated almost all conflicts I may have had with my wife Ellen regarding virtually any issues, large or small, having to do with the kids' education, and it led (if I might say so myself) to pretty spectacular outcomes.

I simply learned to assume she was right. Always.

There you have it. It took a little practice, with my being a veritable "Mr. Know-It-All", with opinions concerning just about everything, likely far too well-read for my own good, and an ego the size of a large rhinoceros. I found out that Ellen was perfectly capable of taking that into account. Early on, occasionally I bit my lip. Later, I don't even think I much noticed. Doesn't mean she *was* always right; only that I learned to begin with the assumption that she was.

Thing is, I realized early that she was much more likely to be most sensitively attuned to the kids' needs and desires, hopes and aspirations. Now, let's be clear: I don't think there was anything biological about it. Nor would it be true that she was better equipped to assist in our children's particular learning quests – we have always had a wonderful division of labor on that front.

It also has nothing to do with that "Women are from Venus, Men are from Mars" claptrap either. Rather the reality is that, to overgeneralize, men in our culture are often banished *to* Mars. We have it drilled into us from an early age that it is a big, bad world out there, and that we must gird up our loins (all right – for some of us, occasionally put on a tie), and sacrifice at least some of our personal satisfaction – and most of our waking hours – to provide for hearth and home. We are trained to put aside our emotions as we go out and battle and scrap for a share of the kill. Many of us get really good at what we do, within a narrow frame of reference. In my case, an overabundance of competitive-edged education didn't help matters any, my saving grace being that, once the kids were born, I was quick to realize it. (No, I am not appealing for sympathy from the female folk, who are also beset by their own cultural mythology – "Having It All" – effortlessly juggling the responsibilities of wife, mother, career, and being thin. A little compassion all around – for all of us – would go a long way).

With effort, I probably could have overcome my miseducation, and to a large extent, I think I have. (As I grow older, it is getting more difficult for me to physically pat myself on the back, so I am getting better in doing so psychically). But for so many of us, it is merely a matter of time. Even though I re-careered, and managed to find a job where I could come home for lunch every day, the reality is that my wife simply knew the kids better than I did, learning from them hour-to-hour, day-by-day. We love our children, but many of us don't have the opportunity to know them as well as we would like.

So, dads, don't let anyone fool you – it is *quantity time* that counts. The idea of *quality time* was invented (in the mid-'70s) at just such a period when the amount of time we got to spend with kids, with our families, began to slip away, and has accelerated since. What you do during *quantity time* hardly matters, so long as you are available to your children. You don't have to take them to the zoo or to a baseball game for it to count. Kicking a soccer ball in the driveway, a walk in the snow, or listening to music together will do just as well. Taking them (preferably only one at a time) on your trip to the hardware store to get that missing piece for the toilet (which you've never actually fixed before) will be a great opportunity. Or even just sitting in the same room as the kids are, and reading a book. Pretty much whatever you do, provided you keep the electronic boxes turned off (and there are exceptions to that as well), will give you a better sense of who your children really are.

And now for another little secret: it is always useful when you pay special attention to the developing passions of your children, and help them find new ways to follow their learning quests. You might initially find yourself outside of your comfort zone, but with just the right amount of detachment, you might come to realize that you can appreciate the gymnastics gym or the physics camp like you would a foreign culture (which, to you, they may well be, with their own rules, language, and ritual).

But the real secret is that you get to share *your* passions with them as well. There is more to being a father than being a breadwinner and good husband (don't lose sight of those, of course, but there is, or should be, so much more). Whether it be sports cars, service projects, gardening, woodworking, or just good books, allowing your kids to see that you have particular enthusiasms and pursuits independent of them (but in which you discover ways for them to join in if they choose), will expand their sense of you, and of the possibilities open to them far beyond what they could otherwise conceive. And I promise…fun!

Consider a little fun my Fathers Day present to your family. Happy Fathers Day!

A Grand Spectacle

LAST WEEK, I went to the opera. Well, not quite, but the next best thing. The Metropolitan Opera provides simulcasts to selected movie theaters around the country, and today was *Turandot* by Puccini (or at least most of it – he died before completing the score, and the third act suffers accordingly). A grand spectacle, an opulent Italian representation of a greater China. It is said that Puccini got his major theme from a little Chinese music box.

The theater was almost full, and my first thought was, "Oh dear, I must be the only person here under 60." And then I gulped, recognizing that, by the time you get to read this, *I* will be over 60. My wife says not to worry. Next time I go the opera I am likely to think the same thing, only this time with "70" as the reference number. One of the singers, Charles Anthony, playing the Emperor of China, is over 80, and has been singing at the Met since 1954. In the opera, the Emperor is repeatedly praised, with the universal hope that he may live 10,000 years.

Though the scenery was the real star, the vocal show was stolen by a young Russian woman playing one of the secondary roles (Liu), and everyone knew it. Her name is Marina Poplavskaya.

So when I got home, I hurried over to my trusty computer, and looked her up. She is from Moscow, and tells a wonderful story about how she came to be an opera singer. She had begun singing as soon as she could talk, but her two scientist parents weren't particularly encouraging of her musical gifts. Anyhow, one evening, when she was eight, she heard on the radio in her room that the Bolshoi Opera was auditioning for members of their children's chorus. The next morning, after her mother had gone to work, she left a little note for her on the dining room table. "Gone to audition for the Bolshoi," it read.

She took a train by herself (having figured out with a little help at the station which train she needed to take), then got out and took a bus, and finally arrived at the audition location. There were some 300 parents, with their children in tow, all with sandwiches and other things to eat. She was hungry, but she wasn't going to lose her place in line.

At last it was her turn. The conductor asked her what she was going to sing. "What would you like to hear?" she replied, "I have a very large repertoire."

Almost needless to say, she got in. A star was born. Her mother was very proud (though Marina notes there "was some trouble" when she got home that night).

I shudder to think what might have happened had she been enrolled in an American public school. Actually, in at least one case, I know. We had a friend, Barry, who was a very talented 13-year-old singer (and had sung the role of the Shepherd Boy in *Tosca*). There was a tryout for one of the three sprites in Mozart's *The Magic Flute* with the Portland Opera. His mother wrote a note to the school a week in advance that she would be taking him (no unaccompanied train rides for him!) A note came back – this would be an *unexcused absence*. Oh, the horrors of it! The mother thought, "Wait! I thought I was the one who does the excusing for my own son." On his return, the school threatened to suspend him for a week.

In both cases, I would have preferred it otherwise. In the best of all possible worlds, the school (and Marina's mother) would have thrown a party the night before, and provided a hearty sendoff – a *bon voyage* – as they each sailed off to confront their operatic destiny, or at least a piece of it. And they'd be prepared to help their charges deal with the disappointments that would inevitably occur along the way. If a future career in opera was not in the offing, there would always be community or church choruses, or maybe a flirtation with hip-hop. Who knows?

But I can hear the objection in my ears, as I channel my inner assistant principal. "What would happen if *all* the kids decided to do it?" he whines (not being aware in the least that he is echoing Kant's 'categorical imperative.')

What indeed? The opera companies would be filled with new young singers, who would be assiduously studying Italian, French, German, and Russian for real (not the ersatz variety they often get in school, but the genuine article), and the discipline that operatic performance requires. Communities would be raising funds to send them on trips to New York, Paris, Milan, London, Bayreuth. The opera audiences would be filled with middle school and high school students (I might occasionally be the *oldest* person in the audience), as well as with fathers, mothers, uncles and aunts, grandparents and family friends.

The local orchestras would be replete with an abundance of players as well (there would even be enough bassoon players!), and new ones would be formed all the time. Community theater companies would see a revival, with young people playing and singing alongside older ones (like me). In fact, when bringing their kids to rehearsals, parents would get excited and want to join in as well. The high schools would make money renting out space.

Opera, of course, is just escapist fantasy. I have one in my mind – a tragedy – about a handsome young assistant principal – a tenor – who falls in love with an unfortunately recently widowed homeschooling mom – a soprano – with five lovely homeschooled daughters, (one of them in a 'pants role,' all of them talented in different ways, and each uniquely insightful about the situation and about the world around them), and is brought low because he has been urging his students that they have better things to be doing with their time and energy than sitting in a high school classroom. The villain – an evil, mustachio-ed baritone with a pompadour – is the local school superintendent, who embezzles milk money from the schools in his charge, and who is trying to force himself on the soprano under the threat of finding a way of coercing the kids into the box. Want to write the ending? (send me an e-mail at david@skylarksings.com)

Moving Out

THEY'RE GONE!

Packing up Aliyah for her move to New Jersey took three months, and, in reality, we are still not done.

Upon graduating from college, she shipped five boxes of books down to Washington, DC to her grandmother, for pickup later. Then out came the books from her room. Astronomy books and Tolstoy, endless numbers of Dickens novels, books on constructing northwest Indian baskets, six volumes of Will Durant, books of Renaissance maps, Tamil phrasebooks, Jack London and Alexander Dumas. There were dog books and horse books and bird books and insect books and math puzzles. Dictionaries of musical biography, art books on Gauguin and Cezanne and medieval churches, how-tos on oboe reed-making, embroidery, and weaving. Shakespeare and Cervantes, Garcia Marquez and Jane Yolen. Books in Italian, German, and French

The books continued to be carried out to the living room. The two dogs sniffed at them in bewilderment. We ran out of our local supply of boxes, and called a librarian friend who came to the rescue. We ended up contributing seven boxes full, 278 lbs., to the new community library set up by homeschoolers in southern Oregon after the regional library system shut down for lack of funds. There were still more books. Books related to peace, nonviolence, and social activism were donated to the Quaker Meeting library. After all this, there were still six boxes of books to ship to Princeton (we are grateful for the Post Office's Media Mail), including rare editions of *Alice in Wonderland* in Latin. The Princeton library has only 6.4 million books – these will come in handy.

We weren't close to being done. There were wire sculptures and wire sculpting tools, ceramics, reed-making equipment, and woodcarving sets. A hefty box of wool, silk, and other weaving materials. Then there is the large loom (it is now in the closet, awaiting further instructions). Costumes. Two dozen hats. The giant dragonfly wings from a community Procession of the Species of many years ago are still mounted on the ceiling. The Celtic harp is out on loan. The oboe has been placed with her former teacher, in the hope that a student may be found who may wish to purchase it. The 8" Dobsonian reflector telescope, built by Aliyah and my wife when she was eight-and-a-half (my daughter, not my wife!), still looking like a large cannon painted robin's egg blue, has now found a long-term temporary home with a seven-year-old homeschooler, together with all the lenses and star finders. We now have a lending library of violins and violas.

Clothing! Snowboots from when she was ten, pants from when she was 14. Old unmatched socks. Ragged tee-shirts. A black-and-red English wool cape, purchased at Covent Garden when we went together to London to sing. Mittens my wife had knitted. Indian sarees and salwar kameez (you'll have to look that one up). A dress Aliyah had woven. When it came to clothing, a single old oversized suitcase, with various sweaters, shirts, shoes, and haberdashery tossed in haphazardly was all that was necessary for the trip east. A box of keepsakes and letters given to her when she was one. And some silver wrapping paper, her favorite gift from before she could walk.

Stuffed animals, puppets, and dolls took a trip to Goodwill. We couldn't part with Agi the Raccoon puppet, Aliyah's very first playmate, nor with Susan Cowfish (a stuffed salmon, not of the eating variety). A squash racket in nearly mint condition, a reminder of my lack of success in engaging her in *my* sport, or any sport for that matter, outside of bird watching.

Then there were the papers, plaques, a trophy from winning a music composition contest when she was 12. Since the National Archives isn't open to her memorabilia (yet!), they'll never know what they're missing. Her floor was littered with wood shavings, unbent paperclips, staples, pins, and an occasional earring, all suggesting that it wasn't safe to enter with bare feet. We are still finding traces of Aliyah all over the house, and I expect we will continue to for a very long time.

Moving Meera, in contrast, took all of two hours. Physically, that is. For weeks, lists had been drawn up and discussed, primarily with my wife Ellen, of what was going and what was staying behind. The clothes were all hung neatly, as always, or presorted and folded in drawers awaiting inspection. The shoes were lined up by color. The gymnastics medals and trophies were all neatly stashed in boxes. CDs had all been transferred onto MP3s or the computer. Jewelry in one tidy box.

Meera shipped one box via Media Mail. It contained all of eight or nine books, mostly unread, and kept not so much for their information value, but rather as keepsakes of peace and social action groups she had supported, presents from friends and admirers, souvenirs of her trip to Egypt. Quarter of a box. The rest was taken up with piano music: Rachmaninoff, Chopin, Albeniz, Granados, Schubert, the complete Mozart sonatas.

There was another box. All shoes. 45 pounds' worth. Meera insisted it had to be shipped via Priority Mail – her shoes would set foot on the American University campus before she did.

That was it. The floor was already spotless. The desk was clean, ready for the next user. The drawers were all empty. Her Italian "PEACE" banner in rainbow colors was still draped across the window, and camel's hair rug weaving from Cairo still on the wall – after all, she would still be coming home for vacations, and the room couldn't be left bare if it was to be acceptable to guests and visitors. She is not gone, though. The 6'2" 1926 Mason & Hamlin grand piano will still loom large in our living room for many years to come. Sigh. I still can't play. But Ellen is threatening to take it up, and a call to old friend Mark Almond ("Piano for Quitters" – www.pianoforlife.com/) may be in the offing.

Of course, as we were helping to pack the kids up, Ellen and I were in a certain sense packing ourselves up as well. What have we learned that will help us on our journey, even as our children continue on their own? What mysteries have we uncovered for ourselves in the process, and what mysteries yet await us?

I know one thing for sure: I have plenty more to write.

Expanding the Food Repertoire

MEERA JUST CALLED us from college, three thousand miles away, to announce she had become a vegan.

"Oh" I said, with clear surprise in my voice. "Not for ethical reasons, I assume?

"No. Health." she replied.

I didn't think ethical was likely, given the conversation she had had with a career advisor last spring, preparing her for an internship interview. Somehow the conversation had turned to his commitment to eating only free-range chickens.

"But you kill them anyway," said Meera. "Eat them, too."

"Yes, but they had a better quality of life while they were around," said the advisor.

"But they're still dead, and you're still eating them," replied Meera, who in the past has found it difficult to get her mind around shades of gray. (It should be noted, she was eating meat, and still is, but we'll get to that).

"Health?" I wondered, though I was sure she'd spent some time on the Internet researching the issue. Nonetheless, I was sure there was more to it. "But I thought you have trouble with wheat."

"Well, not really."

Meera went through rather absolutist food phases. Unlike her sister who at 20 months had a hankering after sushi and kidney beans and whatever the adults around her were eating, Meera's diet was always carefully circumscribed. There was a time where she would eat anything, so long as it resembled a hamburger or a hotdog. (This is my Indian-born daughter; the other one loved my curried lentils with hot Indian pickles). Then it was peanut butter and box mac'n'cheese. Sometime before she went off to college, it became a few slices of deli turkey, fruit-flavored yoghurt, a piece of lettuce with an occasional carrot, maybe a fruit, and powerbars. Six foods a day, one more than Gandhi! Oh, and perhaps an occasional bit of cheese.

We'd already scaled back the university meal plan as far as they would allow. Too much food, and at the wrong times. (In the interest of fairness, it should be noted that American University is considered a vegetarian heaven). Meera has always been a grazer. Something in her mouth every two hours, but didn't want to be slowed down by a real meal. We reaped none of the known benefits of family togetherness at dinner time. And by the time she was six or seven, she was in the gym until after 7 o'clock in any case. As for restaurants, if we go teriyaki or Mexican, she still orders the kids' meal, and then asks for a box.

I told my wife from day one that I wasn't going to *do* food issues. I'd had enough of my own in childhood, and can still remember being forced to sit in the corner chair in the kitchen for three hours with my plate of *lungen* stew (beef lungs – my father loved them!), until I would beg and plead with my mother that I really, really wanted to do my homework. I am pleased to report that it is now illegal to sell lungs for human consumption in the United States. ("Yes, Junior, there really is a God, and He listens to the anguished cries of little children.") Anyhow, there would be reasonably nutritious food in the house, and I'm a good cook, and the kids could eat as they pleased. No one was going to starve.

"But, Meera," I felt called to remind her, as if she didn't know, "You don't like bread, couscous, polenta, rice, potatoes, noodles or pasta, either white or whole wheat. You hate all cooked vegetables. You aren't fond of beans or sprouts; you don't eat soybeans, tofu, or tempeh, or drink soymilk. You won't even touch oatmeal."

"All true," she said, "But that's just the point. I have to learn to like them, or at least to tolerate them. And it will also be good for me. My roommate is a vegetarian, and she'll teach me how to cook them."

"That should help," I opined, remaining unconvinced.

"You see, I need to do this for my future business career."

"A vegan?" Now I was really nonplussed.

"Yes," she said, "All over the world, and I plan to work all over the world, they eat different grains and prepared vegetables, and I have to accommodate to local custom."

"Oh? But what if they're eating meat?"

"Then I'll eat meat. Not opposed to meat eating. Or fish. Or eggs. The point is that I have to expand my food repertoire."

And so it goes. My daughter is becoming a vegan in order to expand her food repertoire. We'll see how long this lasts.

I think I'm now supposed to draw an elaborate analogy between the homeschooling need for a prepared curriculum, well-thought through in advance and which must be followed to the letter, and the requirement that our kids eat three balanced, wholesome meals every day....But on second thought, I won't.

After hanging up, Meera went out and bought soymilk and some organic instant oatmeal.

P.S. At last report, Meera is still veganizing.

Seed

ON THE BACK of the package, it said, "Germination in 14 days."

So I prepared the soil, some nice *dirt* (when I grew up, I never heard of 'soil,' only 'dirt'), mixed in a little compost, watered it cautiously, softened it up. I'd made sure it was in a spot that would receive at least six hours of sun a day, and had waited until there had been three sunny days in a row, so that the soil might be at least a little warm.

I placed the seed carefully, at exactly the depth indicated on the package, not too deep, not too shallow. And covered it up meticulously.

And waited. There was a day of rain and wind, but then the sun came out. And then there were three straight days of sun, and I sprinkled some water. And I marked the days.

On the eleventh day (and, yes, I was counting), I examined the soil for signs of life. Nothing (of course), but I was willing to wait. The twelfth, the same thing. Thirteenth – no luck. But I knew, the package said 14, and I figured the people who made the package should know better than I did.

On the 14th, the sky was a brilliant blue. There was not a cloud in the sky. The sun beat down gently. The birds sang, the flowers lolled in the gentle breeze. All was well with the world, after a fashion.

Except – no plant peeked through. And the 15th, still nothing. On the 16th, I was really concerned. Maybe I had watered too much, and the seed had rotted. Or maybe not enough? Had I put the seed in too deeply (even though I had measured)? Had some underground critter enjoyed a good lunch? What to do?

On the 17th…Maybe the particular seed I'd picked from the seed package had gotten packed by accident, and was really of a different variety? Or perhaps it was sterile? I steeled myself, and decided not to dig to find out. If good things were happening underground, I might dislodge the fragile grip the roots had on the soil below. I didn't add fertilizer, as it might burn up the delicate shoot (if there was one). The soil still has a bit of cool dampness to it; it was not time to water.

I went back and read the package. "Germination in 14 days." Maybe it was a bad batch. Or maybe I really wasn't cut out to be gardener, given my impatience, it perhaps exacerbates my tendencies toward nervous anxiety. And young plants can sometimes be so very silent, and so opaque to my probings. Is this something I really wanted to be doing?

On the morning of the 18th day, a small, grayish bend, almost like a hook, appeared on the surface of the soil. I touched it gently, but then decided to leave well enough alone. By the time I came home for lunch, the hook had unbent itself, and a frail, green shoot appeared in its place, and there were suggestions of leaves, folded in upon themselves. The sun beamed down – it was a hot day. By nightfall, the plant was two inches high. I sprayed a little bit of water on it.

And then, in a self-congratulatory mood, I went inside and told my wife. After all, I had done such a good job.

Now when will the plant bear fruit?

SO THIS YEAR, I planted the first real garden of my life. Hey, I'm a New Yorker at heart. Dug up an excuse for lawn in the front of the house, put in four 4' x 10' boxes, each one a foot high. "Use cedar," said my garden advisor, "It will last 20 years." I did, as an expression of a commitment I wasn't sure I really had.

Filled the boxes with "mushroom soil," a kind of mix between dirt and the remains of last year's mushroom medium from some commercial fungus farm nearby. Filled some extra pots, too. Set up a very large compost bin. (Actually, my wife did). Now we were feeling very virtuous.

Started all my vegetables from seeds. Broccoli raab, Belgian endive, red romaine lettuce, green romaine, mustard greens, microgreens. They all grew. They all bolted. Microgreens became macrogreens. I learned from a friend that we could eat them all anyway, just not as salad. Made great stir fries, chopped them into spaghetti sauces, put into bean stews.

Part of my plan was to grow the usual stuff, but in unusual colors or shapes. After all, I could get all the more standard fare at the market. So I planted yellow and purple bush beans, scarlet runner beans, lemon cucumbers, round purple eggplants, pinkish-and-white striped (Rosa Bianca) eggplants, and Japanese eggplants, purple peppers. Round Parisian market carrots, dragon (purple) carrots, red atomic carrots, icicle radishes (ugh). Golden beets and red cylinder beets. Purple and pink flowering and red Russian kale.

Then there was my Italian series. I found an importer of seeds from Italy . (growitalian.com) Purple Sicilian cauliflower (it's actually more like broccoli, and you can eat the leaves)., escarole biondi (blonde), Italian golden horn-shaped peppers (Corno di Toro Giallo) and Italian red roasting peppers, Broccoli Romanesco (good for a review of fractal geometry), fennel of Parma, Venetian broad beans (they're yellow), Roman broad beans (flat green ones – I intermixed these with the Venetians and let them go to war), and the "marvelous beans of the Piedmont" (Mereville di Piemonte – yellow with purple blotches, and good!). Italian red Concerto artichokes, red Verona radicchio and Italian basil and flat-leaf parsley, and Greek oregano (what is that doing here?)

Most everything grew, despite the coldest, wettest summer in 20 years. I fretted, and they grew. I didn't fret, and they grew anyway. Got some real favorites, and some, well, one learns with experience. This is my kindergarten, complete with my vegetable children.

Then there were tomatoes. The world of tomatoes is quite extraordinary. There are so many! I got seeds, lots of seeds, and babied them, and gave away lots of extra tomatolings to all my friends. Let's see, I have: Sungolds (orange), Brandywines (red), Giant Belgians (pink), Yellow Pears (blue – just thought I'd see if you were really following), Green Zebras (green and yellow), Blacks from Tula (in these climes, they should be sort of brownish), Black Cherries (ditto). Stuck 'em in the ground in late June. Didn't grow – too cold! And then around the second week of July…they all became seven-feet tall! Forget tomato cages, they spilled out over everything, and climbed, and put half the other vegetables in shade. (Surprisingly, they grew anyways).

It's now the third week in September, and I have hundreds and hundreds of green tomatoes. My neighbor who shares a fence just harvested his first red tomato. "What kind?" I ask. "Early Girl," he says, a variety that is usually just about finished the first week in July.

It has rained for the past five days. On the sixth day, I go out to take a look. There are black leaves and stems everywhere. It's "late blight." No cure. Thousands of Irish peasants starved to death (potatoes and tomatoes are in the same family, and get the same diseases). At least I have access to supermarkets.

I decide to go out and prune away as much of it as I can. (Not that I really believe it will make any difference). And then, after two or three hundred cuts, I notice something really interesting (maybe all real gardeners already know this). Of the hundreds of affected branches and stems, not a single one has a tomato on it.

Even tomato plants know to protect their young.

A Little Conversation

I RECENTLY RETURNED from southern India where I continued to work on the land reform and community development efforts I have been involved in for more than 30 years. I was talking with the 83-year-old engine behind these efforts (Krishnammal Jagannathan, the person I call my "Indian mother"), and she told me a fascinating story about growing up in her village as a Dalit "untouchable".

"You see," she said, "We had a tradition. Even though we were all very poor, we weren't allowed to sell 'white foods' – cooked rice, milk, yoghurt, eggs. We had to give them away. When we had any leftovers, my grandmother would get up very early in the morning and seek out people who were poorer than we were. In that way, we could begin the day anew."

I have pondered on this tale for a long time. The obvious moral is that it is a good thing when entire communities embody a generosity of spirit that is shared by all its members to the extent that it becomes second nature. (It has, however, in this case been broken down in the face of outside market forces beyond the community's control, which unfortunately is a generally common occurrence worldwide). But less obvious is the reality that without someone ready and willing to receive, the giver is up a creek!

While I was in India, I spent most of my time begging. (I gave myself a nickname, "The Fat Beggar.") We are launching a housing movement to replace 5,000 leaky, rat-infested mud huts with beautiful four-room houses (367 square feet, with detached bathrooms, and biosand water filters to ensure clean water). I begged for cement, sand, truck transportation (to carry fly-ash used in the making of bricks to our brickmaking site, and to carry bricks to the villages), windows, doors, a huge (70' x 35') open-sided shed. I also begged for, (with great success I might add), a truckload of organic manure to grow vegetables to be used to feed the village brickmakers while they are working. Six dollars equals a bag of cement (70 to a house); one brick costs a dime (we need 15,000 of them – I've got labels for you to keep a dime jar at home – just e-mail me at david@skylarksings.com)

There was a time when education embodied a spirit of generosity. (And, in places, it still does). In traditional Indian practice, teachers (called "gurus") would take students into their families free of charge. Education consisted of treating the student as simply a member of the family, sharing in its work, joys, sorrows, and conversation, while the master went about the business of his own educational and spiritual journeys, of which the student became a living witness.

The apprenticeship system of medieval and Renaissance Europe at its best had similarities, though there were also financial interests involved. Apprentices were a source of cheap labor. At the same time, however, with average life expectancy being much shorter than today, this was the workman's opportunity to pass along his skills and knowledge, something upon which the community depended.

The example of Michelangelo is particularly instructive. Having lost his mother at age seven, he was adopted by a stonecutter's family. At 13, he was apprenticed to a painter who, in turn, passed him onto the care of Lorenzo d'Medici, who moved him into the palace, where he had the opportunity to mix with artists, writers, and philosophers. The core of his education, beyond the skills that he learned to practice his trade, was simply good conversation.

What child development experts beginning with Lev Vygotsky (he is worth googling) have long known, and which is now being confirmed by a myriad of research studies, is that adult-child conversation, and the mutuality and respect that adheres to it, is at the core of higher learning, and the model for "inner speech," or what we more commonly call, "thinking."

I like to think that good conversation is by its very nature an act of generosity, the best opportunity you and your child (and those around you) ever have of sharing of yourselves.

You could do worse than to think of homeschooling simply as a long conversation that you and your children will have with each other long into adulthood.

When we think fondly of teachers (in school or out) that we have had in our lives, it is almost always because of the quality of conversation with which we were graced. And these same teachers will almost always tell you that they received as much in return as they gave.

Sadly, what passes for education these days has so often sacrificed conversation (when it occurred at all) for a regimen of force-feeding. It doesn't work for geese (unless you are seeking liver pâté), and it works even less well with children. If higher learning depends on the quality of conversation, depriving children of it in the name of education represents an actual decision that results in mental retardation.

We could all be so much more! And, if we homeschoolers do this right, our children will be. In fact, they already are.

Accepting that invitation to your six-year-old's tea party may be more important than you know.

Noah's Problem

IT RAINED LAST winter. A lot. It rained for 35 straight days. Then there was a sunny day. Then it rained for 15 more.

Storm drains were flooded. Gutters were stuffed up. Streams overflowed their banks. Salmon swam on highways. Cows waded through puddles-turned-swamp like ducks. Ducks, for their own part, didn't want anything to do with it, and nestled under whatever overhangs they could find. Horses weren't allowed out of barns. I almost broke out a 20-year-old raincoat that has been gathering dust in the hallway closet, dating from the time before I lived in the Pacific Northwest, but, no, it stayed put, refusing to embarrass me for whatever weight I've put on since.

I heard more Noah jokes than I can ever remember. Folks who would have nothing to do with organized religion of any kind prattled on about arks. There were cartoons in the newspaper. Politicians began speeches by thanking people for floating in to hear them, and people asked how many quarters were required for arks at parking meters.

As a child, I loved the story of Noah's Ark, as did many of my friends. At some point, as I'm sure many of you with seven-, eight-, or nine-year-olds have become well aware, the story provokes a rain of questions, the kind for which you are not equipped with pat answers. In other words, the best kind of story.

"Mom, were there dinosaurs on the ark?"

"Joey, as far as I know, there weren't any brontosauruses."

"Oh, mom. Of course there weren't any brontosauri. You know that brontosaurus wasn't a real dinosaur, right? You must mean brachiosaurus."

"Mom, with all those animals on the ark and it raining for forty days and forty nights, what did they do when they had to go to the bathroom?"

"Oh, Timmie, if God could make it rain for forty days and forty nights, I'm sure He could arrange it so that nobody had to go."

"Mom, if there was only two of every animal that came off the ark, what did they do to prevent inbreeding?"

And so on and so forth. Some questions are not really meant to be answered, like that prompted by one of my daughter's first favorite song *MacArthur Park*: "Dad, who left the cake out in the rain?" (I'm afraid this one might date me, but if you look up the lyrics to Richard Harris' greatest hit, you will either be richly rewarded or profoundly disturbed – www.lyricsdepot.com/richard-harris/macarthur-park.html).

At a certain point in our growing up, we all come to realize one way or another that life itself is an open-ended question. Sometimes things just aren't that simple, and we learn to appreciate that there can be as much beauty and wonderment in the new-found complexity of the universe as in its simplicity. An important piece of learning. We grow to expect the unexpected. We take a deep breath, and wade into the water.

Like ducks. Like cows last winter.

HE LOOKED OUT the window, and he knew he had a problem.

The ark had taken him a hundred years to build. Three hundred cubits long, 50 cubits wide, bigger than a football field. Three stories high. Ribs of cypress, just as the blueprints specified. Reed roof. No one had ever seen anything even remotely like it. By the time he finished, the forest by the side of the barely running stream was a grassy field, the reeds were all gone, and the earth was flat.

His neighbors, what was left of them, occasionally came by, shaking their heads. What was this about a flood? There wasn't even a reasonably sized lake within 200 miles. And who had ever seen anything so humongous? How could anyone possibly believe it was going to float? And who could presume they were ever going to get the opportunity to find out?

Noah slept on the ark that night. It was the first night it was finished. He knew the ark was supposed to contain two of every kind of animal on the earth, one male, one female, but he had no idea how he was supposed to gather them up. He slept that night without dreams, amidst this cavernous empty expanse, a night marked by an eerie and unusual silence.

He awoke early that morning to the most awful racket he had ever heard in his life. He limped over to the window, his legs and arms still sore from a hundred years of carrying, and hammering, and sawing, the plaiting of reeds for the roof, and the spreading of pitch on the ark's bottom and sides, all without access to a single power tool.

Yes, now he knew he had a problem. As he looked out the window, there were animals covering the field, miles of animals, as far as his eye could see or ear could hear, if he could manage to hear anything at all. There was roaring and quacking and bleating and buzzing and yowling and screeching and squawking and bellowing and belching and trumpeting and squealing and every sound he could ever imagine an animal making, and some he couldn't even imagine. There they were, a coiling, wallowing, teaming, sweating mass of undifferentiated animality that stretched out to the treeless horizon, beyond anything he could possibly envision fitting on his vessel, which suddenly seemed absurdly small.

Noah clambered up to the top floor of the ark, and looked out. Once he could pull himself away from simply being overwhelmed in surveying the roiling sea that produced this cacophony, and the smell! his attention was drawn to his left, down front, within spitting distance of the ark itself. Elephants! He had heard about them from travelers who had come through to see him at what they thought to be his absurd labors, but he had never seen one himself. But, and now he was taken aback, there weren't two of them, but four! He blinked, rubbed his eyes, and looked again. Sure enough, four of them, 16 legs and eight tusks in all. Patient in all their enormity. And now he began to look more carefully. The ears! Two of them had ears that were barely a cubit across. But the other two had ears that were almost big enough to be wings, four cubits wide, flapping in the growing heat of the day. One of the travelers had told him once, he now remembered, that there were two kinds of elephants, one from Africa and one from India, and that one could tell them apart by the ears, but Noah had let that information slide from his consciousness, especially as he had no idea what or where Africa and India were.

He had figured on a pair of elephants. He knew each would be larger than any animal he had ever seen, and had made a special space in the middle of the boat, bottom story, with specially reinforced flooring. But what was he going to do with *four* of them?

He looked over to the right a little bit, in back of the elephants. There were cats. They took up an entire hectare. Lions and panthers and cheetahs. Ocelots and leopards. Three different kinds of tigers, one pair with teeth that gleamed like sabers. Fluffy ones and hairless ones. Cats with big ears, and cats with almost none. Cougars! Maine Coons and Siamese. Havana Browns, Egyptian Maus, and Ragamuffins. Striped ones and orange tabbies. A Cheshire cat lay on his back, hoping to get his tummy scratched. His youngest son Japheth, he reminded himself, was allergic.

And snakes! There were coiled cobras, waiting to strike, clearly uncomfortable in all the surrounding commotion. Pythons, like long glistening pipes, sunned themselves in the grass. Tree snakes searched in vain for an overhang. Garter snakes hunted for holes in the ground so they could cool off. Water moccasins remained indecisive as to whether to remain where they were, or slither their way down to the water's edge, along with the Komodo dragons, duckbilled platypi, two walruses and 66 other pinnipeds, and a group of miscellaneous caimans, to be joined by an unnumbered party of bullfrogs.

Cows. Oh, there were cows all right. More cows than Noah had ever conceived of. Brahma bulls and Holsteins and Long-Horns. Little mountain cows and Jerseys. Brown cows and brindled. Red heifers, and even a pair of blue ones – yes, there were blue cows back in those days. And yaks, oxen, water buffalo, and, what are those with the big, woolly heads? Bison! And there was a cow giving birth! Now which one was he supposed to take – the mother or the baby? Under foot were 7,923 pair of differentiated dung beetles.

Noah sat down on the gangway, and stroked his red beard fast turning gray even as he confronted his problem. In the west, beyond the brightest sunshine he had ever witnessed, he saw a very small cloud appear, like a bare puff of smoke, peeking out between the heads of the two giraffes.

It was going to be a *very* long day.

The Curriculum of Abundance

WELL, ANOTHER HOMESCHOOLING book almost done. I can see the finish line, and it's been a good ride for me. Thank you for joining me on this journey.

By now, you, dear reader, should know me better than I know you. That's a writer's fate. Lucky for me, I get to travel around a bit so I can meet at least a few of you, and give thanks for your willingness to share some of your voyages with me. As I am always telling my kids, there are no such people as complete strangers, only friends we have yet to meet.

Nonetheless, when I think of all of you who have picked up this book, I am reminded of a story (I am *always* reminded of a story) about the Sufi wise fool Nasruddin.

It seems that Nasruddin was invited to address a large gathering, and he began by asking: "Do you know what I am going to say?" His audience replied, "No." "Well," he said, "I have no desire to speak to people who don't know what I will be talking about," and walked off.

Embarrassed, his hosts invited him back the next day. He asked the same question, "Do you what I am going to say?" "Yes," shouted the audience. "Well, in that case," he said, "Since you already know what I am going to say, I won't waste your time," and again, he walked off.

Perplexed, a week later his hosts invited him to come back. "He began again, "Do you know what I am going to say?" This time, the audience was prepared – half said yes, the other half no." "So, replied Nasruddin, "Let the half who know what I am going to say please explain it to the others."

And so it is with you. Some of you have been homeschooling for a long time, and what I've had to say perhaps has not struck you as particularly surprising, though I hope you have found something that has confirmed you in your commitment, and a few extra 'tricks of the trade,' or just some new ways of seeing. And some of you are new to homeschooling, and are asking yourselves, "what happens next?" And some of you are just contemplating the leap, and want to know, "where do I start?" And some of you aren't homeschoolers at all, but simply have picked up this book (and actually read this far!) because you are intrigued.

If I had you all together in a single room, we could have a great conversation. And, after a time, you wouldn't need me at all. Some sooner and some later, many of you will eventually be among those "explaining it to the others." But failing that, this book has to serve as the next best thing. I hope I haven't disappointed.

Anyway, my reputation, is that I'm a provocative sort of guy, make unexpected connections, and whether folks like what I have to say or not, the usual comment is, "Well, he made me think." I take credit as an "agent provocateur," and one of the best ways of ensuring that reputation is by choosing to address a taboo subject, one that requires a little "truth and reconciliation."

So here goes.

I weigh ten pounds more than I did ten years ago. There, it's on paper. How many of you will admit to the same? Let's see an inward show of hands – come on now, don't be shy.

To be totally honest, it's more than ten pounds. Now, back in the Dark Ages, having been a skinny, runty kid, the 90-pound weakling who may have gotten sand kicked in his face and could have cared less, the new weight has not been a particular blow to my self-esteem. I tell my kids I earned every last one of those pounds, and that it would be unfair to lose any, because that would mean that, in the global ecology of things, they are likely to be found by somebody else.

It has happened to many of us, in case you haven't noticed. Since they started putting corn syrup in absolutely everything, we've gotten larger. Much larger. And some of our kids are larger, too. Compared to our grandparents, we are almost (but not quite) sumo wrestlers, though, on the whole, and other than having shaken our North American tobacco habit, not in as good shape, though better sanitation and a virtual end to childhood diseases has us living longer.

In case you haven't noticed, doctors have been eager to weigh in on our weight, with not a few taking some sadistic and unhealthful delight in advising us (ungrammatically) that our extra poundage is unhealthy. (They really mean "unhealthful," of course, but doctors aren't necessarily known for their grammar, and definitely not for their handwriting!) They've added the weight of our private guilt to the weight of our public shame, and we lumber around encumbered by a weighty load of both. And thus, here we are, having become the favorite enlarged bullseyes of primetime TV humor and infomercials.

When folks who supposedly know about such things weigh in on our weightiness, we are often told that our extra adipose deposits are, ironically enough, a result of scarcity. I'll bet you've heard it all before:

- There is scarcity: we don't exercise enough, just not enough time or sufficient motivation.

- There is scarcity: we don't possess the right equipment to exercise, and we lack a good health club.

- There is scarcity: we don't have a personal trainer, and, hence, when we exercise, we are likely to do it inefficiently.

- There is scarcity: we lack a proper diet, or we don't have enough income to eat the right foods, or the time to prepare them.

- There is scarcity: we lack good information about what it takes to be thin.

- There is scarcity: we lack proper metabolic balance, or are deficient in the necessary metabolic hormones (and they are folks lining up to sell us some!)

When all the other scarcities seem to lack explanatory power, we fall back upon our hefty superfluity of guilt, and simply conclude that we have a scarcity of willpower.

As a result of all these weighty deficiencies, all of these scarcities, our amplitudes are amplified. Cows have had to be bred larger, to facilitate the manufacture of longer belts, worn on those few occasions that we allow ourselves to be seen in public in anything other than sweatsuits or coveralls. Public health experts seem to think this outsized state of affairs gives them permission to yell at us louder, without any evidence that doing so makes one whit of difference. The U.S. Department of Agriculture now seems to have turned the food pyramid on its side, making it totally inscrutable, though I doubt the old one helped much either (chocolate was always at the top, which means one should eat more of it!)

So, for a little excursion into evolutionary biology. Evolutionary biology suggests that, in fact, our extra poundage reflects an evolutionary memory of food scarcity. Given the Biblical cycle of seven fat and seven lean years, the fittest among our ancestors kept some of those extra bushels from the boom times around their middles, as savings against the bust years to follow. And such years always did. This made our ancestors more likely to survive and to fulfill their evolutionary destiny, that is, to reproduce.

What happened to them afterwards, as far as their primary function to the species is concerned, is pretty much irrelevant. Rotund or thin as fork tines, once we have stopped reproducing and the last child is viable, other than in caring for the grandkiddies or in chewing the buffalo hide to make shoelaces, we are (for better or for worse) evolutionary toast. (Don't share that with your teenager, or she'll remind you of it at every available opportunity). Now, so many of us in our culture are surrounded by a virtually limitless ocean of calories, we've given off hunting and plowing under our own power, and are accordingly experiencing the round-mound consequences of our biological success.

Sigh. Now I bet you wonder where this is all going. Well here it is.

Ivan Illich, author of the groundbreaking book *Deschooling Society* in 1971, defined education as "learning under the assumption of scarcity." Of course, the supporters of public schools would look to such a statement and argue that the scarcity is real, and that there is never enough money to throw down the educational sinkhole. But whatever one's feelings about school funding, it is clear that Illich was making a more fundamental point. This becomes clear when you examine the reality that the practice of public education follows the same pattern, regardless of the level of monetary support. The assumption of scarcity remains in place, rather like the body that, to its own detriment, continues to store fat against the inevitable famine to follow.

Take a look around at the schools in your community. Inside these million-dollar real estate boondoggles, you see scarcities almost everywhere. The manicured football field is off limits to 90% of the student body for most of the year, and the few remaining trees under which one could possibly sit are cut down to make way for the chalk stripes on the ground, or the parking lot for same. The hallways are constructed without any possible area for convivial conversation. The art room has no space for students to leave their projects out for more than a 50-minute period. The windows (when there are any to speak of) restrict the flow of natural light. The doors and furniture are usually standard prison issue (and, in many states, may actually have been constructed in the prison shop). School libraries (and school librarians) are quickly becoming the substance of myth.

There is a general scarcity of attention. Teachers, however well-intentioned, can't really be expected to *know* 30 children, their hopes, dreams, aspirations, individual proclivities, learning styles, and so are expected to follow lesson plans constructed without knowledge of even a single one of them. One size fits all, and that size is a short-answer exam that can be scored by computer, and which is more likely than not to determine a child's educational fate. One can't listen too hard to any individual child's questions and expect to complete the lesson plan.

There is an assumption of a scarcity of time. There are only so many years between five and 18, and so many teaching hours in those 13 years, so they cannot be squandered. There are bells and whistles, reminding one of every passing hour, every ticking of the educational clock. Time spent on one child, on one question, on one unexpected learning opportunity, is time taken away from another, in a neverending zero sum game. Never mind that the child might actually understand the current math lesson next week, next month, next year; by that time, the train will have left the station, and the unlucky child who missed it will at best be confined to the caboose. And forget any possibility of silent time, so that there remains even the remotest possibility that a child, or teacher, has the luxury to think straight.

There is an assumption about a scarcity of intelligence among children. The simplest version embodied in all schools, rich and poor, is that children can never be trusted to figure anything out for themselves. Despite the overwhelming evidence of millennia, the general theory is that "if it ain't taught, it ain't learned," the corollary being, of course, "if it ain't tested for, it ain't worth knowing."

But since the early 20th Century, the supposed scarcity of intelligence among children has been given a hallowed place in our new-fangled "scientism." The pseudo- (and well-funded) idea behind this strange belief system is that the distribution of intelligence within the society (or even the world) should somehow conform to a bell-curve distribution, with it implied that the scarcity of those at the right end of the bell curve reflect the small number of individuals possessing wealth and power.

There is absolutely no external evidence supporting this notion. And since an overt racialist, Francis Galton, came up with this screwball idea to accompany his advocacy of eugenics (and we knew where that ended up[36]), there never has been. Examination-based scales have to be created and recreated to force children into this distribution, with the scales having to be repeatedly reconfigured when children just don't over time perform in keeping with the predicted and, more importantly, *necessary* result. For if there are simply too many smart kids, their parents come to expect too much of a system that exists to ration resources (and social position) to only those found "deserving." In other words, if there isn't a scarcity of intelligence in our children, it has to be created.

We hear this constantly, if we listen hard enough, whenever any discussion of the new standardized tests comes up. The tests help create scarcity, and surpluses at the same time. "Well, if everyone passes the test, it can't be a very good test, can it?" While everyone wants their children, and their local school, to be above average, the reality is that if all children are "above average," none are. We need fewer, not more, above-average kids if we are to ration resources.

But more important than that, we need failures, lots of them, people who are resigned to being failures, and will be willing to exist on the scraps and leftovers that our school systems have educated them into believing are their just desserts. At least until 2014 in the United States, if one flunks 10th grade math, one has no right to health care.

In case you haven't noticed, there is, at bottom, a scarcity of trust. We can't trust immigrants to conform, workers not to rebel, leaders to lead, neighbors

---

[36]   You read about Galton in the first chapter of this book. But lest you all think this is ancient history, at least as late as 1963, my junior high school social studies textbook (it had long been banished from the biology textbook as lacking intellectual respectability) still referenced the Kallikaks and Jukes, two semi-apocryphal families said to suffer from 'hereditary criminality' and mental retardation, used to buttress the argument for forced sterilization of entire families. The author of the work on the Kallikaks, Henry Herbert Goddard, had repudiated his own work (and eugenics as a whole) as scientifically invalid some 40 years before it appeared, presumably with the New York City Board of Education's approval, in my textbook.

to care. Once we as adults created a society that more often than not embodies the qualities of "Lord of the Flies," when it comes to education, we decide to ascribe these same qualities to the kids.

The experts have told us we simply can't trust in what Great Nature has made, and there are any number of experts prepared to tell you (and supported by many of your neighbors) that not having ever met your kids, they are better prepared to provide them with what they need – both educationally and socially – than you are.

Your instincts and intuition can't be trusted, your knowledge of your own children can't be trusted, your family life can't be trusted, your community can't be trusted, your religion or belief system can't be trusted, and, somewhere along the line, someone will come up with statistics to prove it.

All of this fat – the result of scarcity – has consequences. We have become sluggish, less active, less participatory. Our democratic institutions wilt, the marketplace of ideas is surrounded by increasingly impenetrable barbed wire fences, our entertainment requires us to leave it to the entertainers and reinforces our passivity, our family life withers. We store more "energy," but we have become far less energetic. We lose ourselves in increments, often unnoticed. Scarcity thinking has stunted too many children's way to personal identity, and for too many of us, our own as well.

That's enough. School is America's leading preventable cause of mental, physical, emotional, and spiritual retardation, and, as millions of us have now discovered, there's a ready cure.

Let's write a different story. We do in fact have enough. Even in the midst of recession, we live in the richest society in the history of the world and we have enough. Our advances in public health have eliminated 95 percent of childhood diseases, and 90 percent of premature mortality among mothers and fathers raising children. Forget cable, cell phones, or SUVs. The productive wealth of our society has made it possible to meet our very basic needs, with little labor relative to past generations, and much, much less of it dangerous employment.

We have enough. We have vast stores of information, not only in libraries or on the Internet, but in the wealth of our elders, now living to riper and riper ages, willing, prepared, and eager to share what they have learned.

So, when it comes to educating our children, it's time to reap our abundance, with them. The reality is that Great Nature, in its wisdom, has equipped them, and you, with virtually everything needed. So learn to trust the divine without, and the divine within, or whatever is the spiritual or moral equivalent in your life, in both you and your children, and that in the abundance of your lives you have been well provided for.

One of the great mysteries of life is that there will always be some things you will not understand about your child. She is her own soul, and with any luck,

will outlive you, and visit places in space and time that you in this worldly
sphere are simply prohibited from going. Indeed this is one of the great
paradoxes of education – you are preparing your child for a future to which
you yourself are denied entry.

Don't get hung up on subject matter. There is enough time for that. Yes, it is
wonderful to know lots of stuff. Sometimes even useful, though you can
almost never predict in advance what, in the ever-expanding cornucopia of
stuff, that is likely to be.

But what's really important is how, as parents, we can foster our kids'
intelligence. Before he became famous for his advocacy of homeschooling,
John Holt wrote in *How Children Learn* that "The test of intelligence is not
how much we know how to do, but how we behave when we don't know
what to do."

In a world that in some respects is changing so fast (and in others seems so
stuck in paralysis), this ability to operate in a new environment becomes ever
more critical. I have come to believe that there are (at least) nine "elements of
intelligence," nine behaviors and qualities that impact our ability to flourish in
the face of the unknown. I think that if you were to observe how people
generally considered to be intelligent behave, you would instantly recognize
these characteristics to a lesser or greater extent. And, if I'm correct, you'll
both begin to understand your kids better, and better think how best to
nurture them for a world of which we ourselves have only the barest inklings:

Focus and centering – The capacity to clearly understand and conceptualize what
is known and what it is unknown, and to pare the latter down to its essentials
is a mark of intelligence, as is the ability to center on the problem on hand
rather than spinning our wheels.

Drive and perseverance – Whether we are attempting to learn a new violin sonata,
master a difficult gymnastics move, or solve a mathematical conundrum,
success is unlikely without inner drive and a willingness to stick to it until the
goal is attained, knowing that once that waystation is reached, there will be
further mountains to climb.

Organization – Confronting the unknown requires the ability to organize
intellectual, material, and human resources in a concerted, articulated way.
Some of those resources will come from past personal experience, others
from our analytical and creative abilities, still others by drawing upon the
expertise and abilities of others. But if we can't organize it for ourselves,
chances are we are not going to find the solution.

Analytical ability – When we don't know what to do, we often engage in a
rollicking game of trial and error. In doing so, we have to evaluate the results
of our experience, narrowing the behavioral options from which we then can
choose, and make decisions as to whether more information is necessary
before an intelligent choice can be made. Analytical ability itself has two
components; *working memory* – the ability to draw upon that which we already

know or have experienced, and *processing speed* – the ability to readily run through all the possibilities to formulate the most useful hypothesis or elegant solution.

Intuition – In life, as in science (and contrary to what they taught us about the so-called 'scientific method' in junior high school), exploration doesn't start with either observation or hypothesis. There are endless universes of objects and phenomena to be observed, and scores of potential hypothesis for any situation, and the choice of which to explore, or which direction to proceed when faced with the unknown, is more often than not an act of intuition, which we build up as a result of increased experience.

Creativity – Creativity is, in essence, the capacity to organize that which is already known or experienced in application to new challenges. We learn by analogy, to make connections among phenomena that might not seem inherently obvious, in confronting what is yet to be unearthed, discovered, understood, or created.

Capacity to learn from others – Sometimes when we don't know what to do, the best way forward is to draw on the resources of others, not just their experience, but in joint application to the problem at hand. Teamwork, leadership skill, the ability to listen well, the initiative to seek out mentors and learn from them, and the capacity to evaluate and make use of the best attributes of those around us enables us to solve problems with a far higher level of creativity that we might otherwise, in a synergistic pooling of intelligence.

Flexibility, humor, and a sense of proportion – While we confront dangers in an uncertain world, the reality is that, in exercising our intelligence, we are rarely faced with life and death decisions. There are few lions in the forests, waiting to pounce as a result of a single misstep. The latitude for error – for *learning* – is usually quite wide. Intelligence requires that we pick ourselves up with a smile when we've gotten off track, ready and willing to seriously yet playfully exercise our capabilities in facing the next set of trials we find along the way.

Courage – Of all the components of intelligence – the ability to face-off and tame the unknown – courage is likely the single most essential, and perhaps the least appreciated. Without courage and a willingness to undertake risk, we draw back from new challenges, or we fall back into ruts, using the other elements of our intelligence in the same old ways. We become competent, perhaps, but dull. Without courage, we are less likely to trust our intuition, less likely to analogize creatively from past experience, and less likely to persevere.

Once we understand that the ability to figure out what to do when faced with what we don't know is the true hallmark of intelligence, with our abundance we can begin to organize the education of our children, and our own way of being, in order to bring it forth into a world deeply in need of it.

So if you are a new homeschooler, and didn't know what I was going to be talking about, trust me: you have that abundance, and are equipped with everything you need. *Your children wouldn't have chosen you otherwise.*

If you are an experienced homeschooler, and I have met your expectations of what I was going to say, trust me: within that abundance you have uncovered, you have also discovered that you were born with that same energy and potential that you are now realizing in your children. So take this as an opportunity to maximize it. There is nothing more important you can do for your child than becoming, fully, the person the Great Creator meant *you* to be.

And you have an abundance of time. I say that somewhat wistfully, with both of my daughters now having left the nest and venturing forth into new challenges and new careers. You will all find out soon enough that your children's lives with you will not last all that long, and will be gone almost in the twinkling of an eye. But, if you go about this right, it will leave behind memories that will nourish both of you for the rest of your earthly sojourns. And you will all still be there – you will have a lifetime together ahead, if you simply grab onto all of this love that is available to you, and that you are! And you will be blessed with abundance.

The math problem that is unsolvable today will still be there next week, next month, or next year – or may simply never be solved at all. History won't have changed if your plans around it – if you have any – don't get accomplished on Friday. Newton's laws have already been discovered, and most of your kids rediscovered most of them before the age of three, even if they don't have their names memorized. So relax, and bask in that light of abundance that is the utter miracle of becoming.

The light of abundance gives you the opportunity to tell new stories. When people are depressed, or we feel in a state of scarcity, we often fall back on old ones. We focus on what we don't have. We focus on our past failings, and expect future ones. We assume we won't get our needs met, because there isn't *enough*. And our focus becomes narrower, shallower, meaner than it could be otherwise, if we only could find a way to stretch our wings.

So tell new stories. Don't make homeschooling a school story. Instead of thinking about it as reading, writing, math, and science, all fitting into neat little boxes, think bigger. Fluffier! Shinier! Dream for better, desire better, (not more, but better), and plan for it.

Try, for example, the story of the Shoshone Medicine Wheel, the story of the four directions, and the four virtues: courage, fortitude, wisdom, and generosity. The Shoshone would tell you that each and every person is naturally gifted with one of them – and the purpose of education is encourage the other three so that they will shine equally on the wheel of this world. How would your homeschooling story look different, feel different, be different, if you told it in these terms? Once you overthrow the school story, what is that you truly want to hold dear to your hearts?

Or perhaps adopt *Woope Sakowin* – The Seven Laws of the Lakota – as your curriculum. Think explicitly how your children can learn to be a living expression of the Seven Laws:

> *Wacante Oganake* – "To help, to share, to give, to be generous."
>
> *Wowansila* – "To have pity, to be compassionate."
>
> *Wowaunihan* – "To have respect, and honor our relations."
>
> *Wowacintanka* – "To have patient and tolerance."
>
> *Wowahwala* – "To walk quietly, be humble, and seek humility."
>
> *Woohitke* – "To be guided by one's principles, to be disciplined, brave, and courageous."
>
> *Wooksape* – "To seek understanding and wisdom."

Try hanging these on the refrigerator, or by the mirror in the bathroom.

Now for the benediction. All homeschooling books should have a benediction, rather like a commencement. It's not an end, but a new beginning, to welcome you to a new start, even while you welcome more abundance into your homeschooling story.

I've chosen one from Saint Augustine:

> *Once and for all, a short rule is laid down for you:*
> *Love, and do what you will.*
> *If you keep silent, do so out of love.*
> *If you cry out, do so out of love.*
> *If you refrain from punishing, do so out of love.*
> *Let the root of love be within.*
> *From such a root, expect nothing but great things to come.*
> *They will.*

Give thanks, and give your kids a big hug for me.

The Tenth Intelligence

DARN! I THOUGHT I was all done with this tome. Time to go pack up my marbles, play with the new puppy, do some of the endless paperwork tasks that my non-governmental organization Friendly Water for the World (www.friendlywaterfortheworld.com) seems to spontaneously generate (it may not work for maggots, but it sure does for paperwork!), chat on Facebook, cook a nice meal, go for a long walk.

But…but there was something still niggling. Something else. Something missing. I had more for the last chapter, but the last chapter, on rereading, seemed too complete and self-contained to reopen. So I guess we'll have to call this one an addendum, postscript, appendix, supplement, P.S., add-on, afterthought, or rider. Whatever it is, here it is. Hope you don't mind. If you do, you have my permission (as if you needed it), to skip ahead.

> *That best portion of a good man's life,*
> *His little, nameless, unremembered acts of kindness and of love.*
> *- William Wordsworth,*
> *Lines written a few miles above Tintern Abbey*

I HAVE ON occasion wondered what it might have been like to go through life as a Robin.

I never had the opportunity to find out. In the second month of the first grade at P.S. 131½, my public elementary school in New York City, we were separated into "Bluebirds and Robins." (I have since discovered that in other schools there were also "Sparrows," who were "Special Ed" kids before Special Ed was invented, those destined to ride "the short bus."[37]) I don't remember any test being involved; we were just told we were either Robins or Bluebirds and that was that.

All of us Bluebirds got to sit together, and do reading together. Same for the Robins. Bluebird books had words in them; Robin books had only pictures. I remember being at least mildly miffed about that at the time, as I had friends among the Robins, and why couldn't I have a book with nice pictures in it?

But by the second grade, there were no longer any Robins in my class. No one bothered to call us Bluebirds anymore. But we knew. We were the chosen *smart* ones – 90 percent Jewish (this *was* New York City in the 1950s, and

---

[37] See Jonathan Mooney's *The Short Bus: A Journey Beyond Normal* (New York, NY: Holt, 2007). It's a great read!

almost all our teachers were Jewish – you should have heard them try to teach us Christmas carols), and the few Catholics and precisely one Protestant were sons and daughters of schoolteachers. We spent absolutely no time with the Robins any more. We didn't eat lunch with them, go to the schoolyard at the same time, walk home with them. Soon, our friends were no longer friends.

Actually, there were four classes per grade at P.S. 131 1/2 in Queens. We were the "top" class. By the time you got to the "bottom" class, there were lots of Protestants, and no Jews. When the schools were finally desegregated, all the bused-in Black kids were automatically placed in the bottom class. [38]

Now, to be honest, I have absolutely no idea what happened in those other classes. We never had even a single glimpse of what went on there. But I do remember something that intrigued me then, and fascinates me to this day. There were students in my class who struggled mightily, received "Ds" on their report cards, had their parents called to school. They were "underachievers." But in the six years of this "ability-tracked" system, not a single member of the Bluebirds ever became a Robin. And not a single Robin ever became a Bluebird. It didn't matter what grades you received, how you scored on standardized tests, what your teachers thought of you. A Robin could be an "overachiever," but never a Bluebird. Once a Bluebird always a Bluebird; once a Robin…

It didn't take long before Robins were entirely out of our consciousness. We never questioned the incontrovertible *fact* that they really were less intelligent. We never learned what kinds of problems they might or might not have had in school, and there was certainly no sense of *noblesse oblige*. We somehow had joined the elect, "deserved" to be where we were, and never imagined it could be otherwise. This "socialization" is the closest I have ever been able to come to understanding being part of a caste system, and I learned my caste position well.

LIKE ALL THINGS schoolish, phenomena that are not part of the curriculum often have greater long-term consequences than those that do. Or, more accurately, they are part of the curriculum *of* school, rather than simply *in* school.

As scholars have begun to note, and as I noted in the first chapter, the Flynn Effect (increases in IQ in every generation, a common feature of the 20th

---

[38]   A friend of mine from Pittsburgh recently told me about enrolling his multiracial son in the 2nd grade (in 1980!). Seeing that he looked Black, they immediately made him a "Blackbird" (which meant, everyone agreed, he was doomed to failure; and all the kids were Black. Yes, really – they called them "Blackbirds"!) When my friend wrote to the school that his son was unchallenged (they had no books!), they moved him up one group. Still unhappy, he went to see the principal. The principal took one look at his white complexion, and without a single word being necessary, moved his son up one group more. So much for the "science" of education).

Century) – seems to have come to a halt around 1990, and IQs have perhaps been declining every since, with an acceleration since 2000. The media has been quick to harp on the reality that the creativity of young people – the ability to produce something original and useful – is declining as well, likely a result of mindless "education reform"-induced conformity in thinking.[39]

But that's about the population of children as a whole. Maybe there are more Robins. Maybe there are more Robins because they are increasingly being poisoned – by toxic chemicals, toxic environments, and relative, if not absolute, poverty, and by toxic schools. Maybe it's worse being a Robin than it was in my day.

But why should I care about Robins? I was "carefully taught" to pretty much ignore them and their existence, and any attempt I have had to make to reacquaint myself has required significant effort. Happily, I believe I have been up to the task.

However, wouldn't I want to know what happened to the Bluebirds? Of course, I know in the aggregate: having been awarded false privileges as a group, we learned to value individualism, and as a group take great enjoyment in being accorded individual recognition for social accomplishment, as we have often been placed in positions to control other people's lives to our own advantage.

Yup. That's what we were carefully taught to understand is the essence of Bluebirdhood – we "earned it." I got more of the same in my elite post-secondary education, enveloped in the individualist, amoral values of the larger social system where I could live on the backs of others, and was trained to become a functionary of that system. And, being a Bluebird and being good at it, I was allowed a large creative space for personal initiative, but only in the service of a system that rationed opportunities for others, i.e. Robins. So much for education being a key element in a democratic society.

I don't want to go overboard. After all, the world has been very good to me – that's the whole point of being a Bluebird, isn't it? But that decision made about me in the second month of the first grade has sure given me enough to stew on all these years.

So what happens to Bluebirds? Well, now we know, and there is evidence to back it up.

Bluebirds go to college. Robins sometimes do. But I've rarely met a Bluebird who didn't. And the result? According to researchers at the University of Michigan, reviewing 73 studies of over 14,000 American college students conducted between 1979 and 2009, college students score 40 percent lower on measures of empathy than they did a generation ago. They are much less likely to be able to look at things from the perspective of others, or to be concerned or even have feelings of compassion for people less fortunate than

---

[39]   www.newsweek.com/2010/07/10/the-creativity-crisis.html

themselves. They are more likely to devalue others, and, to quote one of the professors involved in the study, tend toward being "self-centered, narcissistic, competitive, and individualistic."

Some of the faculty involved in the study have chosen easy scapegoats. Violent video games, social media, on-line networking are all convenient whipping boys.

Everything but the obvious. Maybe we have less empathy because we are *taught* to be less empathetic. We have been rewarded incessantly for being hypercompetitive in a rigged competition. We have been taught that we have succeeded solely on our own merits. We have been taught that we *deserve* our privileges, and those that don't have them, well, the Robins *don't* deserve them. And, as already noted, Bluebirds don't spend much time with Robins in any case, and won't in the future, if we can help it, and so the truth remains as hidden from us as from our Robinish counterparts. In short, Bluebirds have become mentally retarded, and learning disabled.

Don't believe me? Take a look at your government. Liberal or conservative or in-between, virtually all the politicians are Bluebirds. Certainly almost all the social service executives, and all the people in the "think" tanks. Bluebirds 'managed' the global financial meltdown, and send soldiers (virtually all Robins) off to war.

Bluebirds have become mentally retarded, and learning disabled. Don't believe me? Ask the Robins.

YOUNG CHILDREN NATURALLY develop a naïve empathy with the world around them. This comes from the subjective reality that the line between self and others can appear fuzzy. Where do the baby's needs and desires end and those of the mother begin? Who exactly is nurturing whom, and where does one nature stop and the other start?

Children have an affinity for the four-legged people; after all, they were there once. (I would love to understand the cognitive process by which a "pre-toddler" comes to understand she isn't a dog). Children aren't in nature, they *are* nature, though of course we lose that through our processes of socialization. If that process isn't too severe, and we aren't cut off from the wellsprings of our nature, we are likely to carry over some of this naïve empathy for a long time.

It is also natural, however, to engage in our *project* of life, to paraphrase the philosopher Baruch Spinoza (with whom I have great affinity, when I can figure out what he's saying!), to persist in our individual being, and to flourish. When we feel ourselves flourishing, we feel expansive outward into the world, and it gives us pleasure. (When we are depressed, we feel diminishment, as we contract into our little selves, which is painful to our "project.") We desire to grow into our own being, and we are propelled to action toward our lifelong desire to persist and to flourish. And, when young, we don't even know what it is we will require in order to do so, so we learn everything we can (and, sadly, are easily hoodwinked and sold a bill of goods as to what it is we will in fact require). We are specially committed to ourselves and are easily misled. When we are young, adolescents perhaps (I think it better to think of teenagers as incipient adults), we struggle to take control, make good decisions and judgments. We make some poor ones, and make mid-point corrections as best we can.

Don't imagine that this is the same thing as selfishness. We can take pleasure in the thriving of others who give us pleasure, and feel pain when those we love feel pain. They are essential to our feeling our lives are going well. In all these things, we battle against entropy, and experience the emotional ups and downs that accompany our "project."

The problem is that, as a society, we choose to stop thinking about development with adolescence. It is a symptom of societal arrested development. Sigh. Or as the poet Maya Angelou once said, "Most people never grow up. They just find parking spaces."

Back to Spinoza. We can escape this developmentally necessary self-centeredness when, at some point, we come to realize that *everyone else* is engaged in the same expansive mission. We see ourselves ever-more expansively, but our sense of self-importance is diminished. And we begin to understand that others matter every bit as much as we do, and learn to act accordingly. Our identities become merged with those of others. We develop a *mature empathy*.

I HAVE ON many occasions quoted John Holt in *How Children Learn* that "The test of intelligence is not how much we know how to do, but how we behave when we don't know what to do." Once we begin to look at intelligence this way, this business about Robins and Bluebirds obviously goes out the window (as does virtually all IQ testing), and new windows open through which we can see what needs to be nurtured in our children so that they can take charge of their lives in the face of an unknown future. In the last chapter, I cited nine interactive and dynamic elements of intelligence:

> *Focus and centering*
> *Drive and perseverance*
> *Organization*
> *Analytical ability*
> *Intuition*
> *Creativity*
> *Capacity to learn from others*
> *Flexibility, humor, and a sense of proportion*
> *Courage*

But there is a tenth intelligence – empathy. There are clearly certain tasks that can't be accomplished in the world effectively without it. A team leader cannot be effective without understanding why members of the team may be acting less than optimally, and requires a sense of what motivates different individuals to excel. A mentor, teacher, or parent cannot convey skills, tools, or information productively without an inward appreciation of how a child (or adult) will be able to receive them and act. In my experience, the same is true of people in business – good business people can listen intuitively to their clients, and can match their services to meet their clients' needs and desires. Politicians in the best sense of the term require empathy to build consensus. Empathy makes up much of the currency of talented salespeople, doctors, nurses, social workers, pastors. Humbly, may I add writers? And putting aside individual proclivities for a moment, isn't the degree of community-wide empathy one way to assess the true value of a community?

Like other "intelligence muscles," empathy muscles must have opportunity for exercise if they are to become strong. Naïve empathy is particularly easy to exercise, as homeschoolers know so well. From work at the animal shelter to helping at the homeless mission to reading the newspaper for grandpa whose eyes have been dimmed by time, the opportunities are there and around us. Once freed from the exigencies of the day jail, or the very real need to exercise a physical and emotional freedom, sometimes in ways that are unwise, once the doors have clanked open, with the help of their parents, children can find an entire world out there that can well utilize their budding skills, talents, and empathy in helping to make a community whole, and themselves as well.

But there is so much more! For, as incipient adults, and free from the mental constraints of Bluebird and Robinhood, it is possible and, to my way of thinking, even likely that mature empathy may begin to make its appearance even as the project of our lives unfold. If the 'rightness' of our class position, our social status, or our place in society is not drummed into us by other forces in the society beginning with "education," it becomes possible to see our meager share of natural assets, abilities, and strengths as something to be exercised beyond our narrow (and imagined) ends. This is the active component of the tenth intelligence.

Beyond simply protecting youth from "education," is there a way to assist in ensuring that sometime in the future, the tenth intelligence can realize its true potential, so that our children do not remain "underachievers"? I think there is, and the simplest way is to make sure our young people get to spend time with people for whom the tenth intelligence is already well-developed. You can find them everywhere – I like to think of them as "giraffes," people who, as part of their "project," have learned to stick out their necks, look out over the larger landscape of a community and society, and take on the risk that comes with an expansive, empathetic view of themselves. In other words, those who in some way, small or large, have learned to live for others, and have learned in some small measure that living for others is a way of living for oneself. Those with the longest necks and the largest hearts. Those who are engaged in the most expansive project of all.

Every community has them. You find nurses and engineers who volunteer their time in South America. Construction workers who help build the Habitat house down the street. Hospice volunteers. Folks who take funds out of their own pockets and prepare meals at the local soup kitchen once a month. Dedicated foster parents who aren't in it for the money. People who organize their church to support clean water projects in Africa. Individuals who work to preserve indigenous cultures, and cultural heritages. The reality is that you find them everywhere. All you have to do is look.

But you have to make an effort to make sure your kids (especially young teenagers) have the opportunity to rub shoulders with them. Because empathy (like many of the elements of intelligence) rubs off. Or, to use a different metaphor, it's catching. And once you catch it, it immensely enriches your life. It dynamically interacts with the other nine elements of intelligence to make you more than you were. It provides protection against "adult-onset adolescence." And not only is it an expression of freedom, in itself it is liberating, providing entry into a larger world.

Don't assume your pre-teens and teens will just find these folks on their own. You don't do that with the need for a Spanish tutor, or a piano teacher (though kids have been known to find even these by themselves; it just isn't common). Giraffes are usually pretty easy to spot, as their necks stick out over the crowd. The challenge is ensure your kids find a way to meet up with them. In my experience, it won't be difficult, once you overcome your own shyness, and learn to advocate for the maturing intelligence of your children. You just need to learn to think more expansively, get beyond the fetters of your own school-based "education," and reacquaint yourself with what learning should really be all about it. And develop a little more persistence. Start inviting giraffes over for tea.

If I am successful, you may soon find yourself engaged in a whole new "project." Perhaps you will become one of these people other teens – and parents – seek out.

IN SPEAKING WITH many others, I was somewhat surprised at how widespread my school experience was. Give Robins a chance to speak out and the stories I have heard are (to me) somewhat stunning. I have since learned that, in addition to Bluebirds and Robins and sometimes Sparrows, a few schools also had a fourth group – Crows. How ironic that considered lowest of the low in schools, crows are known to be among the smartest, most mutually cooperative creatures on the planet.

May you and your children flourish. Bless.

Two Moments in Time

SOMETIME, MY LESSER self feels it is a disadvantage for me to come to my Quaker Meeting. God often seems to take the opportunity of our worship to volunteer me for new assignments.

Last Sunday, there were no fewer than 11! "Wait, wait," I exclaimed silently, "I need to get a piece of paper!"

To be fair, however, He never volunteers me for things of which I am not capable, even if I feel like screaming that I don't have any more time!

While we are in Meeting, He is busy at His desk, just divvying up the work.

PEOPLE IN INDIA go on pilgrimages to take *darshan* from holy men. The idea is that the light, which shines so fiercely from within these holy personages, strikes those who come to see them and inspires them with a touch of that same divinity.

Most of us feel we don't have time to go visit holy men, even if we believe they exist. So we have to rely on each other. We may think that the light that shines in our neighbor is not quite as fierce. But, when it comes to illumination, let us remember the inverse square law.

The light is right here in this room, or in any room you happen to enter. When there are children in the room, it is often blazing. Proximity counts.

In the Light (or at least trying to wash the windows...),

David

Appendix: The Parrot's Training

Rabindranath Tagore

ONCE UPON A time there was a bird. It was ignorant. It sang all right, but never recited scriptures. It hopped, it flew, but it lacked manners.

Said the Raja to himself: "Ignorance is costly in the long run. For fools consume as much food as their betters, and yet give nothing in return."

He called his nephews into his presence and told them that the bird must have a sound schooling.

The pundits were summoned, and after deep deliberations arrived at the heart of the matter. They decided that the ignorance of birds was due to their unsuitable habit of living in nests. Therefore, according to the pundits, the first thing necessary for the bird's education was a suitable cage.

The pundits were given their rewards and went home happy.

A golden cage was built with gorgeous decorations. Crowds came to see it from all parts of the world. "Culture, captured and caged!" exclaimed some, in a rapture of ecstasy, and burst into tears. Others remarked: "Even if culture vanishes, the cage will remain, to the end, a substantial fact. How fortunate for the bird!"

The goldsmith filled his bag with money and lost no time in sailing homewards.

Another pundit sat down to educate the bird. With due deliberation he took his pinch of snuff, as he said, "There can never be too many textbooks for our purpose!"

The nephews brought together an enormous crowd of scribes. They copied from books, and copied from copies, till the manuscripts were piled up to an unreachable height. Men murmured in amazement. "Oh, the tower of culture, gloriously high! The end of it lost in the clouds!"

The scribes, with light hearts, hurried home, their pockets full.

The nephews were furiously busy keeping the cage in proper trim. As their constant scrubbing and polishing went on, the people murmured with satisfaction: "This is progress indeed!"

Men were employed in large numbers, and supervisors were still more numerous. These, with their cousins of all different degrees of distance, built a palace for themselves and lived there happily ever after.

But whatever may be its other deficiencies, the world is never in want of fault-finders. They went about saying that every creature remotely connected with the cage flourished beyond words, excepting only one – the bird.

When this remark reached the Raja's ears, he summoned his nephews before him and said: "My dear nephews, what is this we hear?"

The nephews said in answer: "Sire, let the testimony of the goldsmiths and the pundits, the scribes and the supervisors be taken, if the truth is to be known. Food is scarce aming the fault-finders, and that is why their tongues have gained in sharpness."

The explanation was so luminously satisfactory that the Raja decorated each one of his nephews with his own rare jewels.

At length, the Raja, being desirous of seeing with his own eyes how his Education Department was busying itself with the bird, made his appearance at the Great Hall of Learning.

From the gate rose the sounds of conch-shells and gongs, horns, bugles and trumpets, cymbals, drums and kettledrums, tomtoms, tambourines, flutes, fifes, barrel-organs and bagpipes. The pundits began chanting mantras at the tops of their voices, while the goldsmiths, scribes, supervisors, and their numberless cousins of all different degrees of distance, loudly raised a round of cheers.

The nephews smiled and said: "Sire, what do you think of it all?"

The Raja said, "It does seem so fearfully like a sound principle of Education!"

Mightily pleased, the Raja was about to remount his elephant, when a fault-finder, appearing suddenly from behind some bush, cried out: "Maharaja, have you seen the bird?"

"Indeed, I have not!" exclaimed the Raja. "I completely forgot about the bird."

Turning back, he asked the pundits about the method they followed in instructing the bird. It was shown to him. He was immensely impressed. The method was so stupendous that the bird looked ridiculously unimportant in comparison. The Raja was satisfied that there was no flaw in the arrangements. As for any complaint from the bird itself, that simply could not be expected. Its throat was so completely choked with the leaves from the books that it could neither whistle nor whisper. It sent a thrill through anyone who saw it.

This time, while remounting his elephant, the Raja ordered his state ear-puller to give a thoroughly good pull at both the ears of the fault-finder.

Thus the bird thus tottered on, duly and properly, to the very verge of utter emptiness. Its progress was deemed extremely satisfactory. Nevertheless, nature occasionally triumphed over nurture, and when the morning light peeped into the bird's cage, the bird sometimes fluttered its wings in a reprehensible manner. And, though it is hard to believe, occasionally it pitifully pecked at its bars with its feeble beak.

"What impertinence!" growled the head guard.

The blacksmith, with his forge and hammer, took his place in the Raja's Department of Education. Oh, what resounding blows! Soon an iron chain was completed, and the bird's wings were clipped.

The Raja's brothers-in-law looked grim, and shook their heads, saying, "These birds not only lack good sense, but also gratitude!"

With textbook in one hand and baton in the other, the pundits gave the poor bird what may fittingly be called lessons.

The head guard was honored with a title for his watchfulness, and the blacksmith for his skill in forging chains.

The bird died.

Nobody had the least notion exactly when this had occurred. The fault-finder was the first person to spread the rumor.

The Raja called his nephews and asked them, "My dear nephews, what is this that we hear?"

The nephews said: "Sire, the bird's education has been completed."

"Does it hop?" the Raja enquired.

"Never!" said the nephews.

"Does it fly?"

"No."

"Bring me the bird," said the Raja.

The bird was brought to him, escorted by the head guarded, with soldiers on foot and cavalrymen on horseback. The Raja poked its body with his finger. Only its inner stuffing of book leaves rustled.

Outside the window, a spring breeze murmured among the newly budded ashoka leaves, and filled the April morning with a deep and heavy sigh.

Lightning Source UK Ltd.
Milton Keynes UK
UKOW051936070213

205992UK00001B/233/P